D0934234

HIMALAYAN ENCHANTMENT

HIMALAYAN ENCHANTMENT

an anthology

Frank Kingdon-Ward

Chosen and Edited
with an Introduction by
John Whitehead

SERINDIA PUBLICATIONS
London

© Jean Rasmussen and John Whitehead 1990
First published 1990
by Serindia Publications
10 Parkfields, Putney, London sw15 6nh

Phototypeset by Input Typesetting Ltd, London
Printed and bound by Biddles Ltd, Guildford

A CIP catalogue record for this book
is available from the British Library

ISBN 0 906026 22 9

Contents

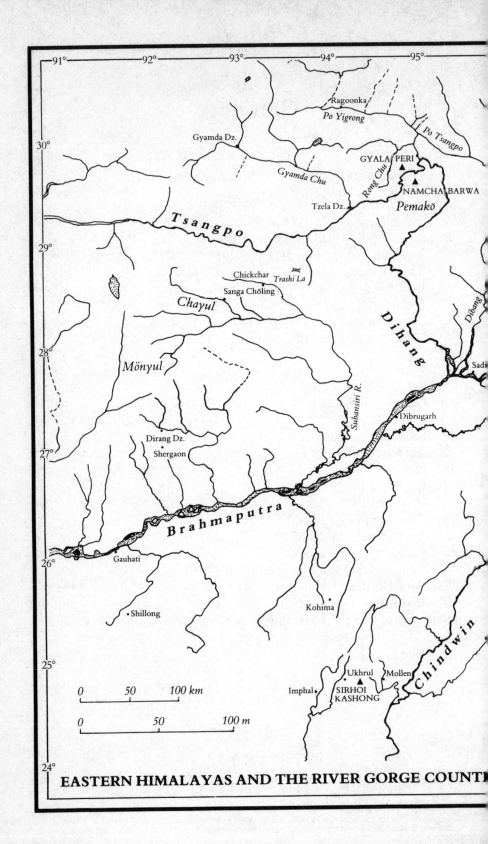

EASTERN HIMALAYAS AND THE RIVER GORGE COUNTRY

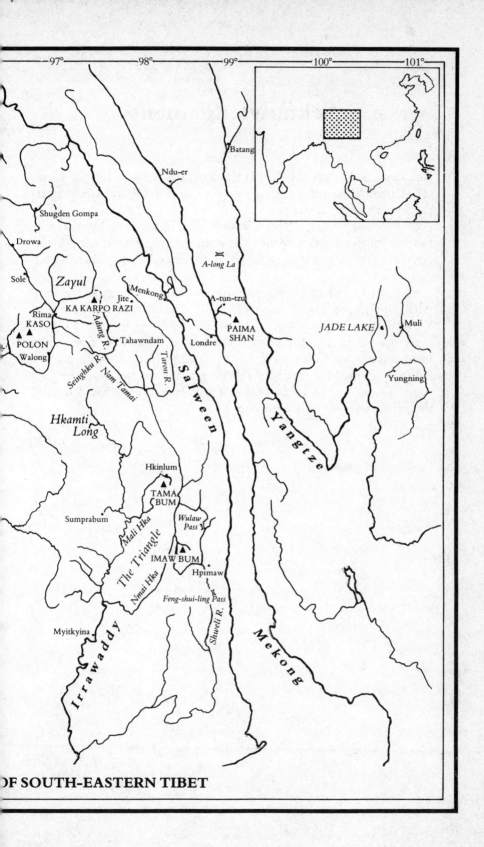

OF SOUTH-EASTERN TIBET

Acknowledgements

Acknowledgements are due to the Royal Botanic Gardens, Kew, the British Museum (Natural History), and the Royal Geographical Society, for assistance;

to Professor Ulrich Schweinfurth and Heidrun Schweinfurth-Marby for permission to use the map accompanying their bibliography (see note on page xviii) as the basis for the sketch-map included here;

to Tom Foxall of Forty-five Design, Much Wenlock, for help with the photographs; as well as to the Royal Geographical Society;

to my wife Ella for converting my handwritten notes into immaculate typescript, and to Mrs Jean Rasmussen (formerly Kingdon-Ward) for carefully checking it and for her many helpful suggestions; and to them both for much encouragement during the preparation of this anthology.

JW

Introduction

Of the three vocations – as botanist, explorer and writer – in which Frank Kingdon-Ward excelled, this anthology is designed to present him as a writer, though the other two naturally provide the subject matter. His profession was that of plant-hunter, in which capacity he undertook more than twenty major expeditions in a career that spanned nearly fifty years; but his interests were far wider than that label suggests and embraced every aspect of the terrain through which he travelled: geology, climate, ethnology, fauna. Before the word had become fashionable his study was ecology, the science concerned with the relationships of living organisms, including human beings, to their surroundings.

The geographical area to which his footsteps were drawn time and again so that it became an obsession is one of the most remote and inaccessible on earth, being that part of the eastern Himalayas where Assam, Tibet, Burma and China meet in a tangle of mountain ranges. Among the snow-peaks of that sparsely inhabited, seldom visited region some of the mightiest rivers of Asia have their sources; and its alpine meadows in spring and summer are ablaze with flowering plants. Its inhabitants, too, are among the most fascinating people in the world.

The key to an understanding of the dynamics of the region, which for convenience may be divided into three sectors, is some knowledge of its rivers. In the westernmost sector the Tsangpo flowing from west to east through southern Tibet turns south to become the Dihang before it swings back on itself and merges into the Brahmaputra whose waters, mingling with those of the Ganges, discharge themselves through multiple mouths in the swampy Sundarbans south-east of Calcutta into the Bay of Bengal. The middle sector comprising part of the Kachin Hills of north Burma includes the Triangle, the watershed dividing the Mali Hka on the west and the Nmai Hka on the east, rivers that meet at the Confluence north of Myitkyina to form the Irrawaddy, which then travels southwards down the central plain of Burma before emptying into the sea by Rangoon; and the Nmai-Salween divide to the east of the Triangle with Imaw Bum rising impressively in its midst. The Salween, Mekong and Yangtze all have their sources in the easternmost sector, at one point blasting their way through sheer rocky gorges less than fifty miles apart, before proceeding on their separate ways: the Salween flowing through eastern Burma and reaching the sea at Moulmein; the Mekong flowing down the length of Indo-China and reaching the South China Sea at Saigon; the Yangtze traversing the massive width of China and reaching the Yellow Sea at Shanghai.

In Kingdon-Ward's day the region was a political Tom Tiddler's ground, loosely administered if at all, much of it unexplored and unmapped; and it was back-breaking country to travel in. The climate was severe, a brief spring being followed by months of torrential monsoon rain before winter brought the heavy snow that closed the high passes. For the traveller there were many deterrents. The local tribes upon whom he depended for porterage were of uncertain temper; their houses were havens for fleas and lice; at lower elevations leeches infested the paths, and mosquitoes and stinging insects abounded. The food available locally was meagre and unpalatable. There was loneliness, too, to contend with, for though latterly Kingdon-Ward took a European companion along with him on his travels he was usually on his own, dependent for company on his native servants and people met casually on the way. To withstand the physical hardships he needed a tough constitution and a stout heart; to overcome loneliness he had deep spiritual and intellectual reserves to draw upon. But above all he had to sustain him the obsession that possessed him. As the title of this anthology suggests, he was a man enchanted, in bondage to the glamour of the mountains and high pastures with their wealth of flowers that persistently called him back.

As he acknowledged in a late essay, he was drawn to botanical exploration at an early age, his imagination fired by Schimper's *Plant Geography* which he read before he went up to Cambridge, where his father was Professor of Botany. Although he had no inclination or aptitude for the teaching profession, he went out to China in 1907 at the age of twenty-one to become a teacher at the Shanghai Public School, his purpose (it may be surmised) being to position himself geographically so as to be able to seize any opportunity that came his way for exploring in the region on which he had apparently already set his heart. His chance came two years later when he received an invitation, prompted by a mutual friend, to accompany an American zoologist on a collecting expedition across central and western China to Tatsienlu and south Kansu.

Less than totally enamoured of the Flowery Kingdom and its inhabitants and with only the sketchiest command of their language, his principal qualification for selection appears to have been his boundless enthusiasm. For he revelled in every moment of the journey which took them upriver by junk and country-boat, on foot and by pony along the Great West Road, over the mountains and through the gorge of the Han river to Mantze, the no-man's-land between China and Tibet. From Chungking they travelled two thousand miles up the Yangtze to the borders of Szechuan and Hopei, and then by stages back to Shanghai. The glimpse he had been vouchsafed of the snow mountains of Tibet was decisive in determining the pattern of his life, and on his return he had no other thought than to go back and explore them.

So he did not hesitate when a year later – a word having been put in for him by an old friend of his father – a Liverpool nursery firm invited him to undertake a plant-hunting expedition on the Tibetan border of Yunnan; and the Shanghai Public School knew him no more. The journey lasting ten months took him for the first time to the area of the Salween-Mekong-Yangtze gorges. Setting out with Chinese mules from Bhamo in north-eastern Burma he made for T'eng-yueh, reaching the Yangtze 2,500 miles from its mouth on the east coast of China. He branched west over its watershed with the Mekong and here had his first encounters with one of the hill tribes, the Lisus, wild people who came up from their jungle villages in summer to tend their flocks, cut wood for their cross-bows and collect wild honey for food and poison for their arrows. From the Mekong he went north to Atuntzu, a large Tibetan village at the head of a valley on the lower slopes of the Salween-Mekong divide, which became his base for botanizing excursions. Now among the Lutzus, he came up against some of the brute realities of Himalayan travel – intractable country, vile weather, inadequate diet, manifold pests, and the unpredictability of the local tribes – but all these were, for him, more than compensated for by the discovery of rare and beautiful plants, the wild splendour of the landscapes and the fascination of the people. For some time he made Gartok, the capital of the province of Kham, his base; and going over the snow passes in October to collect seed from the plants he had marked down in the summer he heard rumours of a great revolution occurring in China. Back at Atuntzu he packed up his collection, which he sent with his followers down the main road to Talifu, while he made his own tortuous way westwards through tribal territory back to Bhamo.

Myitkyina was his starting-point when in April 1913 he again set out for Atuntzu and his former collecting grounds among the glaciers, alpine valleys and screes; and here he learnt of the inauguration of the Chinese Republic. The autumn seed collecting done and his collection sent on its way to Talifu, he was free to go on a winter journey exploring in eastern Tibet. It was an arduous and adventurous trip, and owing to the disturbed state of the country his repeated efforts to get through to the Taron were frustrated. From Atuntzu he was escorted by unruly Chinese soldiers to the Yangtze, passing in a few days from winter to spring, from the austere mansions of the Tibetans to the walled houses of the Chinese, hidden in jasmine-scented lanes.

After only a month's respite he set off again, planning now to explore up the Nmai Hka, cross westwards over the watershed to Fort Hertz, newly established in the Hkamti Long plain, and proceeding down the Mali Hka to the Confluence so complete the circuit to Myitkyina. He first operated from Hpimaw where there was a small Gurkha garrison, then on the slopes of Imaw Bum which he found a paradise of dwarf rhododendron. It was August 1914 when he turned north towards the Wulaw Pass, marching in driving rain and coming suddenly upon a bewitching meadow of flowers beside a stream. When stores began to run low – he had been subsisting for some time on a diet of tea, rice and pumpkins – he made for the fort at Kawnglu manned by Gurkhas under two British officers from whom, over a dish of ham and eggs, he learnt that war had broken out in Europe. When he arrived back at Fort Hertz in September he was in a state of exhaustion and for six weeks was seriously ill, a timely warning that there were limits to the endurance of even his tough constitution.

The Great War imposed a five-year moratorium on Kingdon-Ward's professional travels, an interval during which he served as a captain with a Mahratta battalion of the Indian army in Burma, Mesopotamia and India; but 1919 saw him once more plant collecting in the neighbourhoods of Imaw Bum and Hpimaw, and two years later he revisited old haunts in Yunnan

and Szechuan. In 1922 he took the old trail from Bhamo to
Atuntzu and the river gorge country, on that journey managing
finally to get through to the Taron, which he memorably
described:

> The olive river slid smoothly between tall hills clothed with
> tropic forest, and occasionally broke into tempers of white
> foam where rocks hindered its swift progress –

a description that, as so often in his writings, finds words to
express his grasp of a given terrain as a living organism. On his
way back he recrossed the Nmai-Mali watershed and presented a
curious figure when he arrived back at Fort Hertz: bearded, wearing a stove-in hat, muddy trousers and decadent boots, and
flourishing a butterfly net.

Lord Cawdor accompanied him in 1924 on a year's collecting
expedition starting from Sikkim where the political officer F. M.
Bailey, himself a distinguished Tibetan explorer, sped them on
their way, and making for the Tsangpo; for their purpose –
besides the ostensible one of collecting seeds for horticulturalists
at home – was to try and solve once and for all the riddle of the
rainbow falls. From their base at Tsela Dzong at the junction of
the Gyamda with the Tsangpo they made botanical excursions
on the mountainsides above the fort, then in June moved east to
Tumbatse in the valley of the Rong Chu, thence to Pemakö in a
loop of the Tsangpo. The following month they made a circuit
of a glacier-fed lake from which they obtained a sight of Namcha
Barwa, 25,445 feet, and Gyala Peri, 23,740 feet, massive peaks
only fourteen miles apart.

Their journey through the Tsangpo gorge was hard going, at
times dangerous. Passing the point where Bailey had turned back
in 1911 they struggled on for four more days under increasing
difficulties, and their efforts were rewarded when they came upon
a falls with rainbows dancing in its spray, but not the Niagara of
rumour, for it was no more than forty feet high. The onward
journey was equally arduous, at one point causing the porters –
many of whom were women – to mutiny, but they were persuaded to struggle on to Payi at the mouth of the gorge where,
tired but triumphant, they celebrated with barley-beer and song.
In December they explored the stretch of the gorge lying between
the falls and the confluence of the Tsangpo with the Po, closing

all but five miles of the unexplored gap, and in January were back at Gyamda for the final phase of the expedition before returning to India through Bhutan.

It is necessary to give these brief, inevitably sketchy, accounts of Kingdon-Ward's successive journeys in order to bring home to the reader, not only the completeness of the spell under which he was held in thrall, but the dauntlessness and determination of the man. In no other way can his considerable achievements be seen in their true perspective.

In the spring of 1926, then, he made for the sources of the Mali Hka north of the Irrawaddy-Lohit divide, a range across which the Diphuk La at the head of the Seinghku valley gives access to the Tibetan province of Zayul. From Haita he moved camp further up the valley and made a reconnaissance to the Lohit, along which he proposed to make his eventual way back to Assam. Having time in hand he made a side trip to Fort Hertz before returning to the Seinghku-Adung confluence for the seed harvest. On the return journey he faced a dangerous situation when most of his Nung porters, taking fright at the sight of the deep snow on the far side of a pass, flung down their loads and made off for home. Aided by Lisus, Mishmis, and men from Zayul, he managed to make his way westwards, with his baggage including his seed collection intact, along the Lohit to Sadiya, which he reached in December.

He returned to Sadiya in March 1928 with H. M. Clutterbuck with whom he set out up the Rima road through the Delei valley, making for Meiliang and Peti, Mishmi villages from which they botanized on the slopes of Kaso and Solon. Next year, deserting his favourite territory, he travelled in the southern Shan States of Burma and, as a member of a plush American safari, in Indo-China. By the end of 1930 he was back at Myitkyina, this time with Lord Cranbrook a zoologist, his object – besides collecting seeds for his sponsors – to trace the headwaters of the Irrawaddy. They followed the Nam Tamai, a tributary of the Nmai Hka, to the Seinghku-Adung confluence in the country of the Marus, and for three months operated from Tahawndam, the last Tibetan village on the Burma side of the nebulous frontier. In May 1931 they crossed the border to Jité in Tibet and penetrated as far as the Lachong La. October was spent collecting, cataloguing and packing seeds, and as winter began to sharpen its claws on the mountains they headed back for Myitkyina.

Starting from Sadiya early in February 1933 he retraced his steps beside the Lohit to Rima, taking with him the young Ronald Kaulback, then struck north on his own towards Shugden Gompa. July found him exploring the sources of the Salween. Two years later he went over the Himalayan passes from Assam back to Haita, Chayul Dzong and Sanga Chöling and on to the Tsangpo, linking up with the journey he had made in 1924. On this expedition he fulfilled a long-cherished desire to penetrate into the heart of the mountain range whose snow-peaks he had seen from afar nine years before. He was now fifty years old and had been tramping the Himalayas for a quarter of a century.

Back among the Nungs in 1937 he worked in the Nam Tamai and Nmai Hka valleys and made a side trip to Ka Karpo Razi, Burma's highest mountain, round whose skirts he botanized before going on to the Adung gorge. Next year, after exploring in the Balipara Frontier Tract, he joined the Vernay-Cutting expedition sponsored by the American Museum of Natural History, as its botanist. Its objectives were to collect zoological specimens in the Ngawchang valley and around Imaw Bum in the Kachin Hills and to visit the passes leading to China. To J. K. Stanford, a former Deputy Commissioner at Myitkyina who went along as organiser and ornithologist, we are indebted for a rare glimpse of Kingdon-Ward at work.

We set off down the hill one by one in the wake of the mules. I started an hour behind Frank but overtook him in the first mile. What we called his 'trouser-press' was open on the road and covered with assorted flowers, while Frank himself, with flashing spectacles and his cap-comforter awry, looked as if he were directing the early stages of a film scenario. He was waving his stick and shouting Chinese exhortations, coupled with a few straight-flung English oaths, at Lama Ta, who, forty feet up in the wrong tree, was pointing at every plant in sight and shouting back in Yawyin. It was, we were told later, a *Pentopterygium*. Somewhere behind the scenes the invisible hoolocks yodelled and whooped and applauded in their own tongue, glad perhaps to see us go.

But the expedition was altogether too lavishly equipped for Kingdon-Ward's taste, and he did not much relish the continuous slaughter of wild creatures for the sake of their skins, longing for the solitudes of the high valleys. It was to be his last expedition for several years, because soon afterwards World War II broke out, putting an end to plant-hunting sponsorships for the duration.

Kingdon-Ward was in Burma when the Japanese overran the country in 1942, but had no difficulty in walking out to India along familiar mountain tracks. He spent the war there, teaching jungle survival to soldiers training for the reconquest of Burma. (Another instructor was Jim Corbett of man-eating tiger fame.) After the Japanese surrender he was employed by the American military authorities to locate three transport Dakotas which had crashed in the hills of Manipur while carrying war supplies 'over the hump' to China. While so engaged he noted that the slopes of Sirhoi Kashong offered a promising field for plant-hunting, so when in 1948 the New York Botanical Garden asked him to undertake an expedition to collect ornamental plants for the southern states of America and California he chose to return to Manipur.

He was then sixty-two years old, and it was fortunate for him that on this and subsequent expeditions his wife Jean accompanied him, not only to assist him in his botanical work, but also to look after him when his health, as it now tended to do, broke down after particularly strenuous exertions. Ukhrul in the Tangkhul Naga country was their base, and at first they confined their attention to its environs, then in April made for Sirhoi six miles across the valley to the east. In the slack period before the monsoon was due to break they made a sortie towards the Burma border, and near the Kuki village of Mollen (where wild tea was reputed, wrongly, to grow) they had a glimpse of the Chindwin twenty miles away. They secured an abundant harvest of seeds and plant specimens before going back to India. It had been Kingdon-Ward's seventeenth major botanical assignment in Asia, but still he had not done with exploring, and the most exciting adventure in a highly adventurous life still lay in the future.

1949 saw the Kingdon-Wards collecting in the Mishmi, Khasi and Naga Hills, and the following year took them from Sadiya along the Lohit to Rima. Camping nearby they found themselves, in the evening of August 15, uncomfortably close to the epicentre of the most spectacular earthquake of modern times. Lucky to have survived, they were marooned amid the shattered landscape for three weeks before, aided by a patrol of the Assam Rifles, they

were able to start on their perilous return journey. Undeterred by
their ordeal, they were off again in the winter of 1952, starting
from Myitkyina in now-independent Burma and making for
Sumprabum north of the Irrawaddy Confluence, where they spent
three weeks collecting; but their main objective was the group of
peaks seventy miles further north at the source of the Hrang Hka,
a tributary of the Mali Hka. In the spring they explored towards
Tagulam Bum and Tama Bum and, while at Tibu camp on
the slopes of the former, Kingdon-Ward was granted an instant
recapitulation of a lifetime's travel in the panoramic view presented to him of the mountains of China, Assam and Tibet and,
conspicuous 125 miles to the south, the massive bulk of Ka Karpo
Razi. He spent his sixty-eighth birthday profitably botanizing on
the mountainside.

By now Kingdon-Ward was a figure of international eminence
in his chosen field, the recipient of many honours and much
sought-after as a consultant and lecturer. More than once he had
been offered the security of a permanent official position in the
world of botany, which would have enabled him to take things
easier; but he valued his freedom too much and always declined.
He had been his own master too long for him now to submit to
harness. And as he once remarked, if he had never been able to
make money, at least he had learnt how to live without it. He
was, literally, of no fixed abode and did not even possess a
complete set of his own books, having nowhere to house them;
but he would not have wished for any other way of life.

He was a man of absolute integrity, pursuing his three vocations
with courage, determination, loyalty and a becoming modesty;
and his achievements in the fields of botany, horticulture and
ecology are internationally recognized. Reviewing the course of
his strenuous, dedicated life it is impossible not to conclude that
he was a great man. Certainly, to the last, he was a happy one.

In his early seventies accompanied by his wife he went on his
last plant-hunting expeditions, first to the Chin Hills of Burma,
then in Ceylon, and he was planning further travels in the Cauc-
asus, northern Iran and Vietnam when, on April 8, 1958, he died
suddenly in London.

Kingdon-Ward wrote twenty-five books, published between 1910
and 1960, of which thirteen are travel books describing his botanical expeditions in Asia and four of the rest collections of essays

having a bearing on his work as explorer*. Most of his books have long been out of print, which has meant that a large body of writing of the highest quality has been generally unavailable. The purpose of this anthology is in some measure to make good the default by bringing together in one volume passages from the travel books and essays which best illustrate his literary gifts.

It has been divided into three parts. The Prelude and first six chapters are taken chronologically from the first seven travel books (1910–30). The middle section comprises eight chapters, each containing a group of short extracts dealing with a particular facet of Kingdon-Ward's interests. The last six chapters and the Envoi are taken chronologically from the last six travel books (1934–1960) except that an essay on the Assam earthquake of 1950 has been inserted as chapter 20. The chapter headings in the first and third sections are, with that same exception, the titles of the travel books from which the passages they contain were chosen.

Like any other anthology, this one is primarily intended for occasional reading, but each of the chapters in the first and third sections, if read straight through, will give the reader a bird's-eye view of the particular expedition it covers, and the anthology as a whole presents Kingdon-Ward's entire career as botanist and explorer in a nutshell.

My object having been to demonstrate his mastery of English prose, I tried in making the selection to include only passages that combine intrinsic interest with good writing, and I have given preference to those through which his personality – especially his sense of humour – comes through most vividly. The anthology is not intended as a substitute for the books from which the passages have been selected, but rather to stimulate interest in Kingdon-Ward as a writer, in the hope of creating a demand for them to be brought back into print. Writers of Kingdon-Ward's calibre are not so thick on the ground that we can afford to allow his work to slip into oblivion.

John Whitehead
Munslow

* See *Exploration in the Eastern Himalayas and the River Gorge Country of Southeastern Tibet – Francis (Frank) Kingdon-Ward (1885–1958) – An Annotated Bibliography with a Map of the Area of his Explorations* by Ulrich Schweinfurth and Heidrun Schweinfurth-Marby (Franz Steiner Verlag GmbH. Wiesbaden, 1975).

On The Road to Tibet
1909–10

On the Han river – Among the Tibetans – Approaching Chengtu – Nightfall in the mountains – Tatsienlu – Omi-san – The call of the mountains

On the Han river

The crew, four in number, concealed themselves forward, under the fo'csle deck-boards, and quartered in the after-deck house were the remainder, namely, the *lao-pan* and his wife, and his son, and his son's wife, and his son's wife's baby, and an obscure relative and her child, and a friend. The baby wasn't a bit obscure – she was one of the most obvious articles in the boat, but the poor little thing was sick most of the time.

On moonlight evenings, when the junk was tied up for the night, and the baby girl had gone off into a feverish sleep, it was the strangest thing in the world to sit on deck and listen to the old *lao-pan* calling gently to her soul to come back, come back, before it flew too far away; when sick children fall asleep, their souls leave their bodies and wander abroad into the night.

'*Hwei-lai! hwei-lai!*' (come back!) he chanted, looking up to the brilliant stars.

'*Hwei-lai-liao! hwei-lai-liao!*' (I have come back!) crowed the aged grandmother in reply, taking the part of the baby soul.

It was a pretty thin disguise, but it seemed to comfort the old man, and so the picturesque pantomime went on night after night till the baby was well again.

Among the Tibetans

This mountain village could not have mustered fifty people all told, and the men were chiefly hunters, woodsmen and herdsmen; the people are too indolent, too tolerant of a 'hand-to-mouth existence, to cultivate more than the barest amount that would suffice, and the women were responsible for most of that; but excellent fresh milk could be bought here, a luxury unknown in China.

The men are frequently handsome, tall and slim, but even these peaceful villagers are apt to exhibit a hardness in the lines of the face which betrays them as belonging to a ruthlessly cruel people. The women too are comely, far more than the Chinese, at least when young, and their well-knit figures, undeformed feet and breezy, unrestrained bearing betoken a more exalted social standing than is allowed to their less fortunate sisters. But the strenuous life and rigorous climate age them prematurely.

The scenery amidst which we were now placed was magnificent. All around us rose the mountains, densely clothed on their shaded slopes with silver and spruce fir, giving place in the warmer hollows to masses of willow showing as brilliant patches of purple and ochre amongst the olive-green of the sombre forest.

In the morning the graceful tops of these dark trees were always powdered with fresh-fallen snow, and as the sun rose into the brilliant sky they glowed and sparkled with the charm of a thousand Christmas trees. Behind them, immense pinnacles of yellow limestone, flashing in the sunlight, reared themselves far above the forests, their sharp summits where the eagles nest pricking through the soft snow mists which wrap them round and writhe to and fro as the wind rockets through the scree-fed gullies. Far below in the deeply graven valley the stream went singing over the boulders between its ice-walled banks, bursting through gorge beyond gorge where the arching trees almost met overhead, leaving the jagged rent through which the confused waters splashed heavily from one deep green pool to another, dark and noisy.

In one place the bald cliffs, here hewn into fantastic pillars and impregnable battlements on which even the clinging snow-flakes find no rest, rose upwards till the roar of the torrent was drowned in the clouds; in another place the snow lay deep in the shadow of the fir-clad hills which sloped back tier beyond tier till the river was lost to view behind the forest barrier. But no temples crown these lonely mountains as in China; no prosperous villages cluster in the sequestered valleys, no cultivated terraces chequer the slopes; only here and there a prayer-wheel stands stark and mute, strangled in the iron grip of the ice. There are no green leaves yet, no bursting buds breaking into joyful life, no flowers, though this is April, the sun shining brilliantly in a clear sky, the birds singing merrily in the copses. For out here on the grass hills above the forest, where the dead haulms of a thousand decayed flowers are still splitting and cracking in the snow, we are fifteen thousand feet above the sea.

Approaching Chengtu

Another stage, and we were down on the dead level plain, the road now deeply ribbed, as many as eight or ten parallel grooves, worn by the countless wheelbarrows which for ages have plied to and fro across the plain, cutting up the flagstones for miles.

One of the most remarkable features of this plain is the number of rapidly flowing rivers which traverse it at frequent intervals, spanned by arched bridges of red sandstone, many of them with finely carved parapets ornamented with quaint gargoyles. These rivers, usually from twenty to thirty yards across, are, as a matter of fact, artificial canals, which diverge from the Min-ho at Kuan-hsien, some distance to the north of Chengtu, traverse the plain in a number of parallel arcs, and converge again upon the river south of the capital. Undertaken at the instance of one of the emperors more than two thousand years ago, this tremendous scheme of irrigation converted the previously parched Chengtu plain into one of the most fertile and densely populated regions in the world, teeming with prosperous cities and villages, and cultivated to the last acre under every variety of crop.

On our march of 22nd May, villages became more frequent, gradually merged into one long hive swarming with human beings, and culminated beneath the walls of the capital of Szech-wan. So smothered beneath its canopy of trees and houses is the plain, that the great gate is not visible above the roofs of the interminable street till one is within half a mile of it, already sucked into the vortex of the whirl of coolies and wheelbarrows which gurgles with ever-increasing velocity towards the narrow entrance and, rushing through, spreads slowly out into the vast city; a very different sight to that which greets the traveller as he approaches Hsian-fu, visible for a distance of several miles, and enters the huge gate choked with its roaring mule traffic, to hear through the clouds of dust the grinding and rumbling of wheels on cobbles, the crack of the long whips, and yelling of frenzied muleteers.

Nightfall in the mountains

Though prepared only for summer weather we nevertheless now resolved to ascend the mountains behind Wha-lin-ping and spend a few days in the rhododendron forest. A small wooden temple, some three thousand feet above the village and two thousand feet below the summit of the ridge, seemed a fitting place in which to camp, and thither we repaired on 14th June.

The temple, raised on a small level clearing in the forest, was a well-ventilated shanty which only partially excluded the rain, and was now deserted, one or two priests remaining in residence only when it was in demand as a popular resort for the burning of incense and asking of favours, during the sixth moon. The valley lay almost at our feet, for the ascent had been very abrupt, and the little village clustered above the deep ravine where the torrent flowed seemed but a stone's throw away; however, rain fell in torrents every night, and we felt the cold severely, even after the quite moderate warmth of the valley.

From our platform beneath the summit, we looked across ridge after ridge of dark forests, to a tremendous range of peaks stretching across the western sky, from the great glittering snow-fields of which crept a dozen glaciers, jammed themselves into the black gullies which scarred the mountain face from top to bottom, and spread far down into the valleys. In was the rainy season, and towards nightfall these towering white peaks presented an ever-changing panorama of rock and snow, banded with gleaming cloud where the rays of the setting sun played. Now the clammy night-mist came pouring in a mighty cascade over the pass into the valley, where it lay for a time heaving, smoking fitfully at the edges, while the stars twinkled lazily in the brief twilight, and the gaunt precipices, draped in snow, rose straight up from the pale ocean of mist to meet them, clear-cut against the fading tinges of sunset. Now long lapping billows of cloud came thundering silently up the mountain side, hungrily licking the dark tree-tops as they swept ahead, blotting out the star-lit heaven, and masking the distant peaks behind a seething flood of mist. Only the valleys below were filling with purple light now, and the lower mountains over against the little village were steadily changing from blue to purple and from purple to black as the shadows deepened.

Thus it remained for a minute or two and then the tide was

rolling and swirling out again, leaving crag and glacier and tree-clad ridge yet more sharply silhouetted against the after-glow, where the sky was still dyed with filmy green and turquoise blue, with rose and the deepening purple of night, the magic colours there, of the eternal west.

Tatsienlu

The city was a place of surprises. It was on this jabbering, slouching crowd of the strangest people on earth, which ebbed and flowed listlessly through the narrow streets, that the Chinese shopkeepers, like parasites of Machiavellian cunning, grew fat. Amongst this motley throng were tall, bony men, wrapped in greasy skins, who lived their lives in the saddle, with the terrible rigours of nomadic life in the mountains stamped on their hard-lined faces, bringing musks; derelicts from the monasteries sacked during the recent fighting, bringing wonderful paintings and idols saved from the wreckage; pilgrims from Lhasa; yak herdsmen taking out the tea brought in on the backs of Chinese coolies; and strange primitive men, with nothing save their hardy ponies and long guns.

Many of the Mantze girls look extremely pretty, tricked out with heavy silver bangles, ear-rings, and necklaces of coral or turquoise. Of course that is not all. Dark-blue skirts hitched up behind and hide boots reaching to the knee give them an Amazonian appearance which is rather enhanced by the coils of black hair, closely interwoven with strands of crimson twine, bound turbanwise round their heads, and the handsome, open face with its large dark eyes, from which the light flashes and dances when they smile.

Omi-san

The summit of Omi offers some of the most remarkable sights imaginable, not the least astonishing of which is the view, occasionally to be obtained, of the snow mountains of Tibet, south of Tatsienlu, distant more than a hundred miles. Seen in the first flush of dawn, suffused with a pink glow as the sun rises over the Kiating plain, they seem on fire; no longer are they snow mountains, but burning craters, the glow from which shines through their glassy slopes. While we look, they are transfigured, blanching rapidly as the sun rises higher, and before midday the clouds roll up and obscure them behind massive puffs with gilt edges, piled high one on another.

From amidst this richest cloudland rise two strange table mountains, one of which is called Wa-wa-san. Both are many miles long, their summits, formerly perhaps like those whose rounded peaks rise cape beyond cape out of this sunlit sea, now cut clean off with a giant knife as it appears; and the stumps, mutilated but undismayed, not without a wild beauty of their own, planed to a dead level, falling abruptly away in precipices on every hand.

To the south, green mountains streaked with dark gullies full of rich vegetation melt into blue, and the blue hills grow fainter and melt into the summer clouds of the Lolo country, and fade out of sight. As the harvest moon rises, a great yellow orb seen through the veil of mist hanging over the plain, the rim of the snow mountains again becomes outlined, till at last, under the glare of the moon now riding undimmed, high up in cloudless space, they glitter all across the western horizon. So quiet and peaceful is it, so alike are sights and scenes under the softening and muffling pall of night, that this might be the Alps from Geneva, instead of the savage barriers of Tibet.

All these pictures we watch unrolling before us from the balcony of the temple crowning the huge cliff which stands boldly out like a headland, washed at its base by the imaginary Kiating sea, now a sea of yellow rice- and cornfields, so far below that no sound of breaking waves could ever come up to us. Though the glory of this temple was destroyed more than three centuries ago, never to be restored, pieces remain to testify to its ancient beauty – two miniature pagodas, about fifteen feet high, exquisitely chaste, parts of the bronze altar, studded with carving, and a few other relics. For the famous bronze temple was destroyed by lightning during the sixteenth century.

But the most wonderful sight lies right at our feet, beneath the balcony, where yawns that fearful abyss, the steep ridges green with forest trees which buttress the great cliff dipping down, down, two thousand feet to the silvery wisps of mist hanging in mid-air, and down beyond them to the rolling country, and still down between the spreading capes out on to the wide Kiating plain stretching to the horizon, across which crawl a whole mapful of twisting rivers.

The call of the mountains

At midday on 13th September we were alongside the wharf; a year all but seventeen days had passed since I sailed from Shanghai, and it had seemed half a lifetime. A tram roared down the Bund with a horrid clanging of bells and screeching of wheels, and suddenly, with the sound, the terrible loneliness of a big city came upon me with full force.

Forgotten were the hardship of travel in the interior; desperately cold, hungry, tired we might have been; almost broken in spirit too sometimes, our hearts aching for a sight of civilization. But lonely – never! And it was all forgotten now, the deadly cold that made sleep impossible, the long marches through snow and rain and burning sun, the weary climbs, the lack of food, the torturing heat of the plains with its attendant discomforts of insect life. I only remembered the sights and cities I had seen, the mountains of everlasting snow, the wonderful flowers and birds, and the friends I had made.

And the grand solitude of the mountains out beyond the civilization of China is ever calling to me to return. Some day perhaps the voice will become too insistent to ignore, and I shall find myself again a willing pilgrim on the road to Tibet.

ONE

The Land of the Blue Poppy
1911

The Mekong valley – A Tibetan festival – Praying for rain – The Lutzu tribe – La-kor-ah to Men-kong – A Tibetan wedding – At Atuntzu – Tibetan dancers – A brawl at Ndu-er – Over the A-löng La – The last of the Mekong – A crowded night – Halt at Kai-Tou – 'The Land of Deep Corrosions'

The Mekong valley

The weather had now set in fine, and nothing could have been more delightful than these marches up the Mekong valley, for we took matters fairly easily, making four stages from Hsiao-wei-hsi to Tsu-kou. Sometimes the narrow path was enveloped in the shade of flowering shrubs and walnut trees, the branches breasting us as we rode, the air sweetened by the scent of roses which swept in cascades of yellow flowers over the summits of trees thirty feet high; sometimes we plunged into a deep limestone gorge, its cliffs festooned with ferns and orchids, our caravan climbing up by rough stone steps which zigzagged backwards and forwards till we were out of ear-shot of the rapids in the river below; sometimes the path was broken altogether by a scree-shoot, which, dangerous as it looked, the mules walked across very calmly, though sending rocks grinding and sliding down through the trees into the river.

In one gorge through which we passed, large pot-holes were visible across the river between winter and summer water marks and yet others still higher up, forming a conspicuous feature of the otherwise smooth bare cliffs which dipped sheer into the river; but on the left or shaded bank dense vegetation prevailed wherever tree, shrub, or rock-plant could secure a foothold. The further north we went the more rich and varied became the vegetation of the rainy belt, though the paucity of forest trees, except deep down in the gullies, was always conspicuous.

Shales and slates, dipping at very high angles, and often vertical, alternated with limestone, through which the river had cut its way straight downwards; but at one spot, where an enormous rapid had been formed, huge boulders of a dark-green volcanic rock, like lava, with large included fragments, lined the shore and were piled in confusion below cliffs of slate.

It is at sunset that the charm of this wonderful valley is displayed at its best, for the sun having dropped out of sight behind the western range still sends shafts of coloured light pulsing down the valley, rose, turquoise, and pale-green slowly chasing each other across the sky till darkness sets in and the stars sparkle gloriously. It is long after dawn when the sleeping valley wakens to floods of sunlight again, and the peaks which stand sentinel over it, blotting out the views to north and south, lose the ghastly grey pallor of dimly-lit snow.

A Tibetan festival

The Tibetan festival itself seemed more in accord with the usages of *nat* propitiation than with lamaism, except that it was eminently cheerful, and the people, led by their priests, went to the summits of the three nearest hills to east, north, and west in turn, in order to burn incense and pray; after which they ate cakes. The first day however was devoted entirely to the amusement of the children, for Tibetan mothers, as I frequently observed, are warm-hearted creatures with a great affection for their offspring.

Dressed in their best frocks, and wearing all the family jewels brought out for the occasion, they went up into the woods in the afternoon, picked bunches of flowers just as English children love to do, romped, made swings and swung each other, and finally sat down to eat cakes, which they had been busily making for a week past.

Just as the young of different animals more nearly resemble each other than do the adults, so too are children very much alike in their games the world over; picnicking is not confined to Hampstead Heath, nor picking flowers to botanists.

In the evening they all trooped back to the village to dance in the mule square, and skip. Three or four little girls would link arms and facing another similar line of girls advance and retreat by turns, two steps and a kick, singing, in spite of their harsh voices, a not unmusical chorus; the other side would then reply, and so it went on, turn and turn about.

It was a most delightful parody of that pretty little Christmas game 'Here we go gathering nuts and may', and I enjoyed watching it though I did not understand the words, which were probably less ingenuous than in the ditty quoted. But the girls themselves, in their long frocks of dark-blue cloth buttoned up one side and trimmed with a narrow border of white, long-sleeved jacket to match, scarlet cloth boots, and tasselled queues, looked charming. All wore several silver bangles, besides ear-rings and large brooches, practically all the jewellery they could find room for.

The boys played together, but were less resourceful than the girls and, as in other parts of the world, never seemed to know quite what to do with themselves. They wore smart white coats for the great occasion, but favoured Chinese dress, and probably they are made to do so in the schools in Atuntzu, for one never sees a small boy belonging to the village in Tibetan dress. One boys' game is however worth mentioning. They call it 'eggs' and it is played as follows. One boy is in the middle – a fundamental necessity in nearly all children's romps – and sprawled on all fours over several pebbles, representing a bird sitting on a nest of eggs, which the others, who danced round, were trying to despoil. When a favourable opportunity offered itself, one of the pillagers would dart at the eggs, and if he secured one without being kicked or hit, he was deemed to have been successful; otherwise the mother bird who pivoted round with much agility, kicking out right and left, in front and behind, put him temporarily out of action – metaphorically speaking.

Praying for rain

One night I camped to leeward of a magnificent Asclepias tree in full bloom, which perfumed the night air. The cicadas were chirping all round, the Mekong could be heard thudding over the rocks below the village, and so brilliant was the moonlight that I was able to write my diary in the open air. And sitting there, I heard above the voice of nature yet another sound, the sound of drums being wildly beaten. Presently there came into view a procession of villagers headed by priests, carrying fragrant torches of pine-wood, sticks of smouldering incense, drums, gongs, and red sign-boards on which various Chinese characters were depicted.

Outside the tiny village temple an altar had been erected, and a fire crackled lustily at the entrance, sending a dense column of smoke up into the air. On the altar were trivial offerings of grain to the gods, and no doubt many paper prayers were burned and wafted to them on the breeze. Then the procession marched round and round the altar, and passed into the fields, waving the torches madly, while the noise grew louder. They were praying for rain.

The Lutzu tribe

The Lutzu tribe, amongst whom we now found ourselves, are interesting for the reason that they seem to indicate an irruption of tribes from the west. That they have come *down* the Salween valley from Tibet, representing one of the links in a chain of emigration in that direction, I do not believe, and so far as language is any test, the Lutzu tongue seems to bear no more resemblance to Tibetan than could be accounted for by the fact that the Lutzu are a small tribe enclosed by Tibetans who, being great travellers and traders, have long been in and out amongst them. The English language has been influenced in much the same way by Norman, but is not related to it.

The Lutzu on the other hand are not traders at all, being in the enviable position of having everything they require, hemp for their clothes which are woven by the women during the winter, tobacco, maize, wheat, buckwheat, apples, oranges, and so on. Bamboos and gourds supply them with vessels, and with the cross-bow they shoot game. Though not a drunken people, they certainly drink large quantities of liquor made by fermenting maize; but this beverage, which is of the consistency of pea-soup and is taken warm, is probably more nourishing than inebriating. In the winter men and women sit round the fire for hours at a stretch, chatting, smoking, and drinking. It is meat and drink and medicine to them, and by no means unpalatable.

The men wear their pig-tails down, not bound on the top of the head as do the Tibetans, and their dress, though simple, is not unpicturesque – short breeches (probably copied from the Chinese) and shirt of white hemp cloth, trimmed round the collar and sleeves with light blue, and strips of cloth wound loosely round the calf, like puttees. The women wear a single long-sleeved garment usually of dark-blue cotton cloth, reaching below the knees and tied round the waist, and frequently a hempen cloak, extending across the chest from the right shoulder to the left arm-pit, is added. A hempen bag, decorated with seeds but of plain workmanship, is slung over the shoulder, and it may be remarked that similar bags are carried by most of the tribes west of the Mekong, but not by the Tibetans or Mosos. They usually bind the pig-tail round the head, after the style of the Tibetan women, but there is little jewellery worn. Some of the girls before childbirth are extraordinarily handsome. Their complexion is decidedly lighter than that of the Tibetans, but not so sallow as that of the Chinese; the features are regular, the nose well bridged, the eyes large and round, the high cheek-bones scarcely prominent.

The religion of this people is a modified form of lamaism, but I believe this has been clumsily grafted on to a much older cult, probably *nat* propitiation, for in common with the Lisu and other tribes they hang up special corn cobs in their houses, which are, I think, in the nature of propitiatory offerings to the Penates, a practice which is not observed by the Tibetans at all. How far their Buddhism differs from the degraded form current in Tibet, I cannot say, for the only rite I ever saw anyone perform was when the young lady of the house took up a jug of water, and made the sign of the cross over the household fire by throwing water across it to north, south, east, and west. She did it in a very business-like way, just as she might have fed the chickens, the first shower hitting the wall behind, and the last one drenching me.

I find it difficult to escape the conviction that the Lutzu, now essentially an agricultural people, represent a jungle tribe in a comparatively advanced stage of civilization. Their short stature, their method of carrying loads by means of a strap passing round the forehead, their use of the cross-bow, pre-eminently a jungle weapon for jungle warfare owing to its short range and diabolical effectiveness, their gourds and bamboo tubes, and their rope bridges, all suggest this.

La-kor-ah to Men-kong

La-kor-ah consists of three huts and a temple, in the shadow of which the tent was pitched. It was a sanctified spot, and dozens of prayer-flags made it look larger than it really was, while on each side of the temple stood a row of big leather prayer-drums, much the worse for wear, containing probably hundreds of yards of the everlasting prayer. Each passer-by set them revolving one by one, the rusty spindles groaning fearfully in their sockets. Immediately below, a grey glacier torrent came booming through a deep sword-cut in the mountains and, sweeping down into the mighty Salween, was instantly engulfed in a surge of yellow waters. Up this narrow rift lay the pilgrims' road to sacred Doker La. Here Gan-ton learnt from the residents that the French traveller M. Bacot was at Men-kong with a large number of mules, and I looked forward to meeting him; but in this country one rarely hears the truth of a story the first time of asking.

Next day's march through a terribly arid and totally uninhabited stretch of the valley was a tiring one, though the track was surprisingly good. The river swept in huge S-shaped curves round colossal buttresses, smashed its way through deep gorges, and roared over the boulders. Immense screes, sometimes smoking with the dust of falling rocks, rose bare and lifeless on either hand, and the ceaseless scorching wind, which seemed to suck the vitality from everything, blew throughout the day with ever-increasing violence. Once in crossing a scree I narrowly escaped being hurled into the river by a small avalanche, but hearing a peculiar noise I glanced upwards in time to see a cloud of rocks whizzing through the air, whereupon I turned and ran, reaching safety just as they hummed past.

Under that incandescent sky, stretched like a tongue of fire up the valley, the place became an oven, but the mountains to east and west were as usual buried in cloud. However, from the village of Chia-na we watched the sun sink in a wild blaze of colour behind Men-kong, now only a few miles distant. Above Chia-na a narrow stony valley to the east led to another pass across the watershed. The lama caravans which pass through Atuntzu go this way to Lhasa, joining the main road again at Chiamdo, to the north of Men-kong.

Passing between boulders of granite amongst which grew masses of Opuntia now in flower, we reached the capital of Tsa-rüng before mid-day, and leaving the men to fix the camp Gan-ton and I crossed to the right bank by the rope bridge and climbed the cliff.

Men-kong is built on an alluvial fan washed down from the

mountains by two converging torrents and ending abruptly in a bluff some six or seven hundred feet high, the Salween – here almost continuously interrupted by rapids – flowing in a deep trench below. Scattered down the slope are the big two-storied 'manor' houses, standing amongst fields of waving corn and shaded by magnificent walnut trees; the contrast between the golden barley and the olive-green foliage, from amongst which the white houses peeped out here and there, was charming.

Up on the hillside, almost under the shadow of the forest, stands the ancient monastery, its splendour dimmed by the ravages of time, unheeded by the priests and people, and westwards the neglected road winds away over the mountains to the plains of Assam. The stone-paved courtyard facing the temple is empty now, and the heavy doors of the temple itself are locked. Only the wind sighs gently through the sombre *arbor vitae* trees which spring up here and there amongst the courts and little wooden houses, some of them decked with flowers where the priests reside, and the ragged prayer-flags flutter merrily. Even as I stroll through the deserted courtyard, its red and white walls almost flashing in the brilliant June sunshine, I hear the rise and fall of the flails and the chorus of Tibetans singing perhaps their harvest song.

A Tibetan wedding

Two days later, that is on June 27, we reached Atuntzu, the journey having extended over twenty-five days, and been fairly successful in results. As in the corresponding region of the Salween valley, the weather remained fine coming up through the arid region of the Mekong, though all day long heavy masses of cloud rested on the mountains to east and west, and the usual local wind got up at midday without ever affecting the movement of the clouds. Never more than a few drops of rain at a time – the dregs from the cloud-fringe – fell in the valley itself at this period.

My landlord had gone away to get married during our absence, the ceremony consisting of fetching the woman and bringing her to his house, no doubt after exchanging presents with the parents. He turned up the day after my arrival, driving several donkeys laden with supplies, chiefly presents from his father-in-law.

Behind him came his wife, dressed, I imagine for the first and last time in her life, in new and clean clothes, with a friend on either side holding her hands, while she coyly looked at the ground. Escorting the party came a crowd of shouting children carrying bunches of flowers, while the villagers stood around in groups to see the triumphal entry. In the evening there was a horrid orgy directly under my room, and everybody got gloriously drunk. Two days later I was called in to prescribe for the bride. On the whole, however, it was nothing like such a popular holiday as a funeral we had in the village a few months later, which was attended by the whole community.

At Atuntzu

From the time the snow disappears towards the end of May till the grass withers and winter sets in about the end of September, the herdsmen camp in the big mountain valleys, fattening their flocks of sheep and yak on the rich alpine grassland, from 14,000 to 16,000 feet above sea level. Once or twice Gan-ton and I had been caught in heavy rainstorms when high up in the alpine pastures, and had resorted to these herdsmen's tents for shelter and refreshment.

A small ridge-tent of brown hemp cloth, the sides pegged down and weighted with stones, one end built against a rock or stuffed up with branches, the other open to the winds – this is the home of the Tibetan herdsmen for four months of the year, while his food consists of *tsamba*, tea, butter, and sour milk. There is just enough room for three or four to squat cross-legged round the fire in the middle, which fills the tent with pungent smoke. The remaining space is occupied by the leather bags of *tsamba*, the wooden cylinders for making tea, and the wooden milk-pails, so dirty with clotted curds that milk drawn into them rapidly turns sour. The men dress in the skins of animals and huddle by day round the fire, sleeping at night on beds of pine branches. An altar is always rigged up at the far end of the tent, and here a single butter-lamp splutters, faintly illuminating small offerings of *tsamba* or barley grains, and clay ikons of the crudest form, daubed with pats of butter.

Kin one morning watched a herdsman rush out from a tent with his long gun, kneel, and fire at a dark object which was moving coolly up the mountain slope with a lamb in its mouth. It was a leopard. These marauders, which stalk the mountains in broad daylight, are a constant source of alarm to the herdsmen, though they never dare attack any but isolated animals. At night they descend to the lower valleys, several having been reported in the neighbourhood of Atuntzu while I was there, and in the winter they come right down into the village, though I never saw one myself. Deer, however, and precipice sheep I saw on several occasions, and sometimes when camping in the forest I would awake in the dead of night to hear Ah-poh [his mastiff] barking furiously at the entrance to my tent, as some denizen of the mountains prowled by.

On July 21 a great Mahommedan festival known as the *ho-pa-hwei* was held in Atuntzu in honour of a certain Ming Emperor, called Pei-wang or the White King, who came from Talifu.

Outside many of the houses, torches ten or twelve feet high had been built by tying bundles of pine-sticks in tiers round a central pole, the entire structure being decorated with flowers, branches of green leaves, and paper flags, making a gay show. As soon as it was dark, crackers were fired as a signal for the revels to begin, and immediately afterwards the big torches were lighted at the top; and looking down the street one saw by the light of these beacons which smoked and crackled on either side the black figures of people dancing.

Everyone was out of doors. Processions of boys formed up and ran round the village, and so along the hill paths above the cultivated slopes, waving fire-brands and whirling round glowing sticks snatched from the torches. The principal Mohammedan merchants had decorated and lighted up the family altars, and engaged musicians to beat drums and cymbals to exorcise all the devils which had gathered during the year, and the din went on all night. Large grotesquely-swollen lanterns swung to and fro in the evening breeze, feasting was carried on till a late hour, and everybody got very drunk in honour of the White King. Altogether it was a most successful carouse.

Tibetan dancers

After supper as I lay on my mattress in the tiny room allotted to me, writing up my journal by the light of several pine-wood chips blazing on a stone, in stalked three Tibetans, all of them over six feet high. Their coarse gowns were tied up above their knees, the right shoulder thrust jauntily out exposing the deep muscular chest, and they were bootless. One of them carried a fiddle, consisting of a piece of snake-skin stretched over a bamboo tube with strings of yak hair, upon which he scraped vigorously with a yak-hair bow.

There was little enough room, but my visitors soon lined up, stuck out their tongues at me in greeting, and began to dance, to and fro, up and down, twirling round, swaying rhythmically to the squeaky notes of the violin (there were only about two notes on which to ring the changes), and singing in high-pitched raucous voices. Presently three women joined in, all tricked out in their best skirts and newest boots, with cloaks flung negligently over their shoulders. Thus they went through many of their national songs and dances, and in justice to my sex I must say the men danced with more skill and grace than did the women, though of course it is easier to dance heel and toe, bare-footed like the men, than in the clumsy boots and skirts worn by the women.

I can still picture the scene in that dim little smoke-blackened room, the rain lashing down outside, and the roar of the river just below us, while I lay back on my bed enjoying it hugely, all cares forgotten. Those great giants of men looked strangely weird in the flickering light of the blazing torches which flared up and burnt down alternately; the wail of the fiddle rose and fell, the voices blended, and broke, and ceased, and still they danced on, up and down, to and fro. They danced for two hours in all, and in return for the little present I gave them would willingly have gone on till midnight, had I not told Gan-ton I wanted to go to sleep.

A brawl at Ndu-er

At the next village, called Ndu-er, all the women and children flocked out to have a look at the stranger, dogs barked, and everyone talked and shouted at the same time; then two of the men, in spite of the soldier's orders, insisted on unloading one of the ponies, whereupon he jumped down in a great rage and, picking up two rocks each the size of a quartern loaf, flung them

with all his force at the offender standing but a few feet from
him. The first missed its mark, nearly brained a child standing
just behind, and ricochetted off the ground on to the hind quarters
of a dog, who went off yelping; but the second one caught the
victim fair and square amidships, luckily just where the sleeves
of his gown were tied round the waist, making a thick pad. He
doubled up like a shot rabbit, but apparently no serious damage
was done; still, I should not like to have been the recipient of the
missile. I now interfered and through Gan-ton put a stop to
reprisals. Every man carries a sword here and we should have
seen them bared next minute.

Over the A-löng La

We camped on a grassy flat amidst poplars and firs at an altitude
of about 12,000 feet and awoke to find it snowing.

Once *en route*, riding soon became intolerable, for my feet and
hands were nearly frozen, so I clambered up through the forest
on foot. When we stopped for lunch under some junipers near
the tree-limit the snow was whirling down thicker than ever;
nothing was visible but grey clouds, trees laden with snow, and
a world of falling flakes. Through the heavy mists everything
loomed white and indistinct, and once out of the forest we got
the full benefit of the wind. Granite had given place to the usual
limestone capping this range, but of the fine scenery we were
now coming into I could see little. The valley head was blocked
by a rounded hummock of rock over which the stream poured
in several small cascades, but this obstacle we outflanked, reaching
an open plateau-like valley covered with dwarf rhododendron,
but now buried under deep snow. We could not see more than a
hundred yards in any direction, but presently we entered a narrow
stony gulley with tremendous scree-slopes rising steeply on either
hand to the splintered limestone towers which had given birth to
them. It was a most desolate scene and the going was very bad,
for, the gulley being blocked by large boulders, it was necessary
to traverse the scree itself.

Finally we scrambled up a wall of rock to the actual pass, where
our troubles really began, for we had turned to the north. It was
difficult to arrive at an approximation of the altitude from a
comparison of the vegetation on the two sides, on account of the

snow, but evidently we were somewhere near the limit of plants on both north and south slopes, so that 17,000 feet is probably a near estimate for the A-löng La, which is considerably higher than the Tsa-lei La, marked 15,800 feet on Major Davies's map.

Across the path the snow was much deeper, and very soft; men and ponies slipped on the loose scree, and we had to go dead slow. But it was the wind whistling over the passes and dashing the snow in our faces which made me call myself a fool for coming and vow I would never do such a thing again. Sensation almost left my feet after a time, but I continued to ride my pony, having no desire to slither about on these treacherous screes and roll in the snow as the men frequently did, though more than once the pony looked like turning a somersault.

I noticed a lot of *Meconopsis speciosa* lower down, but somehow the wind rattling amongst the dead haulms gave me a momentary distaste for botany.

The last of the Mekong

This was the last we were destined to see of the great Mekong river. I was scarcely sorry to say goodbye, for the Mekong gorge – one long ugly rent between mountains which grow more and more arid, more and more savage as we travel northwards (yet hardly improve as we travel southwards) – is an abnormality, a grim freak of nature, a thing altogether out of place. Perhaps I had not been sufficiently ill-used by this extraordinary river to have a deep affection for it. The traveller, buffeted and bruised by storm and mountain, cherishes most the foe worthy of his steel. Nevertheless there was a strange fascination about its olive-green water in winter, its boiling red floods in summer, and the everlasting thunder of its rapids. And its peaceful little villages, some of them hidden away in the dips between the hills, others straggling over sloping alluvial fans or perched up on on some ancient river-terrace where scattered blocks of stone suggest the decay of a ruined civilization – all these oases break the depressing monotony of naked rock and ill-nourished vegetation, delighting the eye with the beauty of their verdure and the richness of their crops.

Happy people! What do they know of the strife and turmoil of the western world? We wear ourselves out saving time in one

direction that we may waste it in another, hurrying and ever
hurrying through time as if we were disgusted with life, but these
people think of time not in miles an hour but according to the
rate at which their crops grow in the spring, and their fruits ripen
in the autumn. They work that they and their families may have
enough to eat and enough to wear, living and dying where they
were born, where their offspring will live and die after them, as
did their ancestors before them, shut in by the mountains which
bar access from the outer world.

A crowded night

As it was obvious that we could not possibly reach Lu-k'ou before
midnight, we decided to halt at a hut perched up on the hillside
in front of us, the firelight of which shone out brightly through
the open door. We reached this retreat about ten o'clock, just as
the moonlight flooded into the valley, turning night into day,
and found a number of men lying round the fire, for it was
bitterly cold now. Two boards were soon procured, laid across
two tubs, and my bed made up, but the hut, though well thatched
and eminently capable of keeping out the rain, had not been built
with a view to keeping out the cold. It was, indeed, more like a
rude stockade than a house, the walls consisting simply of tree-
trunks in the rough, planted vertically in the ground and held
together by occasional cross-pieces. Consequently, not only were
there big gaps in the walls, but the eaves at either end from the
top of the wall to the ridge-pole were entirely open, and sleeping
right up against this airy partition I awoke at an early hour half
frozen.

People now began to rise in every direction, and I found that
there were altogether fourteen of us asleep in the one room of
that hut, our own party contributing but four. However, this fact
caused no inconvenience whatever, for the hut was of ample
dimensions and, as already stated, extremely well ventilated.

I was particularly impressed with the manner in which the
womenfolk of the family, who were allotted the other end of
the room, contrived their nocturnal arrangements; for they were
packed into their bed or, to be more precise, under their quilt,
with the skill we are accustomed to associate with the fitting of
sardines into a box just too small for them. That is to say, the

mother had one end of the quilt all to herself, as befitted her position, while from the other end, where one would naturally have expected her feet to be, peeped the heads of her eldest daughter, a girl of about sixteen, and two small children; a confused lump in the middle suggested a tangle of legs, the plank bedstead being no longer than bedsteads usually are.

It fell to the lot of the eldest daughter – who was in the exasperating position of being young enough to do the housework for her mother and old enough to look after her little sisters – to arise first and, having lit the fire, swept the floor, fed the pigs, and washed herself, to get hot water for everybody else. The mother followed half an hour later, but the two small girls having, doubtless for purposes of warmth, slept naked, appeared somewhat loath to get up under the eye of a white man, even though well screened beneath their quilt. Two little heads of towzled hair peeped out from cover, and two pairs of large black eyes, round with wonder, having stared at me for some time, looked at each other and laughed shyly. Presently they also dexterously slipped on a garment apiece and, emerging from their end of the quilt, stood shivering in the cold.

Halt at Kai-t'ou

Pursuing our way we crossed endless rice-fields and at dusk reached the market village of Kai-t'ou, a mean and dirty little place whose inhabitants crowded round the inn door as though even the building itself had been grotesquely affected by my presence. Certainly they could not see me, for, having been free from this type of curiosity throughout my travels, I found it sufficiently unbearable at the end, and hid securely in my room.

In fact the only good word I can conscientiously put in for Kai-t'ou is that, the early mornings being bitterly cold, with hard frosts, everybody was supplied with a small bamboo basket containing an earthenware pot full of red-hot charcoal, to be carried about whether one is engaged in sweeping the room or cooking the food or waiting impatiently for breakfast, as I was. This device, however, is by no means peculiar to the locality.

But if I excited curiosity, it was nothing to the furore created by the appearance of Ah-poh. Never a man passed us without remarking on his size, or the length of his hair, or his entirely

unique figure, and on the following day he had the satisfaction
of stampeding an entire caravan of mules, who doubtless thought
he was some wild animal escaped from the jungle. After this little
incident, Ah-poh meanwhile turning round to me with a pleased
'See what I've done!' sort of expression, I thought it expedient to
lead him by a rope when passing pack-mules, though even then
they sidled past him in the gutter with an eye open for possibilities.

'The Land of Deep Corrosions'

Convinced as I am that with its wonderful wealth of alpine flowers, its numerous wild animals, its strange tribes, and its complex
structure it is one of the most fascinating regions of Asia, I believe
I should be content to wander over it for years. To climb its
rugged peaks, and tramp its deep snows, to fight its storms of
wind and rain, to roam in the warmth of its deep gorges within
sight and sound of its roaring rivers, and above all to mingle with
its hardy tribesmen, is to feel the blood coursing through the
veins, every nerve steady, every muscle taut.

TWO

The Mystery Rivers of Tibet
1913–14

Ominous greeting – The forest of winds and waters – Dinner with Chinese merchants – Madness of the mountains – Hoa village – Last night at Londré – Arrival at Kábu – A dispute settled – A party of Kiutzu – An unruly servant – Truculence of the Lisu – Through the granite gorge – Last stage to Atuntzu

Ominous greeting

The path no longer follows the cliff edge, but winds its way up the steep slope of the mountains. Just above the temple, many hundreds of feet above the glacier, is an unmistakable fragment of moraine, buried in the forest, evidently a continuation of the moraine below.

Numerous streams, at first sliding stealthily down bare rock slabs, presently leap over the precipice on to the glacier below. Finally we emerged on to a natural platform, where, on the very brink of the chasm, stood a second wooden temple. Below, the cliff fell away sheer for hundreds of feet to the glacier, and we had a superb view of the snow-peaks at the head of the valley, and of the wonderful ice-fall opposite: even as we looked there came a crack which brought us all to our feet in time to see a huge ice pillar sway for a moment, totter drunkenly, and fall with a roar that went bellowing down the valley, frightening a cloud of green parrots from the trees. So that was our greeting! and indeed the thunder of avalanche and crumbling sérac was with us day and night, becoming more continuous as the summer advanced. By midsummer the glacier for a long way below the fall was white with splintered ice as a rocky coast with salt sea spray. It seemed to me that the glacier must be moving at a fair pace, to judge by the frequency with which these séracs toppled over the brink.

The forest of winds and waters

Trapped between granite cliffs several hundred feet high, the only way out was up one of the flues which slit the walls of our prison. These flues had vomited out cone-shaped screes which spread fanwise into the valley; below were massive boulders, covered with a dense growth of shrubs; towards the apex the carpet of vegetation was striped with long gashes, flogged raw by the continual rain of stones. To reach the topmost cliffs, one had to buffet a way through the bamboo brake, scramble from boulder to boulder amidst tangled shrub growth, and finally ascend the slipping gravel which grew ever steeper, to the broken rocks; then climb up by narrow chimneys, clinging precariously to dwarf bushes. Everyone's life hung on a chance. I have lain awake in my tent when moonlight flooded the meadow and listened to the roar of the rock avalanche rolling from cliff to cliff; and looking across the valley, all black and silver, when the frantic noise has died away to a whisper, and only the owl is hooting gently, and the stream humming to itself, seen the white fog of dust hovering over our own gully – the very one we had climbed that afternoon. And I have raced across the scree for my life, and ducked panting under the friendly shelter of a cliff.

Dinner with Chinese merchants

One evening I was invited to dinner with the local Chinese merchants. At five o'clock we sat down ten at a table, some thirty guests in all. Everyone was provided with a pair of chopsticks and a china wine-cup, but there were no napkins, and the Chinamen used their sleeves freely. No ladies were present; they are as rigorously excluded from these functions as from a college 'hall' at Cambridge. Half-naked cooks now came dashing in from the kitchen next door with steaming bowls full of chopped liver, sprouting beans, pickled eggs, sea-cucumbers, birds' nests, sharks' fins, bamboo shoots, and other exotic delicacies. Then, armed with chopsticks, we all set to, finicking in the bowls for titbits like a flock of sparrows. Presently the wine began to circulate, and to the business-like clapping of chopsticks and curious noises made by obese Celestials shovelling hot rice into capacious mouths was added uproarious laughter. I say wine, but that is a poetic licence. It is called *shao-chiu* or burning spirit; it is the colour of gin and tastes like methylated spirit. Luckily the wine-cups are no bigger than liqueur glasses, since you must drink; to refuse would be a serious breach of etiquette. Moreover, it is necessary to play for drinks three rounds with each guest at your table: a strange game, showing fingers and shouting a number. Every time you shout the number corresponding to the total of fingers shown, you lose – and drink forfeit. A rapid calculation assured me that I was in imminent peril of twenty-seven drinks; but happily I won several times. The fun waxed fast and furious. Men were shouting across the room to each other, rocking with helpless laughter. At this point the tables were cleared and the cooks came rushing in again with what at first I mistook for clay-coloured pancakes; however, they turned out to be only hand towels dipped in hot water and wrung out. Each guest received one, and now red-faced men mopped their fevered brows. Finally, chopsticks were wiped clean on sleeves and put away, and the guests, talking and laughing noisily, tumbled out into the street; as for me, I went to bed and stayed there quite a long time.

Madness of the mountains

It is evident that the Ka Karpo peaks can best be climbed from the Mekong valley. By far the best climbing season is the autumn and early winter, from the middle of October till the middle of December, when, in spite of the cold, fine weather can be almost guaranteed. In summer, though there is often fine weather for a week or ten days at a stretch, especially in June, climbing is probably more difficult, if not impossible, on account of ava-lanches.

I had no particular ambition to set foot on any of these virgin peaks myself; yet I sometimes wondered, as I gazed on them in the pink glow of sunset, when the lightning rippled across the sky far down the valley, and the setting planets glowed big, whether their future conqueror would ever think of me, follow my routes, and find my camping grounds. Sitting thus, outside my tent under the brilliant stars, I watched the moon rise over the Pai-ma-shan, till, from high in the heavens, it shed a ghastly radiance on the tortured glacier below; and as I mused, the dead heroes of the mountains seemed to wander out of the night into the glow of the firelight, and pass silently before me – Mummery, hero of a hundred climbs, Whymper, whose name is imperishably associated with the disastrous triumph on the Matterhorn, and many others, men whose iron nerve had never deserted them in the supreme moment; they were, I thought, kindred spirits in this madness of the mountains; but looking up from the flickering fir-logs I found myself alone . . . an ice pillar crashed to ruin, with a tremendous roar, and the dog-star rose under Orion, scintillating like a diamond.

Hoa village

Night had fallen before we reached the valley, and it was pitch dark when at last we heard the barking of dogs and lights began to show up in Hoa village.

Guided by a fearful din, we approached the first house; and saw, in the ruddy glare of pine-torches, a crowd of priests and others engaged with drums, cymbals, trumpets and oft-repeated prayers in exorcising the devil from a sick man. The noise alone would have been enough to drag any but a helpless invalid very quickly from his bed.

At our unexpected appearance out of the darkness the noise ceased, and the fact that the crowd was by this time hilariously merry, in spite of the solemn occasion which had brought them together, added to the usual warmth of a Tibetan greeting. We were now escorted to another house and made comfortable by the fire. Food and drink were set before us, and my guides were very soon as drunk as our hosts; but personally, being hungry after twelve hours' marching, I only sipped the raw spirit.

So we sat round the fire while my two men talked as long as they could of the day's adventures, and I cooked myself a meal; it was all very enjoyable and homely – the young wife with a baby at her breast baking flapjacks on an iron pan, our tall unkempt loose-limbed host, the dark room with the circle of faces lit up by the glow of the fire fading into darkness where outlines became suggested rather than seen, and my two tired men sprawling anyhow on the floor.

Afterwards I went up on to the roof and lay down as I was, in a pile of straw, and, covering myself up with a blanket, soon fell fast asleep under the stars; while a warm breeze floated up out of

the Mekong valley and rustled through the trees, and at intervals
the summer lightning flashed out palely.

Last night at Londré

On the last night of our stay I went across to the boulder beneath
which the Tibetans were camped. In the purple dusk the younger
ones went forth to collect firewood and herbs for the evening
meal. Presently someone climbed up on to the rock and sang out:
'Come, friends, supper is ready.' One by one they wandered
back, some carrying bundles of faggots, others with lily bulbs,
garlic and toadstools, and all hungry. A large iron pot bubbled
over the fire, and into this were thrown various leaves, a pinch
of coarse salt, and lumps of butter. Then the wooden bowls were
brought out and each received a portion of soup. Meanwhile,
buttered tea was being churned in the tall wooden cylinders till
it frothed, skin bags of barley flour were untied, butter boxes
opened, and the Tibetans now set about their meal in earnest.

The night was fine. Through the trees one could see the constel-
lations rolling majestically across the swarthy sky. Someone
began to twang a little bamboo jew's harp, to which was presently
added the mournful wail of a reed whistle. Outside, the night
wind blew softly, making the trees scrape against each other as
though whispering secrets; an owl hooted plaintively, and the
torrent grated over the gravel. Suddenly the silence was rent by
a clatter and roar as an avalanche of rock emptied itself down one
of the gullies.

My companions were a strange lot of scarecrows. One girl
with a huge goitre was deaf and dumb, and one of the men,
similarly burdened with two goitres which dangled in a pouch of
his neck, was blind in one eye and stone deaf. There was an oldish
man who was nearly bald, and an undersized thickset little man
with a pock-marked face. One old woman had but two teeth in
her head, and immense eyes like a fish. Finally, there was a tall
man with thick curly hair and a prominent nose, a very good
fellow; and a pretty little girl, slightly disfigured by goitre, who
was the life and soul of the party, always singing, laughing or
dancing. She kept everyone in good spirits – but indeed all were
merry and cheerful. The deaf and dumb carried on a spirited

language by signs, from which I at any rate learnt that hooking the two little fingers together signified firm friendship.

Meanwhile, those swains who were the fortunate possessors of lady-loves pillowed their heads on their mistresses' laps, and had their hair done. The sham queue (made of blue wool, carefully plaited) was first unwound and detached, the hair combed out, buttered and plaited; and the false queue, with its section of elephant's tusk threaded on it, hooked into position. Finally, the whole was rebound on top of the head.

Arrival at Kábu

Over the top of the ridge, only a few hundred feet high, we see huge portals framing the entrance to a wild rocky valley, lying south-west, and it is here that the river finally wriggles its way out of this mountain maze and turns bravely to meet the Salween. In the failing light the view down the valley, girded by giant rock ribs, is wildly imposing. Terrific gusts of wind buffet us in the face as we continue down the river, and I find the greatest difficulty in taking compass bearings. Now the pink glow, which for an hour has lingered, changes to silver as the moon rises into a sky of palest blue, illuminating bands of white road. I feel in the highest spirits, and sing as we march along in the warm darkness under the brilliant dome of night.

Soon I am far ahead of the porters – only my guide has gone on with the ponies, and except for the splash of the river down below and shrieking gusts of wind which whirl up thick clouds of dust, the night is very still. Presently I am standing on the summit of a high spur, a deep gully into which the moonlight can find no way, below. Looking back, a snow-peak is seen glittering in the north, and the moonlight has turned the river to quicksilver.

The descent is steep and stony, I trip frequently, and have to go cautiously. At last I reach the bottom in safety, cross the gully, and ascend a little way up the opposite side. Silence everywhere. For some minutes I stand listening. Suddenly I hear dogs barking, and see lights, though it is too dark to make out the village. So I blow several blasts on my whistle and along comes the 'Monkey' with a torch, followed by two strangers. We are arrived at Kábu.

A dispute settled

November 9th was a blazing hot day, and the march down the arid valley was most trying.

After a couple of hours across stony terraces, in places burst open by deep narrow ravines where not a drop of water trickled, the porters halloed to a village on the right bank to send over a relief. A reply having been obtained, we went on slowly, leaving the relief to catch us up, as soon as they had crossed the river by canoe. However, they were unable to bring ponies with them, so when they arrived I insisted on keeping the animals from Jana. Thereupon a dispute arose, a Jana man trying forcibly to unload a pony which was as valiantly defended by one of the newcomers, at my behest.

Meanwhile, to my astonishment, one of the Jana girls who had supplied a pony, thinking, I suppose, that we were going to annex her animal altogether, and being pushed roughly aside when she attempted to lead it home, burst into a flood of tears and went off stamping and sobbing, to sulk like a child.

In order to settle the matter as amicably as possible, and not promote a fight between the opposing factions, I hit the interfering Tibetan from Jana gently on the nose, so that he lay down and bled freely; harmony was immediately restored, and everybody smiled again. Promising to send the animals back from Lakora, we continued on our way.

A party of Kiutzu

Next morning, November 20th, a party of Kiutzu arrived at Tzuli from the Taron. They were an uncouth crowd. Their hair hung matted over their dirty faces, giving the men a girlish appearance. They possessed only two garments apiece, a sort of hempen blanket worn round the waist like a skirt, and another thrown over the shoulders and tied across the chest. They carried light loads in bamboo baskets, long spears, big Shan *dahs* in open wooden sheaths, and war-bows with a span of four or five feet. The arrow-case is usually made from the skin of a silver-grey monkey, with long soft fur, the legs making the shoulder strap, and the two little paws crossed rather pathetically over the lid. These monkeys are the sweetest little animals, with long tails and

black faces – later I saw one alive which a Kiutzu had brought
over with him.

The Kiutzu come to the Salween for salt, Chinese cotton yarn,
and sometimes Chinese garments, breeches and jackets. Cloth is
of no use to them as they do not know how to sew. They bring
in exchange *huang-lien* [*Coptis teeta*, a root used as a drug by the
Chinese], skins (monkey and black bear), musk, and gold dust.

An unruly servant

About three o'clock in the morning I awoke – the rain was
pouring down and whining over the sodden thatch. All that day
it continued without intermission. First thing in the morning Kao
[a Chinese officer] again came to see me and stayed two hours.
He told us now it would be impossible to reach the Taron before
next summer – and what was worse, there was a strong chance
of our being imprisoned in the Salween valley, unable to reach
the Mekong either. We must stay where we were for the present,
as the Lisu refused to travel in the rain. In any case I was too
unwell myself to travel.

That evening Atung suddenly turned up, and began to make
further trouble. After a preliminary shout, he dashed outside and
presently came in again swearing furiously and dragging by the
arm my Tibetan, who cringed before him like a child. I was
sitting huddled up by the remnant of a fire at the time, feeling
very sick, but this was too much. I went at once to the rescue of
the 'Monkey', hitting Atung in the face, so that he fell back with
a bleeding nose, and let go his hold. Then he sprang past me,
shouting for his *dah* and dashed into the next room, I after him;
but just as I clutched him I tripped in the doorway and fell.

Some women in the next room screamed, two men dashed in
between us, pushing me back, and I picked up a big stone from
the fireplace with which to defend myself, and retreated into my
own room. Atung was pacified somehow and led outside, nor
did he appear again that evening. Later he drowned his sorrows
in drink.

It appeared afterwards that he was desperately afraid of Kao
and had determined to leave me, whereupon the 'Monkey' remon-
strated with him. Hence the scene. Subsequently the matter was
referred to Kao, who promised that Atung should see me as far

as Latsa, when he himself would get me another man. This quite satisfied me, for I had had enough of Atung.

Truculence of the Lisu

The start from Chilanda on the 17th was delayed by the truculence of the Lisu, who, having demanded an exorbitant price for porters, wanted the money down, in advance. As it was these very people who had only done half a day's journey, after receiving a day's wages in advance, I refused, whereupon the chief, a very powerful man, threw down his load in a rage and began untying the bamboo head-strap.

'Not so fast,' I said, and held his arm. He turned on me like a wild cat, and I caught him by the neck as he gripped hold of my shirt. For a moment it looked as if there was going to be a free fight, and it would have fared ill with me, for the chief, though a short man, had the arms, chest and shoulders of a Hercules. Then the angry faces of two other men were thrust menacingly into mine, a fist was clenched, a *dah* was bared, and I let go, while my pacific Tibetan danced round shrieking in an agony of apprehension, and the soldier stood by, afraid to say a word. Evidently these people had not forgotten my hammering Atung, and thought me a dangerous person; on the other hand, there is nothing more to be feared than a frightened tribesman. One cannot hope to succeed with such people till one has gained their confidence.

After this little argument had been settled, we started, the Lisu promising to go as far as a small village just beyond Sukin.

Through the granite gorge

It was evening now, the sky very pale, a chill breeze making the leaves flap and rustle and rattle together in the jungle; the mournful song of the Lutzu came to us from across the water, and down below the sandbank we heard the water raging amongst the boulders.

Presently the canoe returned and we jumped in, the Lutzu women standing up in the bows; the long bamboo rope was also paid out and coiled up forward, ready for immediate use. Away we went with a swish of paddles, beneath the towering cliffs which hemmed in the river, till we came to a big pebble bank over which the shallow water tossed and raced, rattling the pebbles together as a retreating wave does on the steep shingly shores of England. Bump! went the heavily laden canoe, and the ill-clad girls leapt over the gunwale into the icy water and ran ahead with the long rope. The water swirled around their knees and wetted their tightly bound skirts, the canoe rocked and yawed as they pulled this way and that, hauling us slowly through the rapids while the men pushed with their paddles, and the sound of a million rattling dice echoed from cliff to cliff. At last we were hauled and pushed into deep water again, the women being in nearly up to their waists before they came aboard, and shortly afterwards we ran ashore on the right bank where was a sandy cove; the canoe was unloaded and pulled ashore, and all hands went to collect firewood from the forest which thinly fringed the cliffs behind.

A cutting wind blew down the valley, and we sought shelter in a trough of the sand, and built windscreens with faggots, and lit the fires. My bedding was laid out on the sand, and as the stars began to glitter above the great Salween river, the 'Monkey' brought me my supper and we sat down to talk. . . .

Now it is dark; the Lutzu women sitting in a circle round the fire, their knees drawn up, their feet and legs bare, their wet skirts pulled tightly round them and an extra wrap thrown over their shoulders, look like ghouls. How cold they must be! The temperature is down to 38°F. now, and their clinging garments are scarcely warmed by the blaze. Yet they do not seem to mind. So they sit in a ring, from time to time filling their wooden bowls with hot maize porridge from the bubbling iron cauldron in the centre. Gradually the talk flags, then ceases; one by one the ill-clad crew nod, a head droops on a breast, and then another, till, sitting as they are in the cold sand and crowding closer and closer to each other for warmth, they sleep.

Last stage to Atuntzu

Three magnificent black and white eagles circled over the desolate mountains. Lower down, the snow had melted and refrozen, and ever-widening slopes of green ice lay spread out over the valley bottom, making the path difficult and dangerous. Ice in a hundred fantastic forms locked the stream between its bush-grown banks. It was nearly dark when we reached our old camp, and finding that the snow lay deep under the trees we camped in the open where we looked straight down the valley to the east, and beheld a belt of light in the sky in which all the most magnificent stars glittered at the same time.

Eighteen degrees of frost in the night, and the stars shining brilliantly. When I awoke before dawn the fires were down, but it was too cold to crawl out and revive them, and the Tibetans were asleep. It was the last camp of our long journey, on which I had set out three months ago. The veil of night lifted slightly in the east and the long ragged chain of the Yangtze-Mekong divide appeared, black against the coming dawn; the great stars which all night long had patrolled the sky were setting; new ones waned, and vanished as they rose. The stream was hushed, frozen solid; not even a breeze whispered through the forest. Now the Tibetans begin to stir; presently they sit up, and the fires are quickly attended to, while snow is melted in the iron pot for tea. At last I crept out from my blanket nest, pulled off my woollen gloves, slipped into a woollen dressing-gown, wrapped myself in an enormous *chupa*, and sitting by the fire drank cup after cup of foaming tea. Then the sun appeared over the mountain rim like a ball of burnished gold, and by eight o'clock we were off, picking our way cautiously down the steep path and over the smooth green ice-slides which confronted us.

Under the trees where the snow lay the going was easy, but in the open it was terrible, especially where we had to cross the glassy stream which had welled over in broad, smooth steps. Beautiful were the sun shafts shining red through the long tattered strips of bark wrenched from the birch trees, and the streamers of green lichen which danced in the breeze. Lovely little crested tits hopped amongst the branches; and when at last, leaving the dark forest, we emerged into the arid gorge to find ourselves looking down once more on the Mekong, now blue as the South China Sea, it was impossible to feel anything but gay.

THREE

In Farthest Burma
1914

A climb from Hpimaw – A paradise of flowers – Village of the dead – Monkey-scarers – A Maru village – Approaching Laking – An eclipse of the moon – A sudden storm – A day's march – Of leeches – Out of the valley of death – Six to dinner

A climb from Hpimaw

Up and up, still climbing steeply, at one time enveloped in a forest of bamboos so thick that one could not see twenty yards into the brake, and all clothed in green moss; at another, out on the open ridge again, brushing through stiff bunches of Pieris, like white heather. Far down the steeply shelving hillside lies the network of tree-girt veins which gather water from ten thousand hidden springs and, overflowing, fling it into the pulsing arteries roaring out of sight.

Grass and bracken grow on this rock-strewn slope, with bushes of blue-washed hydrangea, golden-leafed buddleia and willow. Conspicuous too were slender trees of Enkianthus, from every twig of which hung bunches of striped red cups. In the long grass there sprang up in June – it was but May, when the rhododendrons blotched the mountains with colour – a beautiful Nomocharis with rose flowers speckled with purple at the base, pink geranium, gaudy louseworts and other flowers.

Suddenly in the forest we came upon a shady bank blue with the lovely *Primula sonchifolia* growing in careless luxury, as primroses do in a Kent copse. The path was strewn with fallen corollas, scattered like jewels. It is a charming plant, with rather the habit of an English primrose, a hemispherical umbel of azure-blue flowers, each yellow-eyed, springing from a thickly clustered rosette of dark-green leaves.

Up here it really was still winter – there was snow in one of the gullies.

And now the cold air of the pass itself chilled us, while borne on the wings of the wind came rushing up on every side from invisible valleys the rain-clouds, melting about us as they wrapped round the trees, twisting and whirling through the branches like smoke.

Drip! Drip! Drip! It was the only sound which greeted us, for the torrent was out of earshot in the depths below, and birds are rare and subdued in these gloomy forests – we saw only some long-tailed jays and gaudy woodpeckers. Perhaps even their spirits are oppressed by the ceaseless patter of the rain and the sour smell rising from the sodden leaves whence in a night spring strange and sickly speckled pilei, spawn of perpetual twilight.

A deep gash in the mountain ridge – the pass itself, dipping steeply over into the warm blueness of the Salween valley, across which the sun shone brightly on the wall of mountains opposite, twenty miles away; and across *those* mountains too, deep down in the bowels of the earth, rumbled the red Mekong, another warrior river of Tibet.

We stood now on the rim of the Burmese hinterland, looking into the fair land of China, the threshold of Yunnan, which means 'Southern Cloudland'.

A paradise of flowers

Emerging next day from an oak forest interspersed with rhododendrons and holly, we reached a big stream, its banks so thickly overgrown with bamboo that we had to wade knee-deep through the chilly water of the stream itself. The mules enjoyed this, splashing lustily, and when the sun broke through the clouds and sparkled on the chattering water, it was delightful, save for the leeches which we collected.

Paddling thus slowly up the stream, we came from time to time into the most enchanting meads, where the little valley broadened. Here the grass was purple with *Primula beesiana*, and the shallow waters dotted with tall yellow cowslips, which were not cowslips in fact, but *Primula helodoxa*, growing on the banks, on gravel islands, on fallen tree-trunks, in careless profusion. And there were flowering bushes all round us instead of forest, thickets of buckthorn and rose, wayfaring-tree, barberry and honeysuckle, amongst which sprang up white lilies, tall as grenadiers (*L. giganteum**), marsh marigolds and grasping coils of yellow-flowered

* since renamed *Cardiocrinum giganteum*.

Codonopsis, sunning itself as it sprawled carelessly over the surrounding plants like a rich exquisite.

Most lovely of all, hiding shyly within the dark bamboo groves, was a meadow-rue, its large white flowers borne singly, half nodding amongst the maidenhair leaves, so that in the gloom of the brake they looked like snowflakes floating through a forest of ferns. I called it the snowflake meadow-rue – there is none more beautiful.

'Why, what a paradise of flowers!' I said to my companion. 'Who would have thought that these sorrowful mountains and dim, dripping forests held such treasures!'

'It is pretty,' he replied. 'I thought you might find something interesting at the Feng-shui-ling.'

'Feng-shui-ling! Is that what they call it? Why, that may well mean "the pass of the winds and waters". Certainly there is water enough' (we were still paddling upstream). 'Better did they call it "Hua-shua-lin" – the forest of flowers and waters.'

Village of the dead

Maintaining the pace down, we were out of the forest in an hour next morning, great volumes of cloud rising from the valley towards the summits we had left. We soon reached the Yawyin village, only to learn that the sick woman had died the previous day. But the old man had recovered, and with tears in his eyes thanked me for the medicine I had given him.

I went in to see the dead woman, and in the darkness of the poor hut just made out a figure wrapped in a white cloth which entirely concealed it except for the hands crossed on the breast.

An aged hag, crouched on the mud floor, was watching over it, wailing hopelessly and wringing her hands; from time to time she ceased crying and muttered incantations; then she would burst forth again in mournful wailing that had in it a note of uncontrollable despair, dreadful to hear. In the heavy darkness beyond, where the embers of a fire glowed, a white-haired old man was cooking food, and several children crawled about, playing in the dust, heedless of the ruin round them. In such gloomy surroundings, with the old witch beside it, the corpse, swathed in its coarse hempen winding-sheet, looked horribly like an Egyptian mummy, and I was glad to withdraw from that fallen house.

Outside some men were hammering a coffin together – next day the dead woman would be buried on the cold mountainside.

Monkey-scarers

The maize crop was now ripening, and many are the devices employed to scare away the monkeys which raid the fields by night. On the very steepest slopes a small hut is built at the top, with a long diving-board jutting out, thus overlooking the entire slope below. In this forward observing-post one or two – generally two – people take up position for the night and, when the monkeys come, sally forth and drive them away by making strange noises and throwing things at them. In the slack intervals between raids they make love.

A more ingenious method is to erect bamboo poles with split tops, here and there, attaching a cord to each. When the cord is jerked the split bamboo clacks lustily, and by tying all the cords together and leading the one line to the hut the clappers can with one tug be set clacking simultaneously. Thus all the sentry has to do is to sit in the hut and give the line a sharp tug every few minutes, when alarming noises start up unexpectedly from every corner of the *taungya* [hillside field]. The disadvantage of this method is that, as only one is required on sentry duty, the prospects for love-making are not so good.

Tins are sometimes used instead of split bamboos, and where a stream runs through the *taungya*, the line is stretched out from bank to bank with a float in the shape of a log of wood attached to it, dangling in the water. The rush of the torrent against the float, flinging it this way and that, jerks the rope spasmodically, which in turn rattles tins or clacks bamboos all over the field; thus a more or less continuous noise is kept up, breaking out now here, now there with whimsical uncertainty.

But the most ingenious apparatus of all was worked by means of a hollow log, pivoted in the bed of a torrent. As the stream filled the reservoir with water, the log tipped up, emptied out the water and returned heavily to its original position, hitting a stretched bamboo cord a shrewd blow as it fell back. This in turn jerked a cord attached to all the clappers, which clacked away out on the *taungya* every few minutes as the trough filled and fell, emptied and rose.

A Maru village

Sliding and tripping we came down a tremendously steep hillside in the open, and saw the village of Che-wen below on the left bank of a considerable stream which flowed in a deep valley.

An hour later we were splashing through the sties and mud-holes of a Maru village, its dozen huts standing amongst little fenced-off gardens, where grew beans, tobacco, opium poppies and a few peach-trees. Pigs grunted and scuttled, an odd cow or two stood uncompromisingly in the fairway, and women seated in the porches looked up from their weaving and stared at us. However, we were well received, and soon shown into a house, whereupon the inhabitants crowded round the doorway to gaze at me.

At last I was able to take off my wet clothes, and having started a big fire in the room placed at my disposal, we set to work drying everything.

These huts, made of bamboo matting, raised on stilts, with hard floors of wooden boards laid across beams, narrow verandas and front porch, are small, like the Yawyin huts, not at all like the typical Maru huts of the Nmai valley. Outside the houses are small box-like granaries raised high on four pillars capped with circular discs of wood, which serve to defeat the rats.

Fields of maize and buckwheat slope down to the river. Beyond, the shadowy outlines of high mountains disappear into the rain mists. Up the valley and across the Salween divide, distant eight marches, lies the country of the Shapa Lisus, an evil tribe according to Maru tradition; but this is not altogether surprising, since they wage a continuous defensive warfare against the Chinese, whose ruthless efforts to exterminate them are calculated to sharpen all their latent cunning and cruelty.

Approaching Laking

It seemed doubtful whether we should reach Laking, the village at the confluence of the Laking Hka with the Nmai, that night or not; but I was determined to try, so about five o'clock we set out again.

Continuing the ascent, we were soon high above the river, which plunged down deeper and deeper into the bowels of the earth, till close upon sunset we stood on the last spur and looked clear away westward down the now open valley; and black against the western glare a high range of softly rounded mountains appeared, drawn clean across the horizon. It was the containing wall of the Nmai Hka – the Irrawaddy itself! Behind us grey storm-clouds were piling up on the mountains we had lately crossed, but in front the sun, wrapped in mackerel sky, had turned the clouds into a broad lake of chequered silver.

Numerous deep gullies spun out the journey, and in places steep slabs of granite lay athwart the mountainside, in crossing some of which we experienced difficulty in keeping our balance, so that one of the porters fell and cut himself painfully. At last a deeper rent than usual yawned below us like a wound in the mountainside, but descending the path into complete darkness far below, there was heard only a feeble trickle of water, as though the torrent, exhausted after its hard work of carving out this canyon, had slumbered.

A growl of thunder in the mountains behind now spurred us on, and climbing up from the depths, we reached the first huts of Laking at seven o'clock, just as the rain began. We had been ten hours on the road.

An eclipse of the moon

That night the full moon rose partially eclipsed into a clear sky, and by eight o'clock the eclipse was almost total; it was extraordinary to watch the glowing velvet sky, in which formerly none but the most brilliant stars had been visible, slowly turning black till stars of the second and third magnitude shone out like lamps being lit in a distant city, and the heavens sparkled with the full splendour of a starlight night.

Meanwhile the villagers had become greatly excited, believing that a devil was devouring the moon. A procession formed up and paraded with gongs, which they banged lustily, shouting as they circled round a barrel-shaped drum on which a small boy operated as it lay on the ground. Finally, the procession moved off through the village, carrying the gongs above their heads and flapping their arms to a sort of cakewalk, while a child not much bigger than the tom-tom staggered along with that instrument for another person to hammer.

After a time the efforts of these merry roysterers were rewarded, the devil grew frightened and sicked up the moon even as the whale did Jonah, and presently its silver rim reappeared, and by ten o'clock the exhausted band stood in the full flood of moonlight, their labours ended. As for me, I went to bed.

A sudden storm

A short climb up the opposite spur soon brought us to a village insecurely perched in an exposed position on the hillside, where some slabs of slaty rock stood on edge like low walls; one hut was built close to the brink of a small scarp formed by one of these outcrops. To the west the mountains, in the form of a small horseshoe-shaped bay, stood up very steep and menacing, as it seemed.

Since four-thirty p.m. I had noticed an occasional growl of thunder, and when I looked out of our hut at six-thirty the wind was rising; before eight it was raining, a strong wind was blowing and frequent flashes of lightning illuminated the dark sky; evidently it was working up for a storm.

Quite suddenly it burst upon us with awful fury, the wind blowing with hurricane force. Now the lightning blazed incessantly, flash following flash with such rapidity that we could see everything – bending trees, whirling leaves, and the dark outline of brooding mountains; and to the continuous roll of thunder, like heavy artillery, was added the shriller rattle of drenching rain as it beat viciously on the stiff palm leaves.

The storm simply crashed down on to the village from the mountains, as though someone was tipping barrels full of water and compressed air on top of us.

Water poured through the thatch roof of our hut, bringing with it dirt and leaves which it splashed everywhere, quenching the fires and soaking our belongings; the hut rocked and shook on its piles like a liner in a gale; people screamed, dogs barked; every moment I thought the hut must collapse. Now the voice of the wind in the stiff-leafed sago palms and amongst the tall clumps of bamboo rose to an angry scream, and above all this tumult could be heard the deepening roar of the torrent below.

There came an ominous crash, and a shower of sodden leaves, dirt and debris from the roof littered the room where I sat, the earth floor of which was already a puddle; but in the furious gusts which came raging down the mountainside I could not tell what had happened.

Then the people of our hut, snatching up torches, rushed out into the darkness, scared and weeping, and in the dim light cast by the quivering flames I saw the hut just above ours lying on the ground, a mass of broken beams, torn thatch, and split posts; the wind had simply crumpled it up like brown paper. Around it stood a group of wailing villagers, who seemed more concerned in rescuing a little food and a few stoups of liquor than in looking to see if anyone lay beneath the wreckage, though that may have been because they knew all had escaped. However, one of my men said there were people in the hut when it was blown down, so taking my lamp I climbed up the shattered roof and dropping through a hole found myself in the midst of a dreadful tangle through which it was very difficult to crawl; in this way, partly on my belly, partly on hands and knees, I explored such of the interior as was not absolutely razed to the ground. However, there were no victims. The villagers were somewhat concerned for my safety, as they feared a further settling down of the huge mass, for their huts are enormously long, and it had been simply doubled up. As a matter of fact, little of it could have been laid much flatter than it was already.

Luckily for us this hut stood near us and to windward, otherwise *ours* would have gone! As it was, fragments had beaten against our roof, sending showers of debris into the rooms.

Close by, a second hut, in which less than an hour before a dozen people had been seated round their family hearths, lay a shapeless mass on the ground, but from this too the inhabitants had escaped just in time, so that our further explorations led to no sad discoveries. Had anyone remained in the wrecked hut he must have been crushed by the falling beams, or suffocated beneath the weight of sodden thatch.

After paddling about in the mud outside and delving amongst the wreckage till I was festooned with soot and leaves from the thatch roofs (for chimneys there are none, and the interior of the hut is black with the smoke of generations of fires), while people shouted to me as I crawled here and there to hand out bite and sup which they specially prized, I returned to my quarters, thankful they were safe. The fire had been lit again and T'ung was preparing my dinner, though even here, so much water and

rubbish were scattered about, it looked as though there had been
a small earthquake.

It was nine o'clock and the storm was fast disappearing in the
south-west – you could still hear it, growing fainter and fainter
as it died away down the valley. By nine-thirty it was all over,
the wind hushed, even the thunder too faint to be heard. A great
stillness seemed to come upon the wrecked village as suddenly as
the storm itself had fallen on it.

A day's march

September 21st. – Minimum 62.7°F. It rained steadily all night and
continued most of the day, the longest and most trying march
we had yet done, ten hours in the sodden jungle.

First we continued the descent of the previous evening, crossed
a big torrent, and traversed for some distance, winding our way
round gully after gully. The whole region was a perfect maze of
mountains, cut up by hundreds of streams flowing deep in their
jungle-hidden ravines, and the road was marked by the skeletons
of mules and broken pack-saddles. All the time we were squelching ankle-deep in mud, tortured by leeches which dropped on us
from the trees.

My feet and ankles were now covered with dreadful sores
brought on by being always wet and the bites of leeches which
easily got through my worn-out boots. Every night the continuous irritation would awaken me, or even prevent me getting any
sleep at all sometimes.

A long climb brought us to the top of a ridge, and this we
followed up and down for mile on mile. A gleam of sunshine at
one o'clock was a false alarm, but another gleam about four
proved less fleeting. At five, when I was tramping along mechanically, noticing little, I saw something better than sunshine, for
the white mist between the trees suddenly gave place to a deep
indigo blueness, and I knew what that meant – it was the blueness
of distant mountains. The plains at last! I thought. At the same
moment we began to descend into a deep valley, and presently
the fretted mountains on either side of the ridge showed up
momentarily through the changeful mists; far below we distinctly
heard above the patter of raindrops the unmistakable chatter of a
river.

It was now getting late, and we raced down the almost precipitous path as fast as we could go. Down, down, several thousand feet, till the whirr of cicadas filled the air again, and it grew perceptibly warmer. At last we could see the valley below us, and at six-thirty we reached a considerable river, the Shang Wang, a tributary of the Nam Tisang, which flows into the Mali.

Crossing by a bamboo trestle bridge, we reached a small hut at dark, built by the expedition in the previous year. Never had I been so tired as I was that night. Next day I anticipated an easy walk down the river valley to the plains.

Of leeches

The land leeches, however, were dreadful.

These little fiends are about an inch long and, at a full stretch, no thicker than a knitting needle. They progress similarly to a looper caterpillar, though they are not, of course, provided with legs. Fixing one end, which is expanded into a bell-shaped sucker, the leech curves itself over into a complete arch, fixes the other extremity in the same way and, releasing the rear end, advances it till a close loop is formed. The process is then repeated, the creature advancing with uncanny swiftness in a series of loops. From time to time it rears itself up on end and sways about, swinging slowly round in larger and larger circles as it seeks blindly, but with a keen sense of smell, its prey; then suddenly doubling itself up in a loop, it continues the advance with unerring instinct. There is nothing more horribly fascinating than to see the leaves of the jungle undergrowth, during the rains, literally shaking under the motions of these slender, bloodthirsty, finger-like creatures, as they sway and swing, then start looping inevitably towards you. They have a trick, too, of dropping on to the traveller from above into his hair and ears, or down his neck. Cooper★ says there are three kinds of leeches in Assam, including the red or hill leech, and the hair leech. I do not recollect coming across either of these last two on the North-East Frontier, but I have no doubt that if they are found in Assam they are also found in the Burmese hinterland.

Poor little Maru [his puppy] suffered most of all. I halted

★ *The Mishmee Hills*, by T. T. Cooper.

continuously to relieve him, on one occasion pulling six off his gums, two from each nostril, several from inside his eyelids, and others from his belly, neck, flanks, and from between his toes. Sometimes his white coat was red with blood, or rather with a mixture of blood and mud.

As for me, leeches entered literally every orifice except my mouth, and I became so accustomed to the little cutting bite, like the caress of a razor, that I scarcely noticed it at the time. On two occasions leeches obtained such strategic positions that I only noticed them just in time to prevent very serious, if not fatal, consequences. I also ran them down in my hair, under my arm-pits, inside my ears – in fact everywhere. My feet and ankles were by this time covered with the most dreadful sores, the scars of which I carry to this day.

Out of the valley of death

There is perhaps no more lovely experience on earth than to awaken slowly to life after a long illness, much of which was a dark blank, with vague shadows projected on it from time to time; to see again the blue sky overhead, the golden paddy-fields, green forests and distant snow-clad mountains; to wake in the radiant dawn at the cry of gibbons shrilly calling from the jungle, when the mist hangs over the river and the first rays of the rising sun are sparkling across the blue mountain-tops; to hear the birds whistling and trilling and the silver-throated gong vibrating in the monastery. A vast peace seems to have enfolded the whole world in its embrace. You tread on air with winged feet, and sing, nay shout, for the very joy of living. Every leaf and flower, every bird and beast, every cloud in the sky, is revealed as an object of beauty, welling life and love. Happy the man to whom such revelation is permitted.

Therefore shall I ever remember with gratitude those convalesc-ent days at the end of November in Fort Hertz, when, having emerged from the Valley of Death, I walked a little farther, and grew a little stronger, each day.

Six to dinner

We had only ten miles to do, starting with a long climb up from the valley till we stood over 3,000 feet above the river. A few miles more and then from the ridge just above the Nsop stream we had a clear view southwards of the Mali Hka, blue as the cold-weather sky, twisting through the forested mountains; the bare, white-barked trees striping the green wall of jungle made a very pretty scene, bathed in the golden afternoon sunshine. A precipitous descent brought us down to Nsop Zup, splashing over its bed of jagged slate rocks; and crossing by a bamboo trestle bridge we reached the military police post above.

That night we sat down six to dinner – two P.W.D.* men, an officer of the 32nd Pioneers at work on the new mule-road, a military police officer, the doctor and myself. The talk naturally ran on exploration at the sources of the Irrawaddy, of dead and dying mules, of trackless forests and strange beasts, of rations and ammunition abandoned and buried in the jungle for lack of transport, of wild savages and wilder mountains, remote valleys and unknown rivers. It was a picturesque gathering on a far frontier of the Empire, while Britain was fighting for her life in Flanders.

* Public Works Department.

FOUR

From China to Hkamti Long
1922

Great rivers of eastern Tibet – Yangtze-Mekong divide – High pastures – A Tibetan welcome – A wealth of rhododendrons – A makeshift bridge – No quarter asked or given – In the Irrawaddy jungle – 'Great land of gold' – Rainy season in the jungle – Mishmis encountered – Sunrise at Fort Hertz

Great rivers of eastern Tibet

There is no more remarkable strip of crust on earth than that where the great rivers of eastern Tibet almost jostle each other in their eagerness to escape from the roof of the world. They issue from Tibet through a grooved slot in the backbone of Asia, and are squeezed between two of the mightiest uplifts in the world. Deep down in their troughs they rage. They cannot get out, neither can they spill over.

To the east flows the Yangtze. In the west, million-throated Irrawaddy gulps down inexhaustible waters, wrung from the misty hills. Between these two, the Mekong and the Salween force their way. The gap is narrow – barely 70 miles wide – and through it the four loud rivers rush. So they must hustle. There is no waiting. They pour through together in one roaring, bouncing flood, and the iron-shod alps which hem them in lift their heads to heaven as they plant their feet in the howling water and brace themselves to the storm.

The Yangtze rolls along with pompous might, for it has come a thousand miles hotfoot. Already it has reached adolescence. To frolic would be undignified. But its solemn dignity is but a pose. It has nearly 3,000 miles yet to flow, before it attains to the wisdom of the sea, and is absorbed into the oneness which all rivers attain. So, having shed its pose for a time, it breaks into riot.

The Mekong rumbles by in muffled laughter. It is as though it has slipped through unobserved, and had chortled at the trick ever since. It is a merry river, but often gusts of fierce anger seize it.

The Salween is neither so majestic as the Yangtze nor so trivial as the Mekong. Nevertheless, it is sedate. And then, with little cause, it is roused to a cold fury terrible to see. Emerging proudly from the stark gorges of Tsa-rong (the gateway to eastern Tibet), it plunges headlong into the monsoon valley. Henceforward it is peevish and perverse.

But the Taron is the darling of them all. From aloft you may look down the frightful slopes, over forest and lawn, to the river shouldering its way through the velvet-coated gorge, 3,000 feet below. How puny it looks! – a weak and wayward river, inaudible, crawling along at the bottom of its deeply eroded valley. And then you come to it, and behold, it is a savage river, yet beautiful, with that ruthless beauty which compels grudging admiration.

Yangtze-Mekong divide

The Yangtze-Mekong divide is here fissured longitudinally. Overlooking the Mekong is the snowy Pai-ma-shan range; on the other side, towards the Yangtze, is a high, undulating grassland plateau. Between the two is a deep ice-carved trough, which collects the water from both sides. The range trends north and south, between the two rivers; and the road on the summit plateau also lies north and south, or nearly so, seeking a way down to the Mekong. It follows the foot of the high, bare limestone escarpment of the grass country, with all the rhododendron moorland and the milky glacier-fed stream between it and the snowy range.

This rhododendron moorland, though now drab, is in the spring a many-coloured sea of bloom. What heather is in Scotland, the dwarf rhododendrons are in the Chinese alps; but instead of an endless haze of purple, the hillsides here are chromatic with many colours. They grow ankle-deep, no more, thick and twiggy, covered with wee crusty leaves; but the flowers are large in comparison. Pale gold and lavender blue, plum-juice, wine-red, and flame are some of the favourite colours. On Pai-ma-shan the carpet consists largely of *Rh. chryseum* – one of the few yellow-flowered 'Lapponicums' – and a purple-flowered 'Lapponicum'.

Only solitary blooms of these lingered on till August. One of the aromatic leafed 'Anthopogons' is also common. The under-surface of the young leaves is covered with a scurf of silvery-white scales, which turn a deep rust-brown as the leaves age. At higher levels I noticed the crouching bushes of a 'Saluenense'.

The view of the snowy range from the point where the road switchbacks over the high downs is wonderful; but though only a few miles distant, they are rarely visible during the summer. The plateau summit, on which the topmost ridges stand, is then swathed in mist. It comes rolling up like a sea-fog out of the Mekong on one side and the Yangtze on the other, and then for an hour the cold, pricking showers rocket through the high valleys, and rumple the blue glacier lakes, and blot out the snow-peaks. Then out pops the sun, and for ten minutes you can see the whole coloured, tortured world around you, while the battery is being recharged for a fresh onslaught.

High pastures

One day I ascended the limestone escarpment, by a defile. The stream was fringed with flowers, fragrant Cremanthodium, and nodding primulas. Abundant in boggy places were P. wardii and P. chrysopa. The latter has purplish mauve or lilac flowers, with deep orange eye, and is delightfully fragrant. Calyx, bracts, and scape are heavily crusted with snow-white meal, which shows up the flowers well. The plant stands some 10 inches high. Other species were P. pseudosikkimensis and P. secundiflora, neither of them, however, in flower. On either side the chalk-white cliffs, with their feet buried in rubble, towered up to airy spires; and on the rubble slopes were more flowers. But the cliffs were almost naked.

After reaching the top of the corridor, which pierced right through the escarpment, I emerged dramatically into wide and wonderful pastures. On every side an uncharted sea of rolling downs, 16,000 feet aloft. Innumerable rills oozed from the shallow, bowl-shaped valley heads – it was amazing the amount of water wrung from these Elysian fields – and swelled into brooks girt with flowers. Where the hillsides were not emerald green they were bright red with the stain of manganese. The wind raced splendidly out and across the plateau, and over the ridge and back

again it sang the song of the free; then swooped on and whispered
to the meadow flowers till they nodded their heads. It came
rollicking over the passes and stirred the tufted rock-plants; or
whistled coldly through the corridors, till it reached the open
heights. It buffeted the stolid yak which dotted the slopes in their
hundreds, and spun out their long shaggy hair and fluttered it
bravely. And everywhere water sucked and gurgled as it collected
into rills.

Nowhere as far as the eye could see to north or east or west
was there a rock or a tree to break the smooth, even sweep and
heave of the plateau; only behind me the glazed white girders of
the world, grinning defiance, poked through the green plush
lining.

The setting sun flared on the red ranges, and a sheet of white
mist sailed solemnly up from below, shrouding the valleys one
by one. Then I climbed a thousand feet up the pale screes to the
crest of the escarpment. There were golden saxifrages in flower
on the cliff, widely scattered tuffets, but glaringly obvious in the
wastes. Most of the flowers here were over, but I recognized in
fruit plants of such characteristic form as *Meconopsis souliei* and
Primula dryadifolia. Finally, as the mist floated up, I crept back to
camp with the sting of the rain and the cuff of the wind in my
face; and sweet night came down over the immeasurable earth.

A Tibetan welcome

The people are friendly to strangers. Behold our arrival at a
Tibetan house. 'Arro,' shouts 'Joseph', my interpreter, and the
good wife comes forward. Seeing me, she pulls down her queue
(a mark of respect), spreads out her hands, bows and smiles. The
Chin-t'ang, or family chapel, is swept and garnished, and there I
repose. Later the headman himself arrives, puts out his tongue –
also a mark of respect, not defiance – smiles and bows. He exam-
ines my property. Presently buttered tea is brewed in one of the
tall wooden brass-bound churns, of which there are several in the
spacious kitchen. The butter, more or less aged, is emulsified
with the tea by means of a perforated wooden piston, which is
vigorously worked up and down in the cylinder; a generous pinch
of salt is added, and the clay-coloured liquid is poured frothing
into wooden cups. Everyone sits cross-legged on the floor round

the fire, over which bubbles a huge cauldron. The kitchen is the chief room in the house – it is living-room, dining-room, and bedroom as well. Going to bed is a simple matter, as the people lie down on the floor, covering themselves with a rug or a couple of goatskins; a block of wood serves for a pillow.

There are plenty of other rooms in the house nevertheless, mostly store-rooms, padlocked and as sacred as Bluebeard's closet. The stables occupy the ground floor. On the roof is a shed for straw and grain. A chimney-like structure crowns the parapet, and here each morning green branches are burnt, sending a pillar of smoke up to heaven.

A wealth of rhododendrons

Now the valley began to open out. The slotted cliffs on either flank came into view, and conic wedges of boulder scree spread themselves out below. We clambered over the piled-up ruins and, towards evening, camped under a colossal block of granite which offered convenient shelter. Indeed, so ample was the protection afforded by it, there was no occasion to set up my tiny tent, and I slept on the ground by a welcome fire, 3,964 feet above the Salween.

We were now in the midst of the most wonderful wealth and variety of rhododendrons it is possible to imagine. They grew everywhere. Bogs, boulders, cliffs, forest, and meadow existed for them. In the forest, they were trees with glass-smooth, chestnut-coloured trunks. In the meadows, they formed bushes, gnarled and compact. On the steep granite platforms, smoothed by the scour of ice, they formed patches of interwoven scrub, not a foot high. On the alpine cliff, they changed again to little scared creeping things hugging the rock like ivy. There was no end to them. Every thousand feet of ascent they changed completely. It would have been worth a year of one's life to have seen that valley in June, with the caked snow lying about, water gurgling in a thousand brooks, and everywhere clots of rhododendron romping into flower – gamboge and carmine, snow-white, ivory, purple, crimson, and lavender. I counted twenty-eight species here. The most interesting was a small shrub whose shoots, petioles, and capsules were covered with dark, stiff bristles. The under-leaf surface was furred with a thin coppery red indumentum (K.W. 5427).

Before dark one of the Lutzu porters – Sere, that is to say, 'Gold', by name (he spoke a little Chinese) – cooked my evening ration: boiled rice, some potatoes, and a slice of meat; and I brewed myself a mug of hot cocoa to finish up with. By eight o'clock the men, muffled up in their cloaks, were fast asleep round the fire. I sat in my corner for an hour, writing my diary, and packing specimens collected during the day. The stars blazed fiercely in a jet sky. The shrill gurgle of many torrents was interrupted only by the hoot of an owl or the occasional squeal of an animal. Then I crawled into my 'flea-bag', and presently fell into an iron sleep.

A makeshift bridge

Presently we camped on a tongue of land between the Taron and another river which roared in from the Salween divide. Across the latter, on a small platform, stood a hut.

We had not been here long when visitors began to arrive. First a fat little woman with a basket of firewood, and scanty clothing. Her round, chubby face was woefully tattooed with blue spots and criss-cross lines; it formed a mask, sharply defined, extending from the angle of the eye, down the cheek to the chin, and round the mouth. She wanted to cross the smaller river, and we were introduced to the 'monkey bridge' for the first time. Three or four separate cables, made of twisted bamboo, each no thicker than a skipping-rope, were tied to trees on either bank. The sportsman who wished to translate himself from one side to the other tied himself to a wooden slider, which he placed on this collection of ropes, and proceeded to haul himself across, hand over hand. Of necessity he hung underneath the apparatus, and so could push with his bare feet at the same time. The Nung woman, after trussing herself up, with basket, proceeded to give us a demonstration.

It appeared an undignified position for a lady; but her clothes, though inadequate, were adapted to this form of athletic exercise, for she wore a very small and tight pair of bathing-drawers underneath her abbreviated skirt. Anyhow, she hauled herself and her basket of faggots across while we stared in dumb admiration at her brawn and courage.

No quarter asked or given

The forest was most imposing. The trees were immense, with massive trunks ending in candelabra of gnarled limbs, and so smothered under vegetation as to render identification very difficult. Easily recognizable species were oak, Pseudotsuga, and Castanopsis. Each was a wild garden unto itself. A mane of lichen fringed every branch, waving like seaweed in a tideway. Bushes of rhododendron foaming into bloom, creepers, ferns, climbing plants, and orchids – especially orchids – fought and struggled in ruthless dumb determination for light and air. There was no quarter. Nature asks none, gives none. The weak, the wounded, and the dying went equally to the wall in the fierce competition for a place in the sun; and the result was certainly beautiful.

The variety of orchids, their strange colours and bizarre forms, were a perpetual source of wonder. A sweetly scented Pleione frilled every tree-trunk with its purple blooms. Another species, milk-white with a chocolate lip, formed drifts of snow, high up. Many hung down from the branches in festoons, or beaded threads; or lolled in corners; or stood up in stiff haughtiness. But all of them, plain and coloured, proud and humble, had the craftiest, daftest flowers, tuned to the tricks of the insect world.

A colony of belligerent caterpillars created a certain amount of disturbance. They had recently emerged from dormitories, made by weaving together two leaves with a silken web; several such dormitories, crowded with kicking caterpillars, were still intact, but the plants were also speckled with the little black chaps, who resented my mere approach. Their displeasure was so acute that they stood up on their hind legs, so to speak, in protest, lifting their heads with a jerk. The curious thing was that they did it simultaneously, like a company sloping arms; the effect was extraordinarily odd. The leaves seemed to shudder under their efforts, and any faint-hearted bird, seeking a succulent morsel, might well be daunted by such combined action. There were, perhaps, six or eight caterpillars on each leaf. Did I approach, they would suddenly jerk up their heads at me in unison, and repeat the movement; did I touch the leaf, those on other leaves would join in the agitation; till finally the entire bush, containing maybe half a hundred larvae, would be twinkling as the outraged inhabitants jerked up their heads and let them fall, repeating the manœuvre while the danger lasted. However, they seemed to grow weary after a little while, till at last they could scarcely lift a leg.

In the Irrawaddy jungle

Oh, but the smell of the jungle as it rose richly to my nostrils! The perfume of flowers in the boscage, mingled with the sour odour of decay, and the shapeless musty patches, where some creature had crossed the path, breathing infection! And the queer cries and noises, the sudden fearful silences, the long hush in the misty dawn, before the valley rang with the hoot of the hoolock monkey!

The cry of the hoolock, the white-faced gibbon, as it greets the dawn, is the most joyous cry in the world. When the sun slants over the ridge, splitting the forest with golden wedges, and the hills begin to harden out of the nebulous vapour, the jungle gives tongue. '*Wa*-hu! *Wa*-hu! *Wa*-hu!' cry the gibbons in chorus; the yelps quick and short, like the yapping of a puppy, the second note almost lost. And then comes the answer, 'Hu-wa-a-a!' in a long-drawn wail, and – silence. Suddenly the chorus breaks out again wildly, and the glad shout is taken up by more and more of the troop, till cutting crisply through the babel comes a clear, shrill whistle, repeated at intervals; and once more abrupt silence. And presently the cry is heard more faintly, far away in the jungle.

Perhaps during a lull you may hear a movement in the tree-tops, and see the branches shaking, and hear a splash of foliage; but rarely do you catch sight of the gibbon, for he is a shy creature, being much persecuted by the hunter for his skin, and no doubt for food also. It is the exception to hear him cry after noon; at dawn, when the shredded mist hangs over the valleys, he yelps with joy, and so goes away and hides himself in the jungle.

During the heat of the day, insects and birds keep up a monot-onous vamp. The whirr of the scissor-grinders is heard every-where, and the whistle and steady chirp, chirp of crickets. A sudden clamour of birds, quarrelling under the bamboos, breaks through the stifling peace, and then the maddening twonk, twonk, twonk of the coppersmith bird, or barbet, repeating itself on one note for as long as you care to listen.

As the sun gains in power, silence gradually steals over the jungle; the drone, and clack, and tick of insect life ceases, and even the birds are dumb. Then it is that the jungle begins to whisper to itself, and swift noises stab through the afternoon rest, loud and clear, leaving the silences between more tense. A fruit drops to the ground with stunning violence. A leaf snaps loudly, and comes crackling down through the branches. Bamboos, rubbing against each other, grunt and squeak dismally, and even the stiff palm-leaves twitch noiselessly in a stray eddy. In the hill jungle you are always within earshot of tumbling water, and the splash of the torrent as it drops from pool to pool is as refreshing as it is musical.

At night is heard the minatory bark of the muntjac, and perhaps the scream of an animal in deadly terror, which dies away in horrible gurglings, or ceases abruptly.

'Great land of gold'

As the morning mist dispersed, there was a slight fall of rain – just enough to keep the vegetation fresh; but the gibbons yelped in derision till the sun drove off the mist, and the forest was striped and dappled with light and shade. In the rocks in the stream-bed grew masses of curious but beautiful begonia, with snow-white flowers, and very regular, lanceolate leaves. In the forest a large species, 2 to 3 feet high, was also in flower, the flowers in this case being blush-pink, the capsule clothed with crimson hairs, and the stems and leaves hoary. The march was an easy one, the path ascending gradually, till at last we came out on to a narrow platform. Below us the last spurs flared away westwards, and at our feet lay the honey-coloured plain, with the Assam ranges dimly outlined beyond; an arc of silver where a loop caught the sun proclaimed the Western Irrawaddy. We raced down the slanting rock rib and so out on to the level plain of Hkamti - 'great land of gold'. Crossing the paddy-land, which is diversified with strips of bog and dense scrub, we came to the village of Kang-kiu, on the bank of the placid Mali Hka, the Western Irrawaddy itself.

A soft peace enfolds the world. Doves coo in the jack-fruit trees about the village; myna birds chuckle to one another in the roofs; and the silvery tinkle of bells from the monastery, whose thatched spire peeps up from the palm-grove, mingles with the lowing of cattle. A calm-faced monk in yellow robe beats a spinning gong, and the high throbbing note calls the neatly dressed Shan women to evening prayer. And when the sun has dipped down behind the purple ranges, bats flit to and fro in the shadows, wheeling through the hut and out again with sure skill.

Rainy season in the jungle

During the rainy season it is, of course, impossible to get along. The scene then is very different. The swollen river fills its bed and comes galloping madly down from the hills; as it rushes along at the foot of the forest, it plasters the lower branches with flotsam. The stagnant air throbs with the roar of flood and the rumble of grinding boulders. Pale wisps of cloud writhe through the tree-tops like wet smoke, and the melancholy drip, drip of the rain from the leaves sounds a perpetual dirge. There is a rank odour of decay in the jungle, though life is everywhere triumphant. Scattered over the dark squelchy ground are speckled pilei in flaring colours, and horrid fungi scar the bloated tree-trunks. Pale, evil-looking saprophytes lurk beneath the creaking bamboos, and queer orchids peep from the bibulous soil. The atmosphere is foul with mould, yet life is at full flood.

The most entrancing ferns carpet the banks with jade tracery, and wave from the tree-tops; filmy ferns cover the nakedness of the lower limbs, maidenhair and polypody frill the rocks, and the great bayonet fronds of the bird's nest fern stick up menacingly from the boughs. Mingled with these are orchids, trailing their spikes of long-lipped flowers; the lounging, leather-leaved stems of Æschynanthus, with pairs of perky scarlet flowers; bushes of Agapetes, hung all over with urn-shaped pink bells, like a Christmas-tree; creepers, arums, and sheets of bright green moss. The vegetation, with the thick sap of youth tingling in its veins, overflows in all directions, sprawling and careless in the bitter strife. The slain are out of sight. That is the curious part of

Nature's war in the jungle; the dying are visible sometimes, though so well nursed by their enemies (not in love, but in hate) that only a practised eye can recognize them. But the dead are not there, or only very few of them. If you search long you may find some newly slain, but they are already forgotten. Millions died that life might surge sweetly through this green forest, with its infinite variety of strange and beautiful forms, its cool colours and daring contrasts, its tangled order and ordered chaos. But they died very young; at birth – nay, before birth, many of them.

When a giant of the forest dies there is a conspiracy amongst its enemies to hush up the matter. Friends it has none. It is each for himself and all against all. New enemies appear, to feed on the remains. They fight tooth and nail, but in a common cause, to hide the dead. Not till that is accomplished do they turn and rend one another again. And then the great tide of deathless life sweeps on once more; the gap is filled; the dead are forgotten.

But the slaughter amongst the young and the weak and the helpless is frightful. It goes on and on without cessation, behind the fairest scenes. Where life is most prolific, death is most active.

In the jungle there is not only the fierce competition of plant with plant, for light and air and water; there is a much fiercer hidden warfare carried on with the myriad insect world. In the hot weather the jungle is filled with strange noise, the whirr and drone and hiss of an unseen multitude. It is the war-drum of the six-footed.

Mishmis encountered

After marching several miles, we began to meet strange men of savage aspect. They were watching some fish-traps, which filtered every sluice in the boisterous river; or trailed from stakes driven amongst the boulders, or from low bamboo fences built out from the shore. These half-wild men were Mishmis, who had come over the Krong-Jong pass, at the head of the Nam Yin, from the Lohit valley, to fish on the British side of the frontier.

In stature they were short, but sturdily built, with a mop of cotton-black hair. Their mahogany-coloured faces were round, with oblique Tibetan eyes, and flat noses. They wore few clothes, yet though we were scarcely 3,000 feet up here, it was none too warm by the river; we had not seen the sun all day, and an ominous snow-mist hid the peaks ahead.

A short kilt of thick red Tibetan cloth covered the thighs of these fishermen. The edges are not sewn together, but overlap in front for convenience in marching; so for decency's sake the savage wears underneath a – well, sporran – tight and tiny. A sleeveless cloth jacket and a long scarf, thrown over his shoulders, completes his costume, which, though scanty, is picturesque. Every man carries a short *dah* in an open wooden sheath, and a monkey-skin bag, in which are pipe and tobacco.

The Mishmis come from the hills below Rima, on the Lohit-Brahmaputra, and were much the most Tibetan-looking tribe we had met with yet. They belong to the Assam stream of migration, which diverged towards the south-west, skirting the Irrawaddy basin.

Sunrise at Fort Hertz

We had just finished breakfast when the sun, roused at last, began to tear rents in the milk-white mist. So we carried our chairs outside and sat down in the waxing warmth, to watch a scene of marvellous beauty unfold itself. The mist, which an hour earlier had appeared solid in its opaqueness, was merely cobweb, after all; it was fraying in all directions. Huge windows opened suddenly, displaying pictures of a world beyond the plain, and we looked out on to the gleaming snow-clad ranges of Assam and Tibet.

The white dome of Noi Matoi, whence rises the western branch of the Irrawaddy, swam to the surface of the milky sea, and remained floating in space. Even the peaks above the Shingrup-kyet, which overlooks the boisterous Nmai Hka, where the sun rises, a hundred miles away, were mottled with snow, while the Assam ridge to the west was heavily furrowed.

Then the last shreds of mist melted, and the tusk-shaped wall, Burma's northern rampart, stood out clearly in harsh grandeur. It towers up there, aloof and scowling, as it has done since the days when it was built, untold ages ago; its rivers shout a savage warning to the hardy races beyond not to venture southwards into the Irrawaddy jungle.

FIVE

The Riddle of the Tsangpo Gorges
1924–25

Flowers and beggars – The day's work – Precautions to ensure cross-pollination – A wonderful day – Pomé royalty – A bleak and dreary spot – Abors at Pé – An awkward climb – The rainbow falls – Through the gorge – Lost on the plateau – Over the last pass

Flowers and beggars

At the end of May and beginning of June we had ten days of really fine weather, and the valley grew hot and close. Blossom burst from the bushes. A clump of butter-golden peony flowered, and so did the dainty tamarisk. We walked through lanes of yellow dog-rose into billowy blue seas of Sophora, whose previous year's seeds still lay scattered over the hard ground like a broken string of coral beads. *Clematis montana*, cool and virgin white in the sultry jasmine-haunted air, trailed over every tree and bush.

One afternoon we went for a walk up the Gyamda valley as far as Pu-chu, about 5 miles distant. There is a small temple here, conspicuous for its golden roof, and noteworthy for its Chinese architecture, with curly corners. This roof was fitted with a system of bamboo drain-pipes, the top of a long bamboo being split and opened out into a funnel to catch the rain-water, while the bottom opened on to a splash-board.

The temple courtyard was almost deserted save for a few diseased beggars. One horrible leper, his hands replaced by stumps, sat on the steps in the hot sunshine working two prayer drums ceaselessly round and round by means of a rope.

The day's work

The day's work in camp was as follows: We rose early, and I usually spent the hour before tea was ready writing descriptions of new plants discovered the previous day. Then came tea and biscuits, at which meal we discussed our plans, or, since it is not always safe to talk to an Englishman or Scotsman before breakfast, read our books in stony silence. While the men were breakfasting round the fire, we dressed and went on with our work. Then we had breakfast, usually about 10 o'clock – porridge occasionally, curried chicken or scrambled eggs and *chappatties*. The only things that weren't severely rationed were flour, rice, *tsamba* and butter, all of which could be obtained locally, so that when we were hungry we demolished quantities of buttered *chappatties* – that is, thin baked cakes of flour and water. We had no bread, of course. After breakfast we went out on the day's excursion exploring, botanizing or taking photographs, according to the weather, usually making some peak our objective. We returned to camp about 4, changed our wet clothes, had tea, and worked or read till supper-time. Supper – menu as at breakfast, with soup instead of porridge and a cup of cocoa to finish up with – was at 7. After that we talked and read by candle-light, recorded the events and observations of the day, and turned in at 10. How peaceful it all was! No train to catch in the morning, no unsatisfactory play to criticize, no income tax form to fill up, no income, no broadcasting, no hustle, bustle, and boost.

All the same, June is a strenuous month for the plant-hunter, and I often worked ten or twelve hours a day in order to keep abreast of the times. For in June all the flowers are coming out with a rush, and moreover one finds oneself fresh and eager for the task in an astonishingly new and beautiful world. Naturally, one tries to make the most of it. After the long journey by sea and land, it is immensely refreshing to settle down to a serious job. Of course, the pace does not – cannot – last. At the end of two months, altitude and weather – unceasing rain – begin to tell on the nerves. Reaction sets in, and you feel peevish. Then it is you know that the crisis is come, that if you are to get through the long season successfully, you must keep yourself well in hand, and keep a firm grip of things. August is the critical month. It is long and wet. The spring flowers are over, the autumn flowers are not yet out. If you can get through August with your flag still nailed to the mast, you are all right. Things begin to mend. The worst of the rain is over by September, and the weather is getting finer every day. Seeds are ripening, autumn flowers are blooming, and that shapeless shroud which for three months has

muffled a dead world is being blown away to reveal the quick
form reincarnated beneath.

Winter comes with its biting winds, its clear cold skies, its
sunshine and snowstorms. By this time one is tired with a tiredness which knows no equal; not the tiredness which can be cured
by a night's rest, or a week's rest. Every cell and fibre in one's
body seems worn out, and it takes months of gradual rest and
change of scene to renew one's strength. It is the effect of prolonged living at high altitude, of course, not of late hours.

Precautions to ensure cross-pollination

A close heath of purple-flowered 'Lapponicum' covered large
patches of oozing lawn, where the ground flattened out at the
foot of the steep forest; and just within the forest, lining a burn,
we found one of our very best rhododendrons, a bush 'Oreotrephes', hung all over with masses of rosy-purple flowers. The
colouring was rich, and luckily we had found the plant in a good
year, at its best; the glen was simply glowing with it (K.W.5790).
On dry sunny slopes, particularly on old moraines, amongst
wizened bushes of the Mahogany triflorum was an undergrowth of
dusky crimson 'Lepidotum' rhododendron, which bloomed in
July. The precautions taken to ensure cross-pollination in this
plant are significant. The flowers stand on edge, erect on their
long pedicels, and slightly arched, so as to present only their
mailed backs to the rain; a sensible enough provision in a flower
which opens in the wettest month of the year. There are ten
stamens of equal length, the filaments of the five upper ones being
expanded at the base, while the upper edge of the corolla tube is
slightly inturned to form a flange, where honey is secreted. On
the upper lobes of the corolla are painted a number of darker
spots and streaks, all pointing like fingers towards the honey bath,
held up between the flange and the palisade of filaments. Insects
want honey – or, in a few cases, pollen – for food; they don't
care two straws about pollinating flowers. But flowers want to
be pollinated – and the aristocracy want to be *cross-pollinated*; a
little honey costs them nothing, and they willingly pay that
bounty to insects in return for a little solid cross-pollination work.
An insect approaching this rhododendron flower reads the hiero-
glyphics on the corolla, and translating them, 'Step inside; this

way, please', reaches the honey without waste of time. While blindly probing for the concealed honey, it may entangle its legs with the pollen, which is in the form of elastic white threads, and carry some off to another flower. At any rate, these threads may often be seen festooning the lower stamens and trailing all over the flower, as though brought from elsewhere.

The average insect is doubtless a wiseacre; it aims at economy of effort, and goes straight to the point – in this case honey – without creating a disturbance elsewhere, or doing a stroke more work than is necessary to accomplish its purpose. But there is the usual village idiot to be considered – a clumsy oaf which always does everything upside down and inside out. The plant legislates for him, too – it is taking no risks. The device described ensures that the clever insect shall concern itself only with the upper male part of the flower, without troubling itself about the female apparatus – which has nothing to offer; but the clumsy insect would be sure to blunder into that, so the plant cleverly removes it out of the way by bending the style down till the stigma projects between the lower lobes of the corolla.

The most stupid insect, fuddled with honey and entangled with pollen threads, cannot now fall against the home stigma on his way out, and deliver the goods at the wrong door; the chances are it will carry them away and deliver them outside the 4-mile radius, where they will be entangled amongst foreign stamens and eventually blown on to a foreign stigma.

A wonderful day

The day after our arrival we set out from camp to ascend to the alpine region, selecting the avalanche as the best route. Thus, instead of having to cut our way through the dense scrub which clothed the steep slope above the forest, we could walk on the snow, keeping to the open valley, where the torrent flowed beneath the avalanche. Nor had we climbed far when we began to find treasure. There were ruffled seas of 'Glaucum' rhododendron (K. W. 5844), with a pink foam of blossom frothing over it, and brilliant clots of purple 'Saluenense'. Broad bands of sulphur and pink striped the sheltered slope, where two scrub species, a 'Souliei' and a 'Lacteum', made an impenetrable wire entanglement 3 feet deep; and the former became known as

'Yellow Peril' by reason of its aggressive abundance. The slope was steep and difficult, so that we halted often to regain our breath, and to collect specimens. Once, when gazing across the torrent to a steep grass slope, I pointed out to my companion some brilliant scarlet leaves which formed a pattern on a rock; and he, taking out his telescope, looked at them long and carefully. 'Why,' said he, at length, 'they aren't leaves, they are flowers; it's a rhododendron, I believe.' 'What!' I shouted, almost seizing the glass from him in my eagerness; and gazing as he had done, I realized that he was right. They were flowers, not leaves – flowers of vivid scarlet flaming on the rocks.

Straightway we tried to cross the torrent, but finding that impossible, continued upstream to a dangerous-looking snow-bridge; this we might have risked crossing, so great was our anxiety to reach the prize, but at that moment we observed another blaze at our feet, and there was Scarlet Runner, as we called it, laced to the rocks.

For a minute we just stared at it, drunk with wonder. It lay absolutely flat on the rocks, no part of the plant, not even the corolla which is considerably larger than the leaf, rising 2 inches above the surface; stems, leaves, and flowers cling as closely as possible to the ground. Some of the mats were 18 inches in diameter, with stems as thick as a man's little finger, and must have been many years old. But the plant grows slowly and keeps to the sunny side of the slope, sprawling over the barest gneiss rocks, where nothing else will grow. It is the first of its kind to flower and the first to ripen its seed; for the winter sunshine melts the early falls of October snow, when the bushier species of the lee slope are buried alive. Consequently it has to withstand much lower temperatures than Carmelita and its allies; I have seen it lying out on the bare rocks night after night in a temperature which approached zero. Scarlet Runner, in fact, goes through the whole evolution of flower and seed production in the five months, June to October.

Continuing the ascent by a steep gully, we found ourselves ploughing through snow and an inextricable tangle of dwarf rhododendron. There was nothing else but rhododendron in fact, – sulphur seas of Yellow Peril (K. W. 5853), lakes of pink 'Lacteum' (K. W. 5863) and a vast confusion of 'Anthopogons' of all sizes and colours, which completely swamped the few poor little brooms of violet-flowered 'Lapponicum' (K. W. 5862).

Above the rhododendron turmoil there was only snow; we
therefore made our way round the base of a cliff and over the
spur which separated us from the next valley, descending towards
the stream which flowed from the Doshong La. There we hoped
to strike the path and return to camp.

But it was not so easy as it looked. Below us was the valley
under deep snow, vaguely visible from time to time through rifts
in the white cloud which came pouring over the pass; below us
were cliffs whose depths we could not plumb; and between the
bottom of the valley and the path raged a torrent swollen with
melting snow and half-hidden by unmelted snow which concealed
many a trap. We therefore advanced cautiously, in a rapture of
joy at what we found. We were on a giant stairway of smooth
rock, whose steps, ice-carved ledge by ledge, were filled with
dwarf rhododendron in astonishing variety.

At the top on the naked rock was Scarlet Runner in proud
isolation. Sometimes it crawled over the flat and, reaching the
edge of the step, shot out tongues of fire visible a mile away
across the valley. It was already in full bloom, passing over
lower down, and flowered so freely that mats and festoons were
smothered beneath the blaze. The virgin snow, dabbled with its
hot scarlet, spread a bloody sheet over the tortured rock.

A little lower down were the twiggy brooms of R. *damascenum*
or Plum Warner (K. W. 5842), its absurd little plummy mouths
pouting discontentedly at us. Mixed with this, on the sheltered
ledges, grew the more coarsely woven mats of Scarlet Pimpernel,
another fiery 'Neriiflorum' (K. W. 5846). At first sight it looked
like a darker edition of Scarlet Runner; but on closer inspection
it was seen to be a bigger plant, with larger leaves and darker
flowers, borne two or three in a truss instead of singly.

Just as Scarlet Runner was succeeded by Scarlet Pimpernel, so
lower down on a lee slope, Scarlet Pimpernel was succeeded by
Carmelita (K. W. 5847). This plant belongs to another branch of
the family. It is bigger again, with still larger leaves, and flowers
of luminous carmine, in threes. It grows socially, in foot-deep
tangles, and is not really a creeping plant at all, but prostrate with
ascending stems; also, lest anyone should think that it is not
sufficiently distinct from the other two, it may be remarked that
it flowers and ripens its seed a fortnight later than Scarlet Runner.
In October we dug it out of the snowdrifts in order to get seed;
and the crimson conical capsules were found to be scarcely split

at the apex, when those of 'Scarlet Runner', lying prone on the rocks, were wide open and empty.

Next, amongst a chaos of fallen rocks, we found a thicket of Plum Glaucum (K. W. 5843), one of the most striking species of all. The flowers are dark cerise, borne in pairs as in Plum Warner, but formed more after the pattern of Pink Glaucum, which the leaves with their white waxy under-surface recall. In size it is intermediate between Plum Warner and Pink Glaucum, and it looks rather like a cross between the two; but it requires more shelter than Plum Warner.

Thinking that we should find this species abundantly lower down, and finding that we were at the moment in an awkward cul-de-sac, I omitted to mark this spot. We got out of the predicament, and – I never saw Plum Glaucum again! It was only by retracing my route laboriously up the cliff in October, when everything was hidden under a pall of snow, and every landmark wiped out, that at the third attempt I rediscovered the little hollow in which our only Plum Glaucum grew. How well I remember the occasion, for it was in the lilac dusk one frozen night when at last I came on it, excavated it, and triumphantly secured a little seed! As for Pink Glaucum, whose silvered leaves and flat 5-flowered corymbs resemble those of *R. glaucum* itself, it grew everywhere in the bottom of the valley in billowy masses of pale pink and mauve tones.

After crossing the torrent we found the path on the far side under the cliff, and descending through the forest reached camp. It had been a wonderful day.

Pomé royalty

That evening we reached Chunyima, the first village in Pomé, where we were well received by the inhabitants. There was another guest in the house – a servant of the Kanam Raja, or King of Pomé. He was a tall, well-built man with a cheerful cherry-red face, and long, wavy hair falling loosely over his shoulders like a King Charles spaniel. His wife, though a Rongpa (that is, an inhabitant of the *rong*), was a pretty woman, but she declined to face the camera. Pomé women, unlike Kongbo women, do not lacquer their faces, which is an advantage; for the Kongbo women, ugly enough at the best, look absolutely hideous when their faces are hidden beneath a shining black mask. Perhaps the idea is, or was originally, to make themselves less attractive to men; though it would seem unnecessary. But it is easy for a foreigner to get a prejudiced view of these customs, which are largely conventional; and a Tibetan girl with a varnished face may be as popular amongst her set as an English girl, chromatic with powder, rouge, and peroxide, is in hers.

We declined the offer of a room in the house, on account of the excessive number of fleas to the square inch, and elected to sleep in a shed which, by unmistakable signs, proclaimed itself the dairy. Fleas seemed nearly as plentiful here as in the main building, though less brisk, possibly depressed by the odour from bacterial milk pails.

A bleak and dreary spot

Atsa is a bleak and dreary spot. The wind whistles up these bare valleys, and sudden storms swoop down from the heights. The pastures all down the valley were black with tents and yak now, but in a month or two the shadow of winter would fall on the plateau, and the herds would withdraw. Meanwhile we lived in the tiny temple, and were none too warm there with only an earthenware pot of smouldering yak dung.

An excursion to the Banda La proved full of interest. It is a severe climb, but on a fine day the view is worth it. Far away to the north we saw three very high snow-peaks. Much nearer, in the east, was a fine pyramidal snow-peak, forming part of the southern ridge, the true Tsangpo-Salween divide, on which we counted six dying glaciers.

On August 29th we awoke to find it snowing heavily, the valley full of mist, and the hills all round white; but presently the sun came out, and the snow quickly melted. However, we remained at Atsa another day, while all the evening thunderstorms re-echoed from peak to peak, and the thunder rumbled up and down the glen. Next day we started south by the Lhasa road, having given up the idea of going as far as the Salween, since it was clear it would take us another ten days to get there. Passing round the south side of the lake again, we turned up a wide valley and travelled a few miles to a postal station called Kolep. Before we got there, however, we were struck in the flank by a blizzard, and hurled flat, drenched and breathless. The wind blew the rain through us like grape-shot. The animals could not move, and those which did not get under a neighbouring rock, simply fell down. It was very unpleasant for half an hour, but then the wind ceased and it just rained. We reached Kolep, shivering with cold, but some hot tea soon put us right. There were several tents and a few square cabins here.

Abors at Pé

Most of the people we saw in Pé were Mönbas, a few Kampas. But most interesting of all were three Lopas, as the Tibetans call the most surly, savage and benighted of the Assam tribes. These dwarfs (they stood less than 5 feet high) had come twenty-five marches to buy salt and were evidently the folk we call Abors.

It was surprising enough that such small, ill-nourished men should carry loads weighing over 80 lb. over tracks that would break a white man's heart; but to have crossed the Doshong La in deep snow, almost naked, was even more astonishing. For the only garment they wore was a coarse red-dyed shirt of hand-woven cloth, not reaching to the knees, with a small flap beneath for decency's sake. Just imagine it. Bare legs, bare feet, bare hands, bare heads, in that bitter wind. A second garment, like a Tibetan *gushuk*, is worn at night. With such heavy loads they can only travel very slowly. Indeed, while we ourselves were in camp on the Doshong La, they tried to conquer the pass, but were driven back by a fresh fall of snow; the wonder is they did not perish outright. Instead, they hid in the forest for a day, and then, when the storm was over, crossed safely.

These Abors knew no word of Tibetan, and all the resources of the local interpreter were strained to hold a brief conversation with them. They were suspicious of us and surly, scowling at our advances. Their shifty eyes, low bulging forehead, and projecting muzzle gave them a dreadful ape-man look; one wonders if even Neanderthal man looked so utterly simian – if so, he must have been an ugly customer.

For ornament, these Lopas wear bead and chain necklaces and large hollow silver ear-rings, like a back collar-stud, the size of a half-crown and an inch through. A short chopping knife is carried in a basket sheath round the waist, and a bamboo bow with bamboo string and poisoned arrows. We bought an ear-ring for two rupees, but it was evident that they did not want the money; they did not know what it was or what to do with it; an empty sardine tin was more coveted.

An awkward climb

After a minimum temperature of 45°F. in the night, we got away early on the 23rd. There was fresh snow on the trees not very high up, but the day kept fairly fine, with glimpses of sunshine; the clouds, which clung obstinately to the snow-peaks, however, warned us that a storm was brewing.

Almost immediately we were in difficulties, with an awkward cliff to climb, followed by a nasty traverse round the face, along a narrow ledge which overhung the reeling river. The pioneer party went first, and we hauled the women up, the men posting themselves at intervals along the ledge and handing them along. After that, we made our way through the forest for an hour without further adventure, until the way was blocked by an overhanging cliff. Here the main body sat down, thinking that the end had come. A more formidable obstacle at first sight it would be difficult to imagine. It was over the cliff, or back; there was no way round, with the river battering at its foot. Fortunately, there was a chimney or narrow cleft about 30 feet high between the main wall and a detached stack. If we could climb that, the thing was done. At this crisis Curly, the Lay Reader and Shock-headed Peter performed one of the most remarkable feats of rock-climbing I have ever seen; they went straight up the almost vertical outer buttress like cats.

Next they felled two small trees, cut steps in them, and lowered them into position in the chimney – which was too wide and too smooth to climb otherwise – and made fast; two ladders had to be used because there was a block half-way up the chimney, the upper ladder standing precariously on a sloping ledge.

The porters now went up hand over hand. Some of the stoutest even went up with their loads, and Cawdor carried his rucksack up without turning a hair and, descending again, helped the others. But I liked not the look of it, and shed my rucksack at the top of the first ladder, breathing a sigh of relief when I reached the ledge, and safety, above. Tom then tactlessly suggested that,

as it was getting late and the pioneer party who had explored for
another half-mile had not come on a camping-ground, we should
descend the chimney again, camp at the foot and start fresh on
the morrow. I flatly refused. I had got safely up the beastly thing,
and nothing on earth would reconcile me to chimney-climbing
as a habit. Once at the top, there I intended to stay; and to clinch
matters I scouted ahead as fast as I could go. Eventually we
bivouacked in the forest just above the river, having made some
4 miles' progress in seven hours.

The rainbow falls

We camped amongst the boulders, close beside the thundering
river. A quarter of a mile ahead a blank cliff, striped by two silver
threads of water, towered a thousand feet into the air. The river
came up against this cliff with terrific force, turned sharp to the
left, and was lost to view. We scrambled over the boulders,
crossed a belt of trees and a torrent, and made for the foot of the
cliff in order to see what became of the river; but even before we
got there our ears were filled with a loud roaring noise. As we
turned the corner, and before we could see straight down the
river again, we caught sight of a great cloud of spray which hung
over the rocks within half a mile of where we stood. 'The falls
at last.' I thought! But it wasn't – not *the* falls. A fall, certainly,
perhaps 40 feet high, and a fine sight with rainbows coming and
going in the spray cloud. But a 30 or 40 foot fall, even on the
Tsangpo, cannot be called *the* falls, meaning the falls of romance,
those 'Falls of the Brahmaputra' which have been the goal of so
many explorers.

Nevertheless, we stood spellbound, as well we might. The
river here swung round to the west, boring its way between two
mighty spurs which jutted out, one from Gyala Peri, the other
from Sanglung. Cliffs towered up on both sides, so close together
that it seemed one could almost leap from crag to crag; and the
cliffs were smooth as well as sheer. Only high up against the
skyline did a few trees cling like fur to the worn rock surface.
Obviously we could get no further down the gorge; to scale the
cliff seemed equally impossible.

But above our camp the cliffs were to some extent covered

with shrub growth; and up these lay our route, as I was to learn on the morrow.

Through the gorge

The descent down the east flank of the Sanglung spur, at first northwards along the face, and finally north-eastwards along the crest of a minor spur, took us nearly five hours; but there was a track all the way. Passing through conifer forest into oak forest, we soon got down into jungle, and a wealth of new trees; *Rhododendron maddeni* was in fruit and a new species with tiny capsules in threes, which I did not recognize (K. W. 6335). There were big bamboos, giant Araliaceæ with huge palm-like leaves, queer orchids, such as *Cirrhopetalum emarginatum*, in flower on the moss-clad tree-trunks, and many other things. And then suddenly the abrupt descent ceased and we came gently down into cultivated fields, and saw clusters of wooden huts in the distance. We had descended about 5,000 feet from the top of the spur, though we were still a good thousand feet above the river.

Now we were in a new world. How surprising it was to see fields and houses! Nay, the surprising thing was that we were in the world at all! While we had been following the river as it gnawed its way through the Himalaya, wedged between those magnificent snow mountains, nothing seemed more unlikely than that we should ever reach civilization again. Every day the scene grew more savage; the mountains higher and steeper; the river more fast and furious. Had we finally emerged on to a raw lunar landscape, it would scarcely have surprised us, but for one thing. As the river, rushing like a lost soul between the hot hell in the heart of the Himalaya and the cold hell on the wind-swept peaks which guard the gorge, grew more dynamic, as the scenery grew harsher, and the thunder of the water more minatory, the touch of Nature came marvellously to the rescue. Everywhere, by cliff and rock and scree, by torn scar and ragged rent, wherever vegetation could get and keep a grip, trees grew; and so, from the grinding boulders in the river-bed to the grating glaciers above, the gorge was filled with forest to the very brim. Ten thousand feet of forest coloured those cold grey rocks of tortured gneiss; and when the summer rain weeps softly over the scene of riot a million trees will flame into flower and strew their beauty over the ruin.

And so on a sunny afternoon we marched into Payi, or Payul, amidst gardens of Cosmos and tobacco. We felt triumphant, though there was more to do yet – indeed, the hardest part of the job still remained to be done; but first we wanted to sleep, and sleep, and sleep.

Lost on the plateau

From the tip-top of the pass, we gazed eastwards over a bare and gloomy scene. It was 5 o'clock on a grey February evening; nothing was visible but wide earth plains, chequered with tufts of coarse grass, and beyond that the jagged rim of snow-striped mountains; an icy wind snored over the bare gravel. There was no comfort in such a view, except the thought that somewhere out beyond the farthest mountain rim the spurs flared away to the plains of Hindustan, where flowers bloomed. Descending by a vile and ice-glazed path, we turned south again, keeping now along the foot of a lofty snow range, which divided us from the basin of the Trigu Tso, a large unexplored lake to the west. We were ourselves on unknown ground, but it was getting dark, and soon we could hardly see where we were going. We continued to march in glum silence, too tired to do more than tramp steadily on, and much too cold to ride our ponies. Daylight dwindled to dusk, and dusk swiftly hardened to night. The wind still sobbed and moaned through the empty valleys and a pale moon occasionally shone through a rift in the flying clouds. But there was no sign of habitation. An hour passed. No sign yet. Two of the men lagged behind and I with them; we could hear the caravan crunching over the gravel ahead and sometimes see them against the sky as they topped a rise. Another hour passed. Suddenly a dog began to bay long and loud. 'At last!' I thought, much relieved. But nothing happened; we just went on and the baying of the dog, which came from a herd's tent, died away in the distance. By this time the caravan was swallowed up in the gloom, but we did not hasten; I felt sure that we should presently come up with them at a house.

We continued to ascend gradually, the plateau opening out in every direction, the mountains receding. We saw the red glow of a fire not far away, and again I thought we had reached our destination; but again it proved to be nothing but a herd's tent - there were yak snorting and grunting all round us now. At last we saw a house silhouetted against the sky and the men went forward joyfully shouting. A voice answered them – alas! the caravan was not there, it had gone on. The cold was sending me off to sleep and it was all I could do to stumble along; but the men said it was quite near now and that we had not stopped at the first house, because it was quite full. So we went on again and gradually, in the darkness, went right off our course. The wind now mercifully began to draw breath, the clouds were already blown to shreds, and the stars glittered like gems. We found ourselves in the midst of a vast, featureless, undulating plain, surrounded by low hills which gradually receded as we tried to approach them. Round and round we wandered looking for a trail and shouting; but to no purpose. We separated, and searched in every direction; but could not find a trail on that iron ground. We were lost on the plateau at 15,000 feet, on a winter's night.

At last, after two hours, we heard a faint cry. Whooping with joy we went after it – lost it – followed it again in another direction, like the will-o'-the-wisp, and again heard it. Next minute a man holding a torch appeared over the skyline not a quarter of a mile away. We followed him to a small stone house, hidden by a fold in the ground, and there found the rest of our party. It was 10 o'clock, and we were very cold, tired, and hungry. I could not, however, help feeling sorry for the yak and ponies; though there must have been 50° of frost on the ground, they spent the night in the open yard.

As for us, we had a yak-dung fire which filled the small room with vitriolic smoke; but at least we kept warm. The place is called Tating, and consists of two stone houses, or two blocks of houses, about half a mile apart, and a few scattered tents; the altitude is over 15,000 feet.

Over the last pass

February 9th, 1925, was a great day. We rose early and packed. The animals came into the yard two by two, and for a long time we thought we never should get away. In the end everything went according to plan, and we started up the sparkling valley, where crowds had collected to see us off. It was only about 5 miles to the pass, with an ascent of some 2,500 feet, but the snow got deeper and deeper, and the march proved troublesome, especially as we had started so late that the wind began before we reached the top. However, we reached the Pö La (14,900 feet) early in the afternoon, and what a sight greeted our tired eyes!

Behind us the dead plateau, wrapped in its dazzling white shroud, stretched out its frozen limbs to the pale porcelain mountains, all frothy with cloud. Except for the moaning wind and the swish of the driven snow blast, complete silence reigned. There was no tinkle of water, no song of birds, not even the flutter of a leaf; everything was dead, or fast asleep, or gone abroad for the winter.

In front of us, the mountain dropped away steeply to the valley, the snow ceased abruptly, and the dark mysterious forests on the southern slopes of the Himalaya began.

A caravan was toiling up to the pass; but we raced down, anxious to see the forest again, and soon found several kinds of rhododendron, including 'Anthopogon', 'Lacteum' and a bronze-leafed 'Arboreum'. The descent grew steeper and steeper, clearly a glacier had once forced its way through this glen; and suddenly we found ourselves in the valley of the Nyamjang Chu, which flows from the north. Perched on a shoulder 1,000 feet above the river was a small village, and here we halted. We were over the third barrier, the Himalaya, in Mönyul, the land of the Mönbas; the last pass lay behind us!

All that night it snowed, and when we awoke next morning the world looked like a Christmas card; but we had only to go down, down, down, steadily towards the fertile plains, and by evening we were out of the snow for ever.

For transport we had forty-five Mönbas, men, women, and girls; or sometimes a few yak, which can live in the upper valley, though not lower down. The path is fairly good, but too steep to ride a pony in comfort, and there are endless flights of stone steps. We therefore walked the rest of the way to India.

SIX

Plant Hunting on the Edge of the World 1926–27

Nungs of the Nam Tamai – A masterpiece discovered – Hanging gardens of the forest – Shy Mishmis – March to Fort Hertz – Temperate rain forest – The conquest of Polon – Rose of Kaso

Nungs of the Nam Tamai

There is ample cultivation in the valley of the Nam Tamai, considering the steepness of its flanks. Yet we saw few huts, these being usually well screened. The Nungs are timid, gentle creatures, neither truculent like the Mishmi, nor swaggering like the Chingpaw, with moderate physique and great staying power. The children always look dreadfully undernourished. No doubt they actually were now, since there had been a famine the previous year. Many of the bamboos had flowered, and the extra food supplied by their seeds had caused a great increase in the number of rats. The rats had overflowed into the fields, and eaten the crops; and the next harvest was three months hence. Nor was the present outlook promising. The Nungs have only one method of cultivation, and are at the mercy of the weather. A slope is selected and the forest cut down, only the biggest trees being left standing, for want of tools to fell them. After lying in the sun for two or three weeks the tangle of dead creepers and trees is set on fire, and finally the charred branches are carried away, the ground is raked over, and the crops are sown. This must be done before the rains set in properly, in June. Therefore, the forest must be burnt not later than the beginning of May, and what is wanted is fine weather in April or March. If April is wet – as indeed it was in 1926 – the jungle of course cannot be burnt. When one considers under what appalling difficulties the Nungs labour, the marvel is that they do not all die of starvation. A hill clearing can only be used once. After the reaping of the crop it becomes smothered with weeds, which are gradually replaced by a dense growth of secondary jungle. This secondary growth is far thicker than the original forest; if left alone long enough, it would no doubt revert to jungle, but meanwhile it is much more difficult to cut down than the forest, and six or eight years must elapse before the impoverished soil is fit for cultivation a second time. Sometimes bamboo takes the place of forest, just as grass does in temperate latitudes; and then when the bamboos flower, the rats increase out of all reason. And so it goes on. Then again it is necessary to select slopes which are not too steep or rocky; and they must be below the 6,000-feet contour, otherwise the crops will not ripen. Of these, maize is by far the most important, forming perhaps, in a normal year, 75 per cent. of the people's food. Secondary crops are Eleusine, mountain rice, buckwheat, and Job's tears, with such vegetables as cucumbers, pumpkins, beans, and sweet potatoes.

At the end of the third day's march up the river we halted to change coolies again. Here we saw the visible effects of the famine, in a graveyard; the graves were obviously recent, for in this climate they hardly last a season. Mock birds perched on tall poles represented the souls of the departed flying away; it seemed natural to see so pretty a thought amongst so simple and child-like a people. On the graves, as though loath to let the dead depart altogether from their homes, and perhaps to lure them back, the living had placed their daily needs – so few and plain; a pipe, a hat, a cooking-pot, or basket.

Many of the Nung girls of the Tam Tamai tattoo their faces, drawing a few lines which curve round the chin from the angles of the mouth; and a round dot is added on the tip of the flattened nose.

A masterpiece discovered

It was now late in the afternoon. A fine drizzle filled the air, which was noticeably colder. Although we had been climbing for some time we were still in the rain forest. Quite suddenly we emerged from the heavy dripping gloom of the forest into a blaze of light. A wilderness of tall herbs and bushes hid the steep track, and the icy breath of the alps smote us. Even the red glow of rhododendrons was cold and comfortless as the winter sun; for here was snow, not in wads and fraying patches, but in enormous mounds which looked as though they would never melt. The river rushed headlong down the V-shaped valley, whose flanks

rose at an angle of 40°; out of the higher slopes tall cliffs thrust
themselves threateningly. Two huge snow fans, one on either
side of the valley, had united to throw a safe bridge, many feet
thick, across the frantic river; and on a grassy alp, amidst a tangle
of shrubs and rocks where temperate forest and fir forest met, I
pitched my tent beside a decrepit bothy. As soon as the men had
lit a fire, I clamoured for tea, feeling both cold and hungry; I *must*
make a first dash amongst the alpine flowers before dark. With
half an hour's daylight to go – for the cloud rack swaddled the
hills, and the twilight in these latitudes is of short duration – I
ran across the snow bridge and up the steep cone towards a high
bank of earth, which sloped up to the cliffs; but I had scarcely
reached the bank when I stopped suddenly in amazement. Was I
dreaming? I rubbed my eyes, and looked again. No! Just above
the edge of the snow, a vivid blush-pink flower stood out of the
cold grey earth. It was as big as a rose, and of that fresh clear
pink seen in Madame Butterfly. Of course it could not really be
a rose, and I was glad of that; it would too easily account for the
superb colour. Tea roses do not grow just like that, in spite of
all the wonderful things that do happen in this Aladdin's treasure-
house. But what could it be?

I just stood there transfixed on the snow-cone, in a honeymoon
of bliss, feasting my eyes on a masterpiece. The vulgar thought
– is it new? – did not at this moment occur to me, if only for the
reason that I had not the faintest, foggiest notion to what genus
or even to what family it belonged. It was enough for me that I
had never set eyes on its like. However, as long as I stood there,
overcome by emotion, I could state no fact about the plant, apart
from its sheer colour and brilliance. Yet it was with a certain
reluctance that I now approached it more nearly, breaking the
fragile spell I had woven about the Tea Rose Primula - for a
primula I perceived it to be as soon as I realized that the flower
was a head of flowers. And *what* a primula! The rosy globe
resolved itself into a tight head of flowers, eight in number, borne
on a short but sturdy stem. Each flower measured an inch across.
Later the saw-edged ribbon-like wash-leathery leaves grew up,
the stem lengthened until it stood four inches high, and behold
Primula agleniana var. *thearosa*, the Tea Rose Primula! In the
autumn the leaves wither and the spherical capsules, filled to the
brim with coffee-brown seeds, crumble like scorched paper.

There remains only the hard pointed leaf-bud to pass the winter beneath the snow.

Hanging gardens of the forest

Undesirable as the rain forest is as a place of residence, its beauty in spring is undeniable. The rugged wooden pillars which support the roof, support also a world of flowers. They rise from a thin and shallow sea of fern brake. Slender wands of bamboo ringed with stout prickles fill in the background between the heavy timber. Higher up a clump of snowy orchid (*Cœlogyne ocellata*) appears from amongst the dark foliage like a flock of tiny white birds; and a purple Pleione pokes a dainty head out of a mossy hassock, in the fork of a battered fir. This particular Pleione is almost always solitary – a single dainty pouting purple flower speckled and crested with yellow inside. From the next tree hang streamers of woolly rhododendron. Then from over the knotted limbs, all padded and festooned with luscious moss, and a welter of leaves which chime and ring with harmonious colours, lean down strange faces; the stippled cowls of Arisaema, or the thin hungry flowers of Globba. And as you gaze upwards into the dim roof, the canopy grows ever more opaque; a desperate confusion of interlacing branches, leaves, and jostling plants all clogged with moss. But woe to the big trees which must support this burden – the larches, and junipers, and firs, oaks, cinnamons, and many more. Few escape, except those which, like most of the rhododendrons, are so smooth that no moss or lichen can lodge on them, or such as the birch which continually slough great papery sheets of bark, punched with slots like a pianola record. For moisture and darkness have filled the forest with lurking death. The very ground from out of which the tree rhododendrons grow is permanently mulched, the air is rank with the breath of decay, and between the stems of trees and bamboos, silently, caressingly, steals the cool wet mist. Nothing is ever dry. Everything is choked and stifled with moss; the deep silence of the rain forest, save for the kettledrum roll of raindrops on the armoured leaves of rhododendrons, is due to this padding of the interior. And embedded in these cushions are the perching plants. It is almost fantastic to see the limbs of strong trees, bound into shapeless cocoons by this stealthy scourge. From this spongey bed the epiphytes draw their water. Their soil is the vegetable mould derived from the decay of bark and leaves. The rain is sprayed through the tree-tops by wind. Up here in the swaying branches are light, air, and space, never drought; and scores of plants have hauled themselves painfully upwards, out of the wet dusk where the sour odour of decay rises from the earth, to enjoy this new freedom. And here out of sight they flower as they could never flower below, often revealed to us only when their spent corollas come tumbling to the ground.

Shy Mishmis

Almost every day bands of Mishmi youths passed us on their way to Rima, whither they migrate to work, leaving their women and children behind to weed the fields. The climate of the Mishmi Hills is appalling. During the horribly wet summer months, while the crops are growing, there is little enough for the young men to do, nor is there enough food left to go round. Last year's stock of grain is almost finished; this year's will not be ready till August. So the young men seek food abroad. In the winter they migrate by whole families, in the opposite direction; that is to say, down the Lohit valley to Assam, where they are employed by Indian contractors to cut cane.

The Mishmi are short, muscular, almost naked savages with simian features, and long hair tied in a knot on top of the head. It is difficult to say just what colour their skin is, so dirty are they; but it appears to be a sort of light coppery brown. They dress very simply. From a cord round the waist a flap of cloth hangs over double, one half being pulled under between the legs and fastened by the cord behind. Over this is worn a sporran, or a short skirt, open down one side. A sack-like jacket, reaching to the knee, with holes for head and arms, and a long scarf thrown negligently over the shoulders, complete the dress. The ears are pierced for large gypsy rings; hence the Tibetan name for the Mishmi – Na. The usual short knife is carried over the shoulder in a flat wooden scabbard bound with wire rungs on the open side, and rawhide straps support both knife and bear- or monkey-skin bag. Seldom have I come across a hill tribe so uncouth and so unsophisticated as the Mishmi. They fled at sight of a camera, and eyed me from a distance with dark suspicion. Except from that one man who had been to Sadiya, and was quite wordly, I could get no information of any sort from them. They would not open their mouths, and on any attempt to fraternize they edged away from me, keeping close to one another like sheep. No tribe in the Irrawaddy basin bears any resemblance to the Mishmi; and eighteen months later I was to learn how difficult they are to deal with.

March to Fort Hertz

Then came a break in the rains. By day, an oppressive sticky heat troubled us; at night, the stored-up electricity was loosed over the ragged ranges, and the many-echoed slam of thunder drowned even the rage of the river. A party of starving Nungs, who had been up the valley digging for roots, passed us.

Arrived at the Adung confluence on August 12th, I decided to rest a few days. It was a glorious evening, but myriads of insects made life intolerable. The chirping of crickets, the hoot of an owl, the bark of a muntjac away in the forest sounded terrifying in the hot darkness.

I awoke late next morning. The sun was shining brightly, and everything was very still. For several minutes I lay in bed, drugged with sleeplessness, collecting my wits. Something was wrong, of that I felt sure. The silence became oppressive. Why had I woken? Generally I woke when Chokra came in to light the fire, or when Laphai brought tea. I glanced at the table – everything was exactly as I had left it. No one had been inside the hut; yet it was certainly late.

I raised my voice. Chokra appeared, and began to tidy the hut. 'Call Laphai,' I said lazily.

'He has gone, sahib.'

This hardly penetrated my brain. I supposed he had gone out shooting.

'All right, call Maung Ba.'

'He's gone too; they both went in the night.'

So that was that. My staff had deserted. They had packed their belongings, taken as much food as they could carry, and turned back along the path which led to Fort Hertz and civilization. Chokra and I were alone in the jungle.

The day was intensely hot. One sweated continuously, and the

Frank Kingdon-Ward *by E.M. Gregson*
(Courtesy of the Royal Geographical Society)

Nam Tamai

Larch, oak and *Rhododendron bullatum*, Mishmi Hills

A climbing gentian

Meconopsis speciosa

Gentiana gilvostriata

Rhododendron megacalyx

Roadside *mani* stone decorated with *Rhododendron polyandrum*, Mönyul

Chömbo, Tibet

Seinghku valley

Mixed forest, Chömbo, Tibet

sweat rolled down face and back and chest in rivulets. The glutinous air could not hold any more moisture. After taking thought,
I decided to return to Fort Hertz. But first, to find coolies. In the
evening two natives appeared, and I sent them off for help. Their
fellow Nungs had mostly fled into the jungle, and were living on
such roots and fruits as they could find. The villages were empty.

However, next morning my messengers returned with five
others, and having reduced the kit to the barest necessities, we
started in the afternoon for Fort Hertz. The cane bridge over the
Seinghku river was in a terrible state of disrepair, but we got
across safely, and by dusk had covered the first stage. Altogether
the six stages down the Nam Tamai were done in three and a
half days of strenuous marching. Starting soon after dawn and
halting at sunset, we rested only for two hours in the hottest part
of the day. But it was a strain. The heat, which made me feel
sick, the ceaseless torture of insects day and night, the plodding
up and down over steep spurs, along a narrow muddy path
overgrown with jungle, almost persuaded me to give up the
struggle and return to my alpine camp. But there was the difficulty that we had no food; the truants had helped themselves to
what remained of the rations in no niggard fashion. Rice we must
have, not only for the three remaining months in the Seinghku
valley, but for the journey to Assam as well. Better to go through
with it, and ensure my supply; at the same time I must get
assistance – Chokra single-handed was not to be borne. I worked
out a time-table. If I left Fort Hertz on September 1st, and did
single stages all the way back, I could easily reach my camp by
the last week in September, even allowing for halts to change
coolies. That gave me time enough, so I decided to go on at all
costs.

We required only seven coolies, but I had some difficulty in
getting even these at the Tamai bridge, and it was midday August
19th before we left the river and turned our faces westwards
towards the long low ranges and the eerie darkness of the hill
jungle. It is eight hard marches to the Mali river, slogging up and
down several thousands of feet each day. Now the hill jungle
stretched away from us, range beyond range, many days' journey
in every direction. In the clammy embrace of the monsoon, when
all the scuppers of the mountain gush, and the trees weep pitifully
as the white mist soaks through the moss-bound branches, it is a
shambles.

After crossing the first range we dropped down 4,000 feet into the valley, crossed the next range, and doing a double march on August 21st found ourselves the same evening wading through the swamps of the Tisang river. We got covered with leeches here, and the sand-flies were terrible. As a result of exposure and poisoning by infinite torment of flies, I was taken violently sick in the night. At the Tisang we fell in with a runner from Fort Hertz carrying my mail; but he brought no news of our supply.

Next day we had to wade for miles across the flooded valley of the Tisang, so what with the awful heat, and sickness, I could only go slowly, stopping often to rest. It is not nice to be ill in the jungle, with no white man to hold your hand, and to know that you must keep moving at all costs, or fare worse. To rest in a swamp such as the Tisang valley in August is to invite disaster. However, after a night's sleep I felt much better and able to face the biggest climb of all in good humour. We were now only five stages from Fort Hertz, and I expected to do the distance in four days.

Half-way up the mountain we at last met our supply train on its way to our rescue; five coolies, each carrying a 60 lb. bag, four of rice and one of flour. I told them to dump the loads at the Nam Tamai bridge, and we would pick them up on our return.

The monsoon had started blowing again, and we had an uncomfortably wet march. On the ridge-top, 6,169 feet above sea level, a raw wind drove the rain full in our faces.

Another double march, and we stood next afternoon on the last ridge, overlooking the emerald plain of Hkamti Long. That same evening we reached the Mali river. Much of the plain was flooded, so next day I hired a canoe to take me to Putao, which is close to the fort. But the sun came out and bludgeoned us all into a state of coma, so that we made slow progress against the strong current. At last I could stand it no longer, and disembarked to walk across the paddy-fields. These, however, were knee-deep in water, and it took me rather longer to wade the last four miles than it took the canoe to paddle twice that distance against the current. However, here I was, having covered fifteen stages through the hill jungle in ten and a half days, at the worst season of the year; one hundred and fifty miles, going 'all out'.

It was hot and clammy on the plain, not much more than a thousand feet above sea level and closely invested by mountains, and I was glad to lie in a long chair during the worst heat of the day. It was pleasant to sleep in a bed again, and to have regular meals – I dined and breakfasted with the Superintendent, who was at headquarters for the rainy season.

Shortly after my arrival, some Nungs turned up from the Nam Tamai, bringing my truant servants in custody. It appeared that Maung Ba and Laphai, hearing of my whirlwind march down the valley, and believing me to be in pursuit of them, turned aside to a Nung village in the mountains, where they were hospitably received. Next day, having robbed their host of some money he kept under the floor, they took to the road again; it being reported that we had passed. But the Nungs, discovering the theft, pursued and captured them, and conducted them in to Fort Hertz. The man who had been robbed then brought a case against them, they were convicted of theft, and discharged as first offenders! The headman recovered his money, and received a further reward from me. I recovered the articles which the pilferers had seized before their flight, and they all lived happily ever afterwards. At least, I suppose so; there seems no reason why not. And that was the end of Maung Ba and Laphai so far as I was concerned.

Temperate rain forest

It is scarcely light when the clouds in the valley begin to heave restlessly, and to rise; presently the mist is flying by us on the wings of the wind. Half an hour later down comes the chilled rain in drenching sheets. Often it rained for days and nights with a pitiless resolution, as though it would never stop. But sometimes, just before sunset, even when the weather was at its worst, there came a lull. The valley below us would empty itself of cloud as though by magic, and the mountains across the way would loom up all greasy with mist in the dark blue dusk. But this glimpse was too brief, and the rain curtain was quickly rung down again. Sometimes just before dawn the peaks were clear.

As we sat in our summer-house by the smoking fire, with the clouds driving like fine spray over us, we would look down the steep slope and see the twisted trunks of the trees, the interlacing branches of those just below, and then against the white bank of mist the rounded tops of those still lower; all seen through waving curtains of moss. And staring thus into the heart of the forest the scene changed in our minds, and we imagined ourselves in some fairyland under the depths of the sea. A pale green light shone through the canopy of leaves, and against the milk-white mist loomed strange forms. The fan-shaped growth of the Tsuga-trees became branching coral, with the angular red boughs of the rhododendrons for stems. The banners of moss hanging from every tree, swayed gently by the breeze, were ribbons of weed plucked by an idle current; the dark junipers were sinister growths from the bed of the ocean, dripping with mournful weed. The fantastic leaves of Aralia spread themselves out like hands against the ghostly background, till they also stiffened into lobes of coral, and the bare tops of the larches which peeped up in the offing were but the broken masts of sunken ships whose keels lay rotting in the ooze. In the greenish gloom, lit only by a pale phosphor-escence, as though some shaft of light from a world beyond seeking its way had been caught and held captive, and in the faintly threatening silence which wrapped the forest, one sensed the underworld of the ocean. But the silence was unnatural, and listening, one became aware presently of a dull distant roar, as of waves breaking on a barrier reef. It was the torrent in the valley, 6,000 feet below.

Then the rain came down again, and drummed on the great leaves and dripped off the moss tails; the dark mournful junipers wept ceaselessly, and the whole scene dissolved in tears. The monotonous drip from the trees tolled a knell through the dark and twisted aisles of the forest.

The ghostly white corollas of the rhododendrons, perched high up in the trees, drop silently one by one; wads of moss fall softly, branches crack and crumple on the mossy mattress, as the giants of the forest shed their dying limbs. Then the scuppers of the mountain gush, and the voice of the torrent rises a semitone, shrilling like a band-saw. And in the cool moisture everything grows, and grows, and grows.

The conquest of Polon

We got back to camp much pleased with ourselves, after ten hours' climbing. Three days later I determined to carry out the final exploration and reach the alpine region. It was a terrible day, pouring with rain before dawn, and breakfast by candlelight was

a cold and dreary affair. Once away, and quickly wet through, I
made good progress up the familiar trail, reaching the cave in
three and a half hours. Here I dumped the pemmican brought on
from the alpine top, and also a tin of biscuits. The day was still
young, and I started up the steep face, through the bamboo
screen, full of confidence. Then came a sprawling undergrowth
of *Rhododendron arizelum* beneath the last fringe of wind-clipped
firs; thickets of scrub *R. cinnabarinum* fledged with verdigris green,
R. sanguineum and *R. cerasinum*, with rose bushes, and Pyrus
bearing panicles of snow-white berries: next minute I was climbing a rock scupper which spouted water as the rain descended in
sheets. The banks were lined with rhododendron bushes, and all
along the edge grew hundreds of plants of the Gamboge Primula
in ripe fruit. I had to go slowly here, collecting seeds as I went,
but always climbing up and up towards the invisible summit.

Now the trail turned across the face again, converging on the
ridge, amongst rocks and crouching bushes, and quite suddenly
I came out into the open. There were no more trees, no bushes
even, only steep alpine meadow, with rocky outcrops and low
escarpments beneath which clumps of rhododendron huddled,
and dwarf shrubs of rose, Spiræa, and honeysuckle pressed themselves into crevices. On the very first slopes I found the yellow-
flowered *Primula mishmiensis* in fruit; and then, pushing my way
up the slope through the dying meadow, at last the Maroon
Meadow Primula (*P. rubra*). That was a glorious moment! The
meadow plants were dying and rotting all round me, the flying
rain stung my face and froze my hands, and the mountains with
the clouds smoking over them looked utterly forlorn. But for a
moment that scene was blotted out and what I saw lay in the
womb of the future. It was an English garden steeped in June
sunshine, with waving clumps of golden and violet primulas, and
outcrops of white Candytuft, and Oriental Poppies bouncing like
scarlet balls on a sage-green sea; and in the foreground a drift of
scented primula with neat rounded leaves and slender wands,
shaking out clusters of maroon flowers, brought by someone
from the Mishmi Hills years ago!

Rose of Kaso

Rose of Kaso lay at the root of a great ugly sabre tooth, the last
on the ridge until you reached the peak itself. It seemed doubtful
whether it was possible to reach the sabre, much less the precipice
under the crown. But there was one plant in a gap on the ridge
itself. The creepy Cephalanthum grew much farther along, but
there were a few plants on the cracked crown. As I went along
the ridge I plucked the furry capsules of *R. lanatum*, which had
been brusque enough to shake the snow from itself. Its dejected
leaves, twisted into squills, hung down by its side.

Arrived opposite the dent in which Rose of Kaso lay buried in
a thicket of *Rhododendron sanguineum*, I picked up my marks easily
enough; they had withstood the storm. When the Rose was incar-
nate in a bloody sea, you could not miss it ten yards off; out of
flower, on the other hand, you could not recognize it a yard off.
Imagine the difficulty now, when the whole confused tanglement
was buried beneath the snow! Yet, thanks to my marks, a quick
and ready measurement by cross-bearings brought me right on
top of it at the first attempt. I scraped away the snow and revealed
the familiar foliage; next minute I was digging like a badger, until
the whole plant was exposed. And not one single capsule did it
bear! There was nothing for it then but to try the cliff, perilous
though it might be. So I climbed the first fang on the ridge and
slipped down into the next hollow, at the base of the sabre tooth,
beneath whose contumelious lip slept Rose of Kaso.

Although the whole face was snowbound, I knew exactly
where to take off for the traverse. A deep groove or chute was
cut diagonally across the face, from the root of the sabre tooth,
at a steady angle; a thousand feet below, it was broken across by
an escarpment, where the snow ceased. The dark rock showed
up harshly.

It was impossible to descend into the chute from above because
at its head it was lined with tilted paving-stones. But the far side,
though steep, was well covered with scrub rhododendron, and
therefore both safe and easy; it was this bank which I had ascended
in June to the foot of the cliff, working my way along to the
ridge again above the sabre. This was tricky, but not dangerous
– in June; even the chute itself, once you were in it, offered no
obstacle to a cautious climber.

Now everything was changed. Every pitfall hidden under that

dread mantle of snow, which lay at a dangerous angle, was doubly accentuated; and the task had suddenly assumed a fearful aspect. What was the condition of that snow? Was it soft and cloying, ready to slip with increasing momentum down the long chute to where the precipice gaped? Or was it frozen so hard that, without an axe, I could not cut steps by which to cross? The more I looked at it, the less I liked it; to make matters worse, it was blowing hard from the north again, and the air was once more filled with whirling flakes. If I hesitated any longer I was lost from sheer terror; so I took the plunge, thankful that the whole ghastly business would soon be over, anyhow.

To reach the lip of the chute, I had first of all to cross a belt of scrub rhododendron; and if that had been difficult in the summer, it was infinitely more so now. Before I had progressed ten yards, my mits had been torn to shreds, the cold chisel-like branches had lacerated hands and face, and more than one wad of snow had found its way down my neck. However, I got through the tangle at last, and stood shivering on the brink of the chute, not with cold, but with fear. That sleek white slant filled me with an indefinable dread; but when at last I dropped on to it I found a firm crust of refrozen snow overlying puffy snow, in which my heavy nailed boots could kick deep holes.

Immediately confidence returned. I had only to cross twelve or fifteen yards. The cairn I had so laboriously built over the Rose was not visible, but I reckoned I must be almost opposite it; and I directed my steps slightly upwards and across the chute, kicking deep holes for each foot before venturing on another step. Now I felt the want of an ice-axe to steady me. Glancing down the slope, I shuddered; there was no comfort to be got out of that view, so I kept my gaze firmly fixed on the opposite bank.

Half-way across I had to dig my hands into the snow above to increase my grip, and lean back against the slope with the whole weight of my body, so steep was it. Even then I was standing almost upright. Probably it was this which caused the next incident. Or perhaps my foot slipped. I have no certain recollection of what happened. Anyhow, I slipped. Then things happened swiftly. I gave one squawk of fright, and the next second was flying down the slope at a horrible speed, enveloped in a cloud of snow. I shot down for twenty or thirty yards, and then came to rest, mercifully. It seemed a miracle; but I was hardly in the mood to appreciate miracles just then. In fact I was badly shaken.

Besides, I was still in the gully. To go back was as bad as to go on; worse perhaps. So, having rested a minute, and recovered my morale, I continued across the chute and, reaching the far bank, thankfully plunged my arms elbow-deep into the snow and grasped the firm branches of rhododendron which I knew lay beneath.

Meanwhile I had lost my bearings, and search as I would, not a sign of my cairn could I see; it was in fact completely buried under the snow. To find the Rose under these conditions was well-nigh hopeless – three or four plants amongst thousands, and all invisible. I soon gave up the search and started for the ridge; for indeed I was unnerved, and anxious to reach the safety of the ridge, now almost a thousand feet above me. As I kicked my way up towards the ridge, sinking knee-deep at each step, what should I do but tread right on and thereby expose a solitary bush! This was sheer good luck, and moreover I found two good capsules. But although I spent half an hour dredging round this spot for more treasure, not another capsule could I find. The cold then compelled me to abandon the search; indeed my fingers were beginning to show signs of possible frostbite, and all feeling had left my toes.

The climb up to the ridge, above the sabre tooth, was arduous; and if any question yet remained of climbing higher, here was the complete answer to it. Even on the windswept ridge, the snow was two feet deep, and on the flank I was sinking in up to my knees. No bushes were visible. A flock of Tibetan sand grouse were whistling not far from me; apart from that a grim and awful silence reigned here, 13,000 feet above sea level; even the wind had ceased, and the pearl-grey mist hung motionless round the peaks. Below lay a heap of torn and ragged cloud.

The descent of the sabre tooth, never easy, was made more difficult by the deep snow. On the rock ledges of the northern face I found several frozen plants of the creepy 'Cephalanthum' (*Rhododendron crebreflorum*), but all the capsules had aborted, and I got no seed. I reached the bottom of the sabre, went on down the ridge and over the next fang to where the snow had been spun off, and stopped to consider the position. It was late, and I must start back for the cave or I should be benighted in the forest. My hands were torn and bleeding; I was dreadfully thirsty, but neither hungry nor particularly cold now; only rather tired, and terribly disappointed. *Rhododendron crebreflorum* had been lost, and so had *R. pumilum*; Rose of Kaso, Rock Rose, and *Nomocharis aperta* had been barely secured, and the same probably applied to *P. clutterbuckii* and *P. deleiensis*, which anyway were rare plants.

On the other hand, I had got the carmine *R. smithii* – all there was of it, and Glowbell and *R. lanatum*, besides other things. Yet I felt that nothing would compensate for the loss of the creepy 'Cephalanthum'. It was no good claiming that I had got this and got that if I went away from the Mishmi Hills without it. Why, the plant was growing within half a mile of me at that moment! In the years to come I would never be able to look a Mishmi plant in the face, all spick and span in an English garden, without hating myself for a deserter if I abandoned it. But what was to be done? Nothing – now! I turned my tired eyes towards the valley, and as I did so I saw a wonderful vision.

Beyond the nearest ridges, the whole horizon was slowly turning porcelain-blue, and on this faint sea floated the dark keels of ships with all canvas spread. Even as I looked, the ghostly scene changed. An ethereal milk-white mist was gradually dissolving like silver from a photographic plate, and the picture was coming into strong relief – mountains, glazed on the deepening blue of the sky! It was God's sign that the storm was over. Weary days were ahead; hours of toil and effort, of rage and despair, moments of triumph; but always my thoughts came back to that vision, which comforted me a lot. Who could ever forget it, up there on that bitter storm-swept ridge, during the lull, when at long last the veil was torn aside and all the mountains appeared in white apparel beneath the turquoise dome of heaven?

SEVEN

Wild Bestiary

Phayre's leaf-eating monkeys – A black bear – Dogs, pica-hares and weasels – Monkeys – A herd of takin – Pig-tailed baboons – Pack elephants – Yak – Dogs in Tibet – Serow – A cat-bear – Baby yak – Black lizards – A baby porcupine – A flying squirrel – Racoons – Dogs for the pot – A big cat

Phayre's leaf-eating monkeys

I looked down the mountain slope in the direction indicated, to a strapping forest giant that spread aloft a great canopy of branches hanging above the road, and waited. One minute, two minutes; not a leaf stirred; the forest was silent and seemingly deserted; not even the tinkle of a stream disturbed the profound quiet. And then suddenly, as though a breath of air had sighed over the jungle, a shiver seemed to pass through the branches of the tree, and almost immediately a brown shadow appeared out of the foliage, ran along a branch which swayed dizzily, and crouched; he was followed by another, and another, and yet others, now plainly visible, and still the branch swayed rhythmically as it became more and more depressed. 'Phayre's leaf-eating monkey' (*Semnopithecus phayrei*), said my companion shortly; 'watch them travel from tree to tree.'

At that moment the first monkey leapt; there was a splash of foliage in the tree below, the branch, lightened of a portion of its load, recoiled, and as it came down again the second monkey sprang into the air, hands and feet neatly gathered together. And so they went on, the monkeys leaping one by one from the branch end as it swung up and down, till there was but one left, the branch by this time see-sawing to within a short distance of the goal. Down went the last of them, tail streaming out behind, and away into the jungle after his companions, who had by this time swung themselves out of sight.

Yunnan-Burma frontier, 1910

A black bear

One evening I was in the forest later than usual, and as dusk
fell the gloom greatly increased owing to the clouds which had
descended into the valley and enveloped everything in a cold
drizzle. Suddenly I heard a snorting noise not far away, and
peering through the trees I saw a large black animal advancing
towards me with an odd gait, his nose close to the ground. At
that moment he reared up on his hind legs not a dozen yards
from me, and I saw that it was a black bear, about four feet high
as he stood. I was too astonished to do anything but stand and
gape at him, as for some seconds he stared at me; then with a
particularly loud snort of disgust he dropped down and shuffled
rapidly away into the forest. It was a surprise to me to see a bear
within half an hour's walk of Atuntzu, and having no weapon of
any kind I was glad he had run away, though annoyed that I had
not been able to bag him. The black bear must be fairly common
in these mountains, for all the tribes in the Salween and Mekong
valleys use arrow-cases made of bearskin, just as they have saddle-
bags made from the skin of the 'precipice sheep', as the Tibetans
call it, though what this animal is I am unable to say, never
having secured one. Shooting bears with a cross-bow sounds
exciting.

Atuntzu, 1910

Dogs, pica-hares and weasels

After breakfast I went up our valley to the Tibetan tents and
called on the herdsmen, three saplings to which as many big black
watch-dogs were tied bending almost to breaking point as the
fierce animals strained every muscle to get at the intruder and tear
him to pieces. It was a noisy welcome. Then I lay up amongst
the boulders and had shots at the giant pica-hares which flashed
in and out of the crevices like streaks of light, but they were too
quick for me. I also saw a couple of wicked little weasels (*Mustela
sibirica*) moving furtively across the open, no doubt in pursuit of
the woolly grey hares.

Yangtze-Meking divide, 1913

Monkeys

In the distance high mountains were beginning to lift up their heads. The monsoon jungle was full of strange noises, which ceased mysteriously as soon as one stopped to listen. A rustling of dry leaves – lizards scampering about under the bamboos; a deprecating cough overhead – monkeys are watching our every movement.

It is a most eerie sensation to feel that you are being watched by scores of half-human creatures hidden in the trees and quite invisible. If you stand still a moment there will gradually steal over the jungle a dead silence, broken presently by a little purr; if you are quick you may catch sight of a monkey playing peep-bo with you in a tree, but as soon as he feels he is spotted the head is withdrawn behind a branch and a moment later poked carefully round the other side. Suddenly the silent trees are alive with baboons coughing, grunting like pigs and plunging off into the jungle; they seem to spring out of the violently agitated foliage, where a moment before was nothing, as crowds spring from the paving-stones in big cities. I suppose a monkey's first thought is self-preservation; his second is undoubtedly an insatiable curiosity.

Nmai Hka valley, 1914

A herd of takin

Patches of snow still lay melting in the gullies; the mists gathered and dispersed whimsically. I would have given a lot to have seen these mountains bathed in sunshine.

Suddenly my attention was diverted by a loud snort, and looking over the ridge I saw on the opposite scree, 300 yards away, a herd of seven takin [*Budorcas taxicolor*] standing head to wind in the driving mist, like Highland cattle. Their backs were to us, so that we had ample leisure to examine them, as the wind was coming up-valley and we were well above them. There were two big bulls, three females and two quite small calves. It was a splendid sight, and I bitterly regretted having left my rifle in camp.

After watching them through glasses for a time we halloed, and the herd started up suddenly at the sound and made off across the scree, those great lumbering brutes, almost as big as water buffaloes, leaping nimbly from rock to rock like goats. Plunging through a strip of bamboo grass, they reappeared strung out in line on the next scree and were soon swallowed up in the mist.

Imaw Bum, 1914

Pig-tailed baboons

The people of this village brought me a long-tailed harvest mouse and a baby monkey, for which I gave a rupee and some beads. The monkey, a pig-tailed baboon, was the oddest little chap, his tiny face crumpled like a petal in bud, giving him an appearance of wrinkled age, though he was unweaned and his weakness, his childish clutchings, and his piteous cries for his mother, dead or wounded in the jungle, betrayed his tender age. I kept him for two days, forcibly feeding him on well-chewed sugar-cane or corn, copiously emulsified with saliva, and then the newly lit flame of his little life flickered and went out in the night.

I bought another pig-tailed baboon from the village in exchange for some beads. He was older than the last one, and only took to me very gradually – indeed it was several days before he could bear to look at me without facially expressing his displeasure, though he was soon smiling at the natives. He became quite friendly with me and rode on my shoulder most of the way, eating chocolate. He was very fond of maize liquor too, and would fill his cheek pouches with food to be chewed at leisure later on. He had a curious way of sleeping on his belly, all bunched up into a ball, and his little cry of pleasure, his querulous scream and his shrill scream of anger were frequently heard.

One afternoon the monkey ran away into the jungle out of pique because I smacked him. I thought he was lost, but presently I heard him screeching away, and caught sight of him crawling along the branch of a tree farther down the slope. I called and called, but he ceased crying, and I had almost given him up when he reappeared sitting on the path below. When he saw me coming he grinned, ran down the path a little way, I after him, and then sat up again, waiting; when I came to him he climbed up my leg and seemed pleased to be back. I don't think that he liked that five minutes at home, for it was raining hard at the time and he hated rain. Whether it was a momentary twinge of homesickness or a joke he was unable to tell me, but he never ran away again.

The Triangle, 1914

Pack elephants

All round us as far as the eye could reach was dense forest or high grass and scrub. The big elephant, an enormous beast from Assam, found it difficult to get through in places, and the *mahout* was sometimes threatened with decapitation by the branches of trees. However, seated on Jumbo's neck with a foot behind each ear, he guided the wise old beast skilfully, and the pair of them provided us with plenty of amusement, especially the small Hkamti animal, who always insisted on rising while he was being loaded.

'*Bat! Bat!! Bat!!!**' screamed the *mahout*, as the kneeling elephant, with half his load on his back, leisurely proceeded to stand up; then he would slowly sink down again and allow the men to put some more on him. In the hilly country, however, the elephants proved only a nuisance, moving with extreme slowness; indeed the big animal became almost useless, so thoroughly exhausted was he, and at one time we quite thought he was going to die by the wayside.

The Triangle, 1914

Yak

At night the yak were driven home and tethered by the tent where the herdsman dwelt: the cows and calves being kept in a separate pen. These 'woolly cows' (as the Chinese call them) would form a ring round our tents, grunting to each other, and moving with infinite caution, one step at a time. At last one is close enough to thrust his nose through the opening of my tent and see what there is inside this odd bag. He does so, blowing loudly through his nose, and peeping cautiously. Then comes the alarm, and the investigators, standing about in attitudes suggestive of polite but

---

* *Baitho* = sit down.

innocent curiosity, instantly spin round and, waving their short plume-like tails high in air, scamper off.

But not far. Their curiosity is even greater than their timidity. Besides, when they find that no punishment follows discovery, they are more reluctant to retire, and do so only as long as the pressure is applied. The men were adepts at devising new and unexpected stunts. When putting one's head out suddenly and saying 'shoo' in an astonished yak's face no longer held any terrors for them, they would lie low inside their tent till the cattle had gathered round, and then beat lustily on the canvas; and when that too grew contemptible through familiarity, they adopted the ruse of stealing out and opening umbrellas suddenly in the beasts' faces, to their complete discomfiture. But whatever we did the yak always returned. At night, when, as sometimes happened, they were not tethered, they were an unmitigated nuisance. Under cover of darkness they would renew their investigations and, tripping over the tent-ropes, blunder half through the entrance. It was no pleasant experience to wake in the middle of the night from an unsound sleep, with the hot, fœtid breath of a clumsy yak snored over your cheek.

Muli, 1921

Dogs in Tibet

There were two enormous mastiffs chained to their kennels inside the courtyard of the *dzong*; and when anyone approached they set up a deep baying and tugged at their chains, making frantic efforts to get at the intruder. These brutes, though not naturally bad-tempered, are deliberately starved in order to keep them savage, and it would go hard with anyone who was set upon by a dog which stands nearly 3 feet high and weighs close on 200 lb. They are kept only as watch-dogs. Besides the mastiff, there is one other well-bred dog in Tibet, and he is not common. I refer to the Tibetan poodle, a house-dog sometimes seen in monasteries, or in baronial castles. He is something like a Pekingese but larger, not so dish-faced, and without the heavy mane. He has long hair and a curly tail carried over his back like a chow's; the few I have seen were black with a small patch of long white hair on the chest. In every Tibetan village, at least in the river gorge country, the usual loathsome pariahs abound; a surprising number of them are wall-eyed, a condition seen also in Tibetan ponies.

Tsela Dzong, 1924

Serow

In the course of a traverse I happened to look up the glen just in time to see a serow (*Nemorhaedus*) leap nimbly up and disappear over the rise. Ten minutes later I topped the next spur, and almost trod on a female serow. She sprang up, gave one bound, and stood staring at me scarcely ten yards away. I could not understand why she did not go off immediately, though I myself stood stock-still, watching her. Her lips trembled, and she wagged her stump of a tail violently, but did not move until I did; I noticed that she was foxy red all over except for a sharp black line all down the backbone. When I moved, she went off through the shrub in huge bounds, and finally disappeared. She made no sound. Seeing a movement at my feet, I looked down; and then I knew why the serow had held her ground so long. I was almost standing on a tiny baby serow. I picked up the little creature, which neither showed any sign of fear nor tried to get away. Indeed it could hardly stand on its feeble little legs. I carried it back to camp in my arms. In a day it was tame, sucking at my fingers and lapping up condensed milk. It was the same colour as its mother, but had grey ears. One might judge of its age from the fact that it could not quite stand upright on its feeble little legs, and that the umbilical cord had not yet withered. The ends of its hoofs were soft like butter, and of course it had no teeth. For two days we fed it on milk. Sometimes it bleated, but on the whole seemed happy. But on the fourth day poor little William Rufus suddenly became very ill and died in a few hours. The new diet had upset him, I suppose. We had not the heart to eat him, and in the evening I buried him under a great rhododendron tree below our camp, and planted some ferns on his grave.

Kaso, 1927

A cat-bear

The most pleasant encounter I had with a wild animal occurred one day when I was on my way down a steep rocky slope. In the fork of a small tree, somewhat isolated from its neighbours, I suddenly saw, almost level with my eyes, a red cat-bear [*Ailurus julgens*]. On catching sight of me (it must have heard me first) the cat-bear stared, but showed no fear, nor even surprise; still less did it hurry away. Very deliberately, staring at me with its large onyx eyes set in white semi-circles, it followed my move-ments. At first it appeared to be measuring its distance from the nearest big tree, then from the ground. But the tree in which I had startled it was a pygmy amongst giants, and it could not reach a bigger one without first descending to the ground. The cat-bear took in all this at a glance, without change of expression, and moved without haste. Not for a moment did it take its eyes off me.

Knowing that it could be easily tamed and would make an amusing pet, I set about capturing my cat-bear. We played a jolly game. I pretended to climb the trunk, and as I swarmed up, the cat-bear retreated along the main branch which overhung the slope, and made as if to come down; but as soon as I slid down, very leisurely he climbed up among the foliage again. At last I laid hold of the slender trunk and began to shake the crown. The cat-bear retreated backwards farther and farther, and the thin branches rocked and swayed under its modest weight. I threw a faggot at the little animal, but it only eyed me reprovingly. It was driven into an impossible position, though, now, and could not scramble back: no longer would the bent branches give pur-chase to its claws. After a short struggle it stopped trying, and hung there swaying, not in the least embarrassed, still staring at me with its calculating eyes.

The lethargy with which the pretty little creature moved struck me as curious – as also the fact that it made no sound. Sometimes it hung vertically, head downwards, sometimes in a more upright position. I was wondering how to make it relinquish its hold and trying once more to scale the trunk, when, without warning, the animal let go and dropped a dozen or fifteen feet to the ground. So long as I stood guard by the trunk this was its only possible line of escape; and yet the manœuvre took me by surprise. Moreover, I was at a disadvantage, because I was a few feet away, and it was impossible to move quickly. With sorrow I saw the cat-bear, obviously not at home on the ground, though more agile than myself on ground so steep and rough, shamble rapidly down the slope and disappear in the forest.

Adung gorge, 1931

Baby yak

About a month earlier the yak had calved, so there were lots of baby yak around. They are shy little creatures, not yet having developed the insatiable curiosity of their parents. In fact, so sensitive are they that, whenever they notice a stranger staring at them, they grunt and run coyly for cover. But they are naughty too, and have to be disciplined. They much prefer mother's milk to grass; but after they are weaned, a prickly bamboo muzzle, shaped something like a gas mask, is fitted over the head. This is enough to make them unpopular with mother, who dislikes being prodded in the udder with a sharp instrument, and kicks the little rebel into the middle of next week.

Chösam, 1935

Black lizards

I spent the morning of September 15th with the black lizards down the valley. It had rained in the night, but the sun came out, and the midday warmth tempted scores of these ugly creatures, known to science as *Agama himalayana sacra*. They can run very swiftly, and when frightened betray their presence instead of keeping quiet. Their usual tactics, as one approaches, are to make a dash, then stop, run again, then stop once more. Only when they believe themselves in imminent peril do they bolt into a hole. When running they carry the tail erect. They can climb a vertical rock face, and are not afraid to plunge into a bush which overhangs a cliff; sometimes they will risk a long leap. They love to lie flat on a slab of rock warming their cold blood in the sunshine. When out of one eye they see anything move, they become alert. Up goes the head, and starts to nod like a mandarin. I found it possible to frighten them suddenly into a cul-de-sac, and capture them alive. Stalking them, I would often see the ugly head of one in front of me cautiously raised, to peer over the top of a rock; flat and vicious-looking like an adder's as the head is, and repulsive the black skin, this reptile has a beautiful golden-orange eye. It was now changing its skin, and looked even more repulsive than usual. I could not discover exactly what their food consists of, but they are certainly carnivorous.

Sanga Chöling, 1935

A baby porcupine

Some forest rangers brought in a baby porcupine. The young of almost all animals are said to be pretty; even the young of crocodiles move the sentimental to crocodile tears. But surely it depends on how young and also perhaps on how helpless they are. Neither new-born kittens nor unfledged birds appeal to my aesthetic sense, and young cobras are scarcely disarming. This little porcupine had a face exactly like a guinea-pig's which had got crumpled, and its quills, soft as indiarubber and almost colourless, were so short that much wrinkled pink flesh was exposed, giving the creature an absurdly senile appearance in spite of its youthful face and figure. Whatever its age, it was far from helpless, and it could run with astonishing speed. Porcupine flesh is regarded as a delicacy; I don't know whether this one was destined for the pot.

Myitkyina, 1937

A flying squirrel

The headman brought me a small flying squirrel, a furry little ball of fluff as soft as eiderdown. The overall colour was steel grey. They told me it ate seeds – so it had come to the right place. It made no fuss at finding itself a prisoner in the small bamboo cage I had made for it, nor did it show any sign of fear; rather did it display a philosophic calm and a dormouse-like capacity for sleep; perhaps it did not like so much daylight. Most of its time it slept, its little head sunk between its forepaws, the folds of its parachute neatly folded up and put away, its body hunched up into a sort of rugby football, its long fluffy tail laid flat over its back. It drank milk but would not touch boiled rice

or papaya. Also it greedily ate bamboo shoots and the scarlet
fruits of a Polygonum. However, the problem of feeding it was
of short duration. I was at work in the rather dark room when I
heard a curious intermittent tapping on the bamboo mat floor
and glanced up just in time to see my squirrel covering the last
lap to the door in a rapid succession of jerboa-like leaps. In a flash
it was through the open door. Though the hut was raised a
couple of feet off the ground, the fugitive did not wait to become
airborne; it ran down the ladder. I was on its tail by this time,
but alas! it was too nimble even on so strange a medium as earth
and it quickly disappeared into the nearest patch of jungle. I
looked at the bamboo cage. One of the bars had been gnawed
through – a flying squirrel possesses two pairs of very efficient
chisel teeth. I should have known that for rodents bamboo bars
do not a prison make.

Tamai valley, 1937

Racoons

The march over the lower spurs to the Nung village took nearly
the whole day, and the sun was setting as we came down into
the little hollow. I was walking ahead of the coolies near the top
of the ridge and had just turned a corner when suddenly three
small animals the size of a spaniel came romping up the hill
towards me. They saw me almost as soon as I saw them and
halted abruptly. Head, body and long bushy tail were black but
the breast was yellowish, the colour continuing round to the back
of the neck. The head was long and pointed. I say these creatures
were romping because that just describes it; they appeared to be
playing like puppies, pawing and chasing one another by turns –
I watched them thus for a few brief seconds. At the very moment
they scented danger, one of them had its paw lifted exactly like
a terrier. There was a noise something between a deprecatory
cough and a grunt. Then all three after a brief look at me standing
stock-still within twenty yards of them took fright, turned and
scampered off. They kept to the path at first as offering the easiest
route, then abruptly disappeared into the forest. They were more
dog- than cat-like in appearance; racoons probably.

Munghu Hkyet, 1937

Dogs for the pot

Later we passed two Lisus squatting by the roadside while round them sprawled a dozen dogs, their heads on their paws. The dogs wore wooden yokes round their necks, like chain-gang slaves, or were tied together with the two ends of a stout stick between each pair, to prevent them from biting their masters – or each other. Certainly they were prick-eared curs of no breeding. Yet they were dogs, the friend of man. The fate in store for them was to be cooked and eaten. Their masters had brought them all the way from China and were taking them to the Laungvaw country beyond the Wulaw pass, to sell them. It seemed a long way to go just for the pot. There can be no more moral obloquy in eating a dog than in eating a lamb cutlet; it is sentiment that makes one dislike eating one's friends. But the dogs, if they knew what fate held in store for them, seemed bored and indifferent.

Kangfang, 1938

A big cat

They told us that a Kachin woman of Rawang had beaten off single-handed, and eventually killed, a big cat. It was in the very act of stealing a pig from beneath her hut. She went out and, facing it boldly, smote it with the *dah* she carried. She wanted to sell the skin, and here it was.

This cat must have stood 20–24 inches at the shoulder, and its length, head and body (taken from the dried skin), was about 43 inches, with a tail 22½ inches long. Thus it was about the size of a lynx, and it had pointed black ears about two inches long, also like a lynx. The colouring was peculiar. Perhaps the most distinctive markings, and the ones I picked out first, were the three narrow black stripes, strictly parallel, down the spine – wavy over the neck, but straight elsewhere, and uniting to form a single black line down the tail; between these lines the fur had a bronze tint, repeated as a background colour on the head. Elsewhere, however – that is to say, on the back and flanks – the underlying colour was silver-grey with a network of black, something like a tabby cat; this resolved itself into definite stripes towards the head end, and equally definite rosettes or half-rosettes, like a leopard, towards the rear end. Both stripes and rosettes showed up dramatically against the rabbity silver-grey in full light, but would probably vanish completely in the jungle; while the sandy-yellow throat, chest and belly would be equally non-committal.

Tama Bum, 1953

EIGHT

An Eye for the Girls

*A Moso girl – A Lutzu beauty – Minchia women – Lutzu girl porters
– Lashi girls – Yawyin girls – Maru girls – Lisu women – Duleng
women – Shan girls – Hkanung girls – Daru women – Kampa girls –
More Maru girls – Daisy chains*

A Moso Girl

I can imagine nothing more charming, nothing in better taste,
than a well-dressed Moso girl. She wears a white or perhaps dark
blue skirt, closely pleated lengthways after the manner of a skirt-
dancer's costume, reaching well below the knees; a dark blue
blouse tied round the waist; and a head-cloth of a dull red colour,
above which is bound the queue, probably adorned with jewels
of coarse workmanship, silver set with coral and turquoise, to
match the long pendant ear-rings. Nor is it too much to say that
many a Moso girl is wonderfully pretty, with a round good-
natured face, regular features, a light complexion which is most
readily described as sunburnt, and large dreamy eyes, though the
general expression is one of considerable animation.

Wei-hsi, Yunnan – Burma frontier, 1910

A Lutzu beauty

The path was very steep and we descended at a great pace to a
small hut about half-way down the mountain, where we stopped
for some refreshment. Here I saw one of the most beautiful girls
I have ever come across, a graceful lustrous-eyed creature, with
warm sunburnt complexion. One meets such beauties sometimes
amongst the Lutzu, more often amongst the Moso or the Tibetan
tribes, and instinctively one wonders where they come from, for
they possess no obvious Mongolian feature, neither prominent
cheek-bones, nor almond-shaped eyes, and scarcely even the distinctive colouring, for the complexion may be so light as to

resemble that of the European. Their straight black hair and black eyes alone betray them.

Salween valley, 1910

Minchia women

It was impossible to reach La-chi-mi that day, for the new moon had already set and it had become very dark in the forest. The stars shone brightly in the clear sky, and a cold wind blew up the valley, so that we gladly stopped at the next village, situated in a clearing on the edge of the pine forest. The Minchias – the first specimens of the tribe with whom we had come in contact – received me kindly and made all necessary arrangements for my comfort, though the dogs, being extremely jealous of poor Ah-poh [his mastiff], were not at all friendly. The huts as usual were of wood, with slat roofs kept down by stones, and the women, except for a tall dark-blue turban standing up on the head like a pudding-cloth, much after the manner of the Shan turban, were dressed in the orthodox fashion. There was nothing Chinese in their appearance, however, for they were one and all fine strapping wenches, though not conspicuous for good looks, their large vacant faces putting one in mind of suet dumplings.

East of the Mekong, 1910

Lutzu girl porters

It was pretty to watch my procession of Lutzu girls on the march. Supporting their loads by means of a head-strap, thus having their hands free, they usually walk along twisting hemp fibre, held between the teeth; a supply of hemp, together with food, being carried, not in a basket such as the Tibetan girls of Jana sling over the shoulder, but in a cloth bag like that carried by the Kachin and Maru. When the girls are not so employed, however, they clasp their hands behind the head, elbows straight out and heads thrown back the better to balance themselves: and so they marched now, their bare feet pattering down the steep path.

The Lutzu women are small and slim with merry round faces, and regular features. They wear a loose long-sleeved jacket of blue cotton cloth, and a short skirt of the same material, or sometimes of white hemp, tied round the waist; to this is added a white hempen blanket with striped ends, extending diagonally across the chest from the right shoulder to the left armpit. Similar blankets with fringed ends are worn by the Nung of the Taron, whose dress differs from that of the Lutzu only in its scantiness. And this is owing to the absence of Chinese garments. In cold weather a goatskin waistcoat is added, hair inside. Hardly any jewellery is worn, what there is being of Tibetan workmanship – clumsy finger-rings, or brooches in the form of collar buckles. No natural ornamentation such as the rattan leg-rings of the Kachin or the cowry belt of the Maru is met with, and the pigtail, though bound on top of the head, is never artificially lengthened and tasseled, like that of the Tibetan matron.

Tra-mu-tang, 1913

Lashi girls

Working in the fields, with their already short skirts tucked still higher, were several stout-limbed Lashi girls, who exchanged loud-voiced greeting with my men.

'What savages!' cried Tung-ch'ien, thinking of the demure matrons of China. 'Look at their feet! look at their hair! They are not dressed!'

And indeed his disparaging remarks were merited, for our Amazons were wading in the mud, and had, besides tucking up their skirts, thrown aside their jackets, displaying ample breasts. Their coarse black hair, which so aroused Tung's derision, was cut in a fringe round the forehead, like a mop, and tied in a knot on top of the head; their feet were bare, number eights, rather a contrast to the 'six-inch gold lilies' of Tung's fellow-country-women. Through the pendulous lobes of their distorted ears were thrust large bamboo tubes, supporting in turn heavy brass rings; and clumsy silver hoops loosely embraced their stout necks, hang-ing over the breast, with a tangle of bead necklaces.

Altogether, what with their awkward movements and pre-posterous ornaments, these heavy-featured Lashi women were not very attractive.

The Triangle, 1914

Yawyin girls

The girls have merry, round faces, pink cheeks and large, frank eyes; they show off their figures to advantage by wrapping a long sash round the waist – a Li-kiang habit. Indeed many of them claim to have come from Li-kiang, which suggests a relationship to the Mosos, and through them to the Tibetans. Their dress is extremely picturesque – a harlequin skirt of many colours, or more exactly three, buff, ochre-red and chocolate, arranged in broad stripes, with a short jacket; a sash tied round the waist; and an ordinary Chinese turban worn in place of the scarf affected by the more prosperous Yawyins of the T'eng-yueh district.

The Triangle, 1914

Maru girls

The Marus are not overburdened with clothes, and during the heat of a summer's day they are reduced to a minimum.

The men wore only a short *longyi* and stopped to bathe in nearly every stream we came to. The married women, who are distinguished by a sort of white turban, like a dirty pudding-cloth after a suet dumpling has been boiled in it, perched on top of the head, never hesitated to take off their thin jackets, and the girls sometimes did the same, though generally throwing it over the shoulders to conceal the breasts. The girls, however, always tucked their *longyi* up to their knees at least, in fact the garment is not much longer at its full extent. They wear nothing on their heads, and cut the hair in a fringe round the forehead, after the manner of a Burmese *sadouk*, the rest of it being cut short so as to form a mop.

Laking, 1914

Lisu women

The dress of the *hê* Lisu women is characteristic, and quite distinct from the harlequin skirt of the Yawyin, which latter peculiarity is said to be due to local influence.

She wears a thin, pleated skirt down to her knees, rather full at the waist, made of white hemp cloth with thin blue stripes, and a loose jacket to match. Feet and legs are bare, but below the knee a garter of black cane rings is worn. There is little display of jewellery such as the Tibetan women wear, this being confined to large ear-rings and silver bracelets, while hoops of bamboo or iron are worn round the neck. The ears are not bored like those of the Burmans, Shans and Kachin tribes, nor are masses of beads, such as the Lashis, Marus and others delight in, worn – probably because they are not obtainable. The hair is done in two hanging pigtails, and round the brow is bound a fillet of white shirt buttons, or, in rare cases, of cowry shells, from which dangles a fringe of tiny beads ending with dummy brass bells. Cowry belts like those of the Maru girls were not seen.

Nmai valley, 1914

Duleng women

The Dulengs, both men and women, tie the hair in a knot on top of the head, and wear a coloured handkerchief over it. The only garment worn is a *longyi*, or skirt, usually dark-blue striped with dull red, and fastened rather above the waist. In place of a jacket the women wear coils of black rattan wire round the breasts, drawing attention to rather than modestly concealing them. Indeed, they have rather fine figures, these Duleng women, being bigger than the Marus, and well made; but their looks are nothing to boast of. Very few beads or cowries are worn – a great contrast to the Marus – and practically no other ornaments; a roll of paper or a bamboo tube is thrust through the large hole bored in the lower lobe of the ear, a few rattan rings passed round the calf below the knee, and that is all.

Nam Tisang, 1914

Shan girls

In the early morning, to the throb of the spinning song, a procession of yellow-robed monks and boys, with downcast eyes and slow step, leaves the wee wooden monastery, and starts on its begging tour through the village. Then from each hut emerge the pious women storing up merit with their offerings of rice, which they tip silently into big bowls borne by small boys. We can see

them well now – they are very dainty, in tight skirt of dark-blue
cloth relieved with a few stripes of red or brown, reaching to the
bare ankles, and close-fitting, short-sleeved jacket. Perhaps they
are proud of their neat figures, these charming little Shan girls,
for their clothes are always tight-fitting, and the trick of edging
the trim sleeves of their dark-coloured jacket with brighter red,
and wearing a low turban of white or scarlet, draws attention to
just those points they would have you look at. Often a white
wrap with coloured stripes at each end is flung loosely across the
breast, over the left shoulder.

Like the Tibeto-Burman tribes, the ears are pierced to hold
metal tubes, but the rattan cane rings with which the rude jungle
people adorn their persons are not worn; for the Shans have
emerged from the wood age into the metal age, and naturally
(but silently) despise their uncouth though powerful neighbours.

Hkamti Long, 1914

Hkanung girls

The valley narrowed and we had repeatedly to cross and recross
the river to avoid cliffs. Three times above Hpalalangdam we
crossed by cane suspension-bridges, but the bridle-path continued
quite good. On the second day we met some people, which was
quite an event here. A Chinaman had married a Hkanung woman,
and we met the whole family. Some of the Chinese pedlars from
the Salween, who tour this country selling salt, cotton cloth,
yarn, needles and such things, marry Hkanungs and settle down.
Yet it was Tibetan rather than Chinese influence we found here.
The people wear woollen instead of thin cotton clothes, and both
men and women possess Tibetan silver jewellery, set with coral
and turquoise. Girls usually wear bamboo tubes in their ear-lobes
about three inches long and an inch in diameter. These are not
merely ornamental but useful. One end of the tube is plugged,
and into the cavity are thrust all the gewgaws valued by the
Hkanung maid, that is to say, odd beads, needle and thread, a
slice of betel-nut, or a leaf of tobacco. The ear-tube is in fact the
Hkanung vanity bag, though it contains neither mirror nor lipstick. Nor do the Hkanung belles powder their noses; instead
they tattoo their faces. Sometimes the pattern consists of a few
poetic lines, sometimes of a mere variety of dots and dashes.

Every girl carries a small bamboo comb hanging from her girdle, and often a bamboo jew's harp, which she twangs in the evening while seated round the fire.

Seinghku-Adung confluence, 1931

Daru women

The Darus were with few exceptions exceedingly ugly. Well under five feet in height, with round faces and heavy features, they dressed in rags and were dirty like wild beasts. Their noses are flattened, their prominent lips thick, their eyes dull; their short, matted hair falls in an even fringe all round. But they are pleasant people. Servile to perfection, they are hard-working, cheerful and possessed of almost unlimited endurance.

Though jewellery is almost unknown, feminine charm is supplemented in various ways. Women wear fine rings of lacquered cane round the calf; and on these they thread metal rings, sometimes as many as half a dozen on each leg. They also wear bead necklaces, and occasionally silver charm-boxes from Tibet. But their most interesting effort at decoration is the tattooing of their faces in a pattern of blue noughts and crosses. Tattooing is optional, and by no means all the girls indulge in it, any more than all English girls paint their lips vermilion and their nails the colour of clotted bullock's blood.

Tahawndam, 1931

Kampa girls

The people of the plateau are Kampas, which means simply 'inhabitants of Kam', the name given vaguely to eastern Tibet. They are taller and finer featured than the people of Lhasa, though they are evidently of mixed origin. Few of these Kampas have ever seen a white man before, but having long had contact with the Chinese, they are broader minded and more progressive than the people of central Tibet. They are naturally hospitable and friendly to strangers, though they are liable to outbursts of fanaticism.

Though the severe climate of Shugden is not favourable to good looks and still less to good complexions, many of the red-cheeked girls I saw in warmer valleys were quite pretty. Women do their hair in a peculiar way. After buttering it, they plait it into a number of thin rat's tails. Then these are gathered together at the end and plaited in with blue wool till the thick queue trails almost to the ground. They wear a spindle-shaped silver brooch on top of their head, with a coral in the middle and a turquoise at either end.

Shugden, 1933

More Maru girls

A number of merry Maru girls with bobbed hair and cane belts, on which were strung little brass bells, used to come jingling down from the village each day. They reminded me of the varnished ponies with harness attached we used to play with in the nursery.

Ngawchang, 1939

Daisy chains

At a village where we halted for an hour, our girl porters proceeded to break off a lower branch from a tree which was a tall white pyramid of blossom. Every twig bore its burden of tiny bead-like flowers. These they stripped, and threaded on cotton to make 'daisy chains', which they wore in their hair. We called it the daisy chain tree – and still do, as we have not yet succeeded in identifying it.

The Triangle, 1953

NINE

Gardens in the Wild – 1

Wind-borne seeds – A temperate rain forest – A dwarf rhododendron –
Meconopsis speciosa – Meconopsis wallichii – 'Lemon Bell' – Incarvillia
grandiflora – A perfect garden of flowers – Myosotis hookeri – Cyanan-
thus incanus – K. W. 5545

Wind-borne seeds

On September 1 we went into camp in one of the valleys above
Atuntzu at an altitude of 13,000 feet. Next day the porters
returned to Atuntzu, taking with them the ponies; and leaving
Ah-poh [his mastiff] to guard the camp, Kin and I ascended the
first hanging valley to the alpine grassland above, finding several
species of Meconopsis and primula in seed, as well as many
plants in flower, chiefly saxifrages, gentians, dwarf aconite, and
larkspur.

It is interesting to note that the seeds of a large proportion of
these high alpines living at from 16,000 to 18,000 feet are adapted
for wind distribution. For example, those of the dwarf rhododendrons are winged, those of the saxifrages and gentians extremely
small and light, those of the numerous scree composites provided
with the usual pappus, and so on. It is particularly noticeable at
these altitudes in the case of precipice plants, which may be
compared to epiphytes. Considering that the winds blow *up* these
valleys, the fact that wind-borne seeds should reach such high
altitudes and gradually colonize ground which may have been
slowly exposed owing to the retreat of glaciers is quite natural,
and I have frequently watched seeds of Compositae being whirled
up a mountainside 12,000 feet above sea level. On the other hand
the mere possession of seeds capable of being carried by the wind
does not enable a plant to establish itself on these inhospitable
mountains, for neither Epilobium nor clematis, to mention only
two genera which are common at 12,000 feet, has representatives
in the true alpine region. Nor must it be forgotten that the high
alpine flora is a north temperate one, and has undoubtedly come
from the north, though growing here in the latitude of Cairo; so

that the south winds which blow up the deep main valleys as already described cannot have added anything to the composition of the flora.

Atuntzu, 1910

A temperate rain forest

The temperate rain forest now looked its best. For the most part the trees were evergreen conifers, firs with occasional clumps of Cunninghamia and other species, but down by the stream were birches, alders, and maples, marked as spots of gold, orange, and red which, in the light of the rising sun, seemed to fill the dark forest with a rich mellow glow pervading everything, and very beautiful. With the thaw, the leaves came whirling down in their hundreds, rustling softly, and, catching the first sunbeams, sent shafts of coloured light twinkling and dancing down the woodland glades. Immense skeletons of *Lilium giganteum* rose stiffly on either hand, some of them ten feet high and bearing a dozen or more big capsules which were slowly scattering their useless seeds, for, so far as I could make out, this plant, though producing many thousands of seeds, rarely sets a fertile one. Here and there, too, clumps of terrestrial orchids caught the eye.

Chun-tsung-la, 1910

A dwarf rhododendron

Along the rocky ridge above camp grew a tangle of rhododendron, of all colours; but the most remarkable one appeared to have black or deep plum-coloured flowers. When, however, the sun shone through them, the flowers were seen to be blood-red, which is how they would appear to their bee visitors, since the flowers stand horizontally. Thus they are really far more conspicuous than might be supposed from their small size (the plant stands barely four inches high) and dull colour as seen from above. A rhododendron four inches high is probably a novelty to many people acquainted with the rhododendron as a big bush at home, or a tree in the Himalaya, and is the more remarkable that no one would ever mistake it for anything but a rhododendron. There are a large number of these dwarfs characterized by flowers standing horizontally, borne in pairs instead of in trusses, which gives each flower more room to develop, hence they are usually borne on long pedicels and are not markedly zygomorphic.

Ka-kar-po mountain, 1913

Meconopsis speciosa

We were again in the land of *the* blue poppy. Of this magnificent plant (*Meconopsis speciosa*) I will give some details. One specimen I noted was 20 inches high, crowned with 29 flowers and 14 ripening capsules above, with 5 buds below – 48 flowers in all. Indeed, the plant seems to go on throughout the summer unfurling flower after flower out of nowhere – like a Japanese pith blossom thrown into water – for the stem is hollow and the root shallow. Another bore 8 fruits, 15 flowers and 5 buds, and a third, only 15 inches high, had 6 flowers, each 3½ inches across, besides 14 buds. But for a certain perkiness of the stiff prickly stem, which refuses any gracefulness of arrangement to the crowded raceme, and the absence of foliage amongst the blooms, these great azure-blue flowers, massed with gold in the centre, would be the most beautiful I have ever seen. The Cambridge-blue poppy is, moreover, unique amongst the dozen species of poppywort known to me from this region, in being sweetly scented. On one scree I counted no less than forty of these magnificent plants within a space of a few square yards, but, scattered as they were amongst big boulders, they only peeped up here and there and did not look so numerous.

The natural history of this Meconopsis is also interesting. It is a plant which produces an enormous number of seeds, very few of which ever germinate, for the capsules are attacked by a small grub before the seeds ripen, and cruelly decimated. Of those which survive till October or November to be shaken out amongst the hard, cold rocks, standing like tombstones, witnesses to the slaughter on every hand, how many are fertile? How many perish before spring comes again? How many grow into seedlings, only to form food for some hungry creature awakening from its long winter sleep? Alas, few, very few, hidden away snugly deep down in some dark crevice amongst the snow-roofed boulders, will survive through all these dangers, and live to flower in the second summer! Think what it means, the forty plants counted above, bearing say twenty-five flowers each, with five hundred seeds per capsule, i.e. half a million embryos to be scattered amongst the boulders, for the seeds are not shaken far afield; yet will there be fifty plants here next year where forty are now? I doubt it. Yet if there are, the sacrifice was not vain.

Yangtze-Mekong divide, 1913

Meconopsis wallichii

Then quite suddenly the meadow widened out, and where the tall flowers swayed graciously all round us I came on what I sought. They were standing in a row as stiff as though on parade, just above the edge of the meadow bordering the woodland, a line of glorious poppyworts. So the missing link was found and the flora of the Imaw Bum range definitely connected through that of the Mekong-Salween divide with that of the Himalaya.

This Meconopsis (*M. wallichii*) grew seven feet high, and had pale purple flowers one and a half inches across, massed with a tassel of golden anthers in the centre. The flowers are small in comparison with many of its kind, but they are borne in remarkable numbers; one plant I examined, which had a seven-foot stem, bore 16 buds, 27 flowers and 103 fruits – nearly 150 flowers in all, though not blooming simultaneously. It may be wondered how so many flowers of this size are crowded on a seven-foot stem, but it is quite simple. They are borne in short racemes six to nine inches long, of about seven flowers each raceme, springing from the axil of a strap-shaped, drooping leaf, closely pressed against the main stem, which itself ends in a flower, giving a wonderful concentration of colour. The whole thus· forms an immense panicle, the tall stem studded from top to bottom first with fat ovoid buds, then with flowers, and below with capsules. I collected seed of this species (familiar from the Himalaya), but it was not quite ripe and did not survive the journey to England.

Imaw Bum, 1914

'Lemon Bell'

'Lemon Bell' is a June-flowering species, one of the most delightful rhododendrons met with. A small, loose-limbed tree, it haunts the coppices, scattered amongst larch and oak, maple, fir, and birch. The buds are streaked and flushed with crimson, but when the bell expands it is a pure lemon-yellow as seen at Muli, very regular, with a wide throat. West of the Yangtze, however, occurs a form having a purple blotch at the base of the corolla. This I introduced some years ago under the number K. W. 529, and it flowered in several gardens in 1923. The truss carries few flowers, which hang freely.

Muli, 1921

Incarvillia grandiflora

The ramp below the cliff was gaudy with the crimson trumpets of *Incarvillia grandiflora* and occasional plants of the tall and stiff *I. lutea*. The latter sends up a sheaf of spikes bearing dull yellow flowers, usually more or less stained with reddish-brown streaks. But *I. grandiflora*, despite its aggressive colour, and a certain freakishness due to the large size of its pouting perianth, and the shortness of its stalk, is really quite a fine thing. Maybe it is pert. It struts. Yet it is undeniably fascinating. As for being tropic, far from it; it is an alpine which does very well at 13,000 or 14,000 feet, though there is no denying it comes of good family, tropic in sympathy. It has connections south of Cancer, and has itself never lost that elusive air of good breeding we associate with equatorial birth.

Muli, 1921

A perfect garden of flowers

Entering on a defile between rugged cliffs, we saw the pass ahead, high up on the brow of the mountain. Suddenly we stepped into a perfect garden of flowers, glowing with all colours of the rainbow. A stream from a hanging valley shot over the lip of the cliff on our left, and tumbled at our feet. Here glimmered flowers never dreamed of in Covent Garden. *Primula* (Omphalogramma) *vinnæflora*, and the large yellow globes of *Meconopsis integrifolia*, floating like buoys on a green sea of grass; the chubby flesh-pink flowers and blotched leaves of Podophyllum, frail meadow rue, and purple aster, clumps of bright gamboge Draba, rather leggy in figure, and the nodding violet-blue flowers of *Meconopsis lancifolia*, their short scapes almost smothered by the surrounding vegetation. One pasture was dyed purple with *Iris chrysographes*, a beardless species of the 'sibirica' type, with flowers the colour of a Munich stained-glass window. (It grows no more than a foot high, flowering in June.) Above all, an amazing wealth and variety of primulas crowded the bogs, frilled the streams, and scattered themselves over meadow and lawn.

Muli, 1921

Myosotis hookeri

We had some beautiful days at Glacier Lake Camp in June, and climbed all the neighbouring peaks. On the slate range we found hassocks of *Myosotis hookeri*, which stands out in my memory as the most sumptuous cushion plant I ever met with. Imagine a bath sponge, a foot through, stuck on a rock. The fibrous part is coloured eau-de-nil, edged with silver, while the holes are plugged with the richest sapphire-blue imaginable. The foliage of this gorgeous forget-me-not forms a hemisphere of cloisonné, which on dissection is seen to be made up of tiny silver-lined leaves clasped in each other's embrace; and from this pedestal, the unwinking blue eyes, flush with the surface, stare at heaven.

Muli, 1921

Cyananthus incanus

One of the most enchanting of alpine plants is *Cyananthus incanus*, var. *leiocalyx*, an admirable plant for the rock garden. In colour and form it is first-class. Not till July does it announce itself on the limestone scree, by unfurling its leaves. The crimped foliage, all grey-white with soft downy hair, forms prostrate mats, which spread and sprawl in every direction. Then in August the flowers open, large shining corollas of glossy silk, till presently the green mats are smothered under a glut of icy blue salvers.

The throat of each is at first plugged with a pompon of white hairs; but as the petals spread out more widely, the pompon too resolves itself into five crests, or beards, one to each petal. The five-rayed stigma is also disclosed in the centre of the tube, like a yellow star.

The whole plant is now covered with flowers. Day after day more open, and for a month or six weeks the mats are a picture of health and loveliness. Through the veil of rain the trumpets gleam and burn against the dead white scree. They are a keen, live colour, now bright and piercing, like blue gimlets; now hot and misty, like Bengal lights.

Comes the early autumn snow, and the plants are buried. When it melts on the scree, under the baleful glare of the November sunshine, it is difficult even to find the plants. They are dead, shrivelled, and uprooted, or torn to shreds. The wind tosses them up and down the scree. But the seeds lie snug. We shake them out – hard marbled eggs, and they travel safely to England (K. W. 4730).

Muli, 1921

K. W. 5545

November 13. Minimum 62°F. Only one more climb, up out of the valley of the Nam Tisang. There was a beautiful, dark chocolate-brown, glossy-flowered Cypripedium just opening on the bank, and maple and Engelhardtia trees overhead. Up and still up, through the rustling bamboo forest, to the cold granite ridge, raked by stinging rain. Here we met once more with homely oak trees, and the queerest little fruiting bush, of which it is necessary to say more.

It was perched on an old tree-stump, on the very apex of the granite ridge, but closely invested by large bushes and small trees of oak, euonymus, magnolia, maple, *Rhododendron mackenzianum*, screw-pine (Pandanus), and so forth. I saw it on the high bank above my head as I passed – a compact 15-inch bush with slightly ascending branches, hung all over with bunches of slender scarlet pods.

'Anyhow, it is not a rhododendron,' said I to myself, and passed on to a spot where I could climb the bank. There was a straight cliff on the other side, and I looked down on the tree-tops. I poked about amongst the bushes on the ridge; came back to the fruiting bush; looked at it curiously. Next moment I was on my knees beside it, trembling.

'Good heavens! it *is* a rhododendron!' I whispered shakily, as with numbed fingers I began pulling off the dangling red capsules. Mist and rain swept gustily over the ridge, but I heeded it not till I had stripped that bush – there was only one.

Nam Tisang, 1922

TEN

Insect World

Caterpillars – A hive of suburban life – A butterfly – A remarkable sight – Ambuscaded by bees – More caterpillars – An unladylike ladybird – Forest butterflies – Sociable butterflies – Insect life – Saw-fly larvæ – The moth that squeaked – Moths on Sirhoi – Papilio machaon and Heliophorus – Uncouth larvæ – A host of butterflies

Caterpillars

Pushing through the thick growth in the stream bed hard by the Yawyin village where we had slept previously, my attention was attracted to the strange circumstance of some tall stinging-nettles rocking to and fro in still air, and turning to them I found that this motion was caused by a number of large caterpillars agitating the leaves. These formidable larvæ, apprehensive at my approach, had raised their heads, snake-like, and darting them rapidly to and fro caused the leaves on which they sat to shiver and tremble in the manner described. The trembling motion became still more marked as I looked closer, and when finally I touched one, several of them ejected at me, with considerable violence, drops of dark-green fluid. Such mummery is evidently designed to scare away some enemy, but whether bird, spider or insect I did not ascertain.

Imaw Bum, 1914

A hive of suburban life

The limit of plant adolescence had now been reached, and everything was growing and spreading enormously. The turgid undergrowth stood man-high, the trees were covered with varied flowers, not their own. The thick pile of fern-like moss which covered every tree-trunk and every bamboo haulm was a hive of suburban life, a world apart from the busy life of the larger forest.

Probing into its green depths, you found the most entrancing creatures in hiding, as when you lift up the fringe of seaweed lining some sapphire rock-pool; and no doubt they were equally astonished at the violation of their sanctuary.

Here I brought to light a quaint green stick-insect cleverly disguised as a sprig of moss, for which, indeed, I mistook him till he showed himself capable of independent motion. Here too in the green underworld of moss were snails shaped like French horns, and slender pink worms, leeches, beetles, spiders – oh! a menagerie of creatures; the hive pulsed with silent life. Beneath an unruffled surface, what struggles took place between creature and creature, each an idea in the Divine Mind, each labouring under a blind impulse to increase its numbers without regard for others; what raids, what devilries, what tragedies!

Hpimaw, 1914

A butterfly

Then there silently arose just in front of me a brown flapping creature which zigzagged through the trees, sawing a little up and down, before it came to rest abruptly, and – melted away. Had it been, as I at first thought, a bird, there was nothing, save perhaps its silent movements, like those of a nightjar, remarkable about it. But no bird I ever met could alight thus on a bush and immediately disappear, noiselessly. Indeed it was not a bird; its flight, its manner of settling, its power of spontaneously blending with it surroundings, all betrayed it for what it was. It was a butterfly; and with the realization at once the incredible size of the insect struck me. But I never captured one of those skulkers, though I saw several.

Hpimaw, 1914

A remarkable sight

Presently we came upon a remarkable sight.

Some carnivorous animal had left its droppings in a rock-pool amongst the boulders, and the poisoned water had tainted the atmosphere for yards around with its rank acridness. From all directions this reeking cesspool had attracted the most gorgeous butterflies imaginable, and they had come in their dozens. The pool was a quivering mass of brilliant insects, and still others hovered to and fro over the unsavoury meal, awaiting their turn to alight; from time to time a butterfly, impatient of waiting, would push itself amongst the already packed multitude, causing a flutter of painted wings as the group rearranged itself like the colours in a kaleidoscope. Is it not curious that such beautiful, delicate, and outwardly dainty creatures should be attracted by such loathsomeness? It is apt to start a cynical train of thought on the corruption which underlies all material beauty and the empty vanities of life.

But it was while watching, fascinated, these heaven-born insects that for the first time I realized the full magic beauty of Mendelssohn's *Papillon*, which ran in my head even as I watched the oscillating wings at the butterfly meet. Amongst them were many swallow-tails of the genus Dalchina, with schooner wings banded with pale green. When the insect settles the wings are folded and in profile resemble the sails of a schooner.

Most lovely of all butterflies are the swallow-tails, of which there are a considerable variety in the hot, sunny valleys. These, as they probe the flowers for honey, scarcely settle or, if they do, touch with so light a caress the damask petals that they seem poised on air; and as they hover over, or tread with fairy pressure, the bell-like convolvulus and trumpet flowers, their wings quiver and tremble like aspen leaves shivering in a zephyr breeze, never still for a moment. One of the most beautiful of these was a species of Leptocircus, with gauzy wings trailing out behind like fluttering ribands. How full of life they look, what restless energy in those slender bodies borne aloft on gorgeous wings! and how exquisitely the first movement of *Papillon* represents to our ears the quivering, restless vitality here seen with the eyes! This music will ever carry me back to the Burmese hinterland, where I shall see again that rancid pool with its burden of butterflies by the thundering Mekh!

Mekh valley, 1914

Ambuscaded by bees

Looking over the cliff, I saw the Nam Ting winding through a stony valley 3,000 feet below. In the afternoon we walked into a trap, and were ambuscaded by bees. The bees were extremely active, and attacked the middle of the line with such vim that half the mules stampeded ahead and half fled back. The Shan dogs (which resemble Chows) bolted through the undergrowth, combing themselves in the bushes and rubbing their heads in the soil – but they did not utter a sound. Altogether a lively five minutes. Eventually we shook off our assailants, and reformed line ahead.

Nam Ting valley, 1921

More caterpillars

More interesting were some nasty-looking corpse-white caterpillars feeding on the leaves of a big Phytolacca which grew in every village. The caterpillars were very conspicuous on the dark-green foliage, and at no pains to conceal themselves. No hungry bird could have failed to see them. What, then, was the secret of their immunity? Chemical warfare!

Along the back of the caterpillar was fixed a double row of papillæ, for all the world like the tentacles of a starfish. On handling it, drops of fluid, of a pure golden yellow, began to exude, not from the papillæ, but from a row of tiny portholes along either flank. The papillæ were merely triggers. You pressed the button, the caterpillar did the rest. If the pressure was maintained, the creature sweated until it was enveloped in a bath of golden syrup. The liquid had a faintly disagreeable smell, and a drop placed on the tongue proved pungent, like pepper, and left a bitter taste behind. Evidently an acid. Now, it is easy to say that no sensible bird would eat such a nasty morsel. But first he must learn, and remember, that it *is* nasty. If the caterpillar does nothing about it till he is touched, and if the first thing that touches him is a large and powerful beak, he will be hurt before the aggressor, smarting from a drop of vitriol injected into his eye, can release him. It would be poor consolation to the caterpillar to reflect, from solitary confinement in the bird's crop, that it – the bird – was going to be sick.

I therefore performed other experiments to discover whether the caterpillar could be induced to exude warning drops without contact. The result was what I anticipated. On blowing on him urgently, or on tickling him up by means of a burning-glass, he reacted so violently as to squirt jets of fluid to a distance of six inches! Obviously, then, a small bird might easily receive a contribution in the eye. True, the caterpillar's aim is erratic; but with the entire battery in action, the chances of a 'bird's eye' are considerable. The merest touch, the stimulus provided by the beat of a bird's wing, might let loose the dogs of war; and though the caterpillar was unable to distinguish between my finger and a twig, he could to some extent distinguish stimuli. Otherwise any chance breeze might open the valves.

Kari, 1922

An unladylike ladybird

There was a curious and most unladylike ladybird here. The dull black wing-cases were crossed by a network of coral-red lines. When molested, it drew in its legs and tucked them underneath; as it did so, from each joint exuded a drop of yellow fluid. If that did not scare away the intruder, the insect permitted itself to roll off the leaf, and be lost like a needle in a haystack.

Bahang, 1922

Forest butterflies

Gorgeous swallow-tail butterflies pranced through the open glades; but those which skulk in the depths of the forest, though the least conspicuous, are the most interesting. Their flight is weak. They fly low, and for short distances only, but with a curious zigzag or dancing motion. They are found in the hill jungle, where the ground is drier, and come out, I believe, mostly in the dry winter months. At that season the sun is lower, and its rays filter into the forest, striping and dappling the slopes with light and shadow; and here it is that the barred and ocellate butterflies hover amongst the dead leaves. On the wing they are conspicuous enough, but no sooner do they settle than they instantly disappear. Their wings are barred with shadows (Melanitis) or edged with rows of pale eyes, resembling the millions of eyes cast on the ground by the sunlight drifting through the foliage. So these dazzle-painted butterflies, as soon as they settle among the dead leaves, wings folded, harmonize with their surroundings and melt quietly into the indistinguishable background.

They do not resemble something else – if they did they would
be visible. They just disappear.

Nam Tisang, 1922

Sociable butterflies

In the course of the day I wandered down to the river bank,
where there were a few poor patches of cultivation. On the damp
sand quivered a vast cluster of thirsty butterflies; they rose in a
cloud, like snowflakes, when disturbed, and broke into dancing
chains which see-sawed through the air. The whites and orange-
tips, which comprised the vast majority, hovered round the same
spot, loath to leave, and frequently settled, though never again
in such a solid phalanx while I remained; but the rarer species –
the panelled swallow-tails and the swift Charaxes – were quickly
scared away, and did not return. A dead butterfly, however,
proved a good decoy, and attracted many curious companions,
who between them pulled it limb from limb; for butterflies, of
course, are hardened scavengers.

It is curious how they insist on drinking in company. They are
sociable creatures, and though there was plenty of room, they all
crowded to the one spot, shoving and butting each other in greedy
haste. When I returned to the place at four o'clock, although the
sun was yet well up, there was not a butterfly left on the beach.
A few, flitting distractedly along the edge of the jungle, were
obviously seeking shelter for the night.

Mali Hka, 1922

Insect life

We had started a collection of insects, mainly beetles, and this
occupation gave us plenty of interest. Whenever we came to a
large log of wood or a stone, we gathered round it armed with
killing-bottles, and proceeded to roll it over if we could. The
sudden light startled the underworld into life. Small beetles scur-
ried this way and that. There were vicious-looking centipedes and
bloated wood-lice running madly about. Little black scorpions
turned up their tails and adopted an aggressive attitude. These
last were more common inside the wood logs than under them

– especially where white termite ants had been at work. Those who are familiar only with English or even with European forests would be surprised at the work performed by the hordes of insects and other creatures which work in the dark in the Burmese jungle. Even at this off-season, prodigious numbers of small sappers and miners were at work. A thick tree-trunk is reduced to dust in a few months by a termite army.

Nor were all the insects we discovered subterranean. Butterflies and grasshoppers, dragonflies and beetles were numerous on warm afternoons in every open place. It was surprising how many of the smaller grasshoppers were one-legged, as though they had each lost a limb during some titanic upheaval, or perhaps only in domestic strife with the more bulky females. Huge locusts with a bright green fuselage, utterly sluggish when the morning mist lies on the ground, became active in the heat of the day, when the shade temperature rose to 70°. These locusts are awkward in the air, flying clumsily and rather slowly when disturbed; but their colour keeps them concealed; often the first intimation one had of their presence was a whirr of wings. They would travel in a straight trajectory, as though loosed from a gun, until they hit against an obstacle. Usually they fell down, but sometimes they clung to the frail support of a leaf or stem. They never seemed to have the power to change their direction while in flight and always kept on their course until stopped suddenly by impact.

Most of the cold-weather butterflies we saw were small, drab, shade-loving insects, their wings dazzle-painted with bars and spots. They are weak and fly slowly, with a zigzag, dipping motion.

Kachin Hills, 1930

Saw-fly larvæ

While walking close to our camp one day, my attention was attracted by the extraordinary antics of some caterpillars, over a dozen of which were herded together on a twig. When I disturbed them, all with one accord, as though actuated by a spring, turned their tail-ends right over till they touched their heads. Thus looped, with only their legs bristling, the pattern resembled a flower or opening bud, anything rather than a cluster of scared larvæ. I prodded one, and instantly it ejected with considerable force a jet of fluid from the anal orifice, the others following suit. Finally, still keeping their heads well down, they all started to wag their tail-ends up and down until sheer exhaustion compelled them to stop. The contortion was disconcerting to some common enemy. There is no doubt that they were the larvæ of a saw-fly. Many saw-fly larvæ squirt liquid when touched, and some wag their heads, but tail-waggers were a novelty to me.

Jité, 1931

The moth that squeaked

One evening I found a large moth, something like a death's head moth, with a similar though not identical pattern. When I touched it gently as it rested, it jerked its body upwards by straightening out its legs, keeping its feet planted; this is did several times, each time giving vent to a queer little rasping squeak. Then, still planted on the same spot, it began to flutter its wings rapidly rather like an aircraft 'revving up'. Not often does one meet with either butterflies or moths which make a sound audible to the human ear.

Mali valley, 1937

Moths on Sirhoi

The nights were short and pleasantly warm, the temperature not falling below 60°, while day after day it reached 75° or 80°. Gorgeous butterflies were abroad, enjoying the sunshine. A yellow and black Junonia looked as though someone had attempted to do poker-work on its tawny wings. A flashing metallic blue-green Heliophorus, when approached, snapped its glittering wings together so suddenly that one expected to hear them clack like castanets; and mingled with these gay creatures were humbler fry like cabbage whites. But the finest butterfly was one I had never seen before. The upper surface of the fore-wing was a rich golden brown with black spots, giving it a leopardish look, in startling contrast with the hindwing, which was midnight blue. The under-wing was a sort of marbled grey, with mutton-fat markings. It was a big insect with a strong, rapid flight, and while settled it fanned gently with its wings, so as to expose both surfaces alternately to the sun.

One evening a magnificent moth flew into Cobweb Cottage. It had a wing-span of three and a half inches, and beautiful fern-like antennae. But its most prominent marking was a kind of peacock's 'eye' painted near the centre of each wing, though it had none of the peacock's colour. The background was a warm chestnut, and the 'eye' consisted of a not quite circular ring, one half maroon, the other lamp-black, surrounding a yellow pupil. Further, the maroon half of the wing had a white paring, like a new moon, on the inner side. Along the trailing edge of each wing was a thin double zigzag of black, and still closer to the edge, but on the under-wing only, a zigzag white line. I renounce all copyright in the above description.

Sirhoi, 1948

Papilio machaon and Heliophorus

The commonest butterfly on Sirhoi was one familiar to many English boys, since it is found in our own Fen district – *Papilio machaon*, the 'English' swallow-tail. Its food plant, a species of Daucus or wild carrot, grew in the meadow, and I found several of its striking black-and-green striped larvæ. This larva has the peculiarity of possessing a pair of soft retractile 'horns', like the horns of a snail, immediately behind the head. When frightened it pushes them out quickly, then slowly retracts them. However, it soon tires of the gesture, and cannot be made to do it more than two or three times without a long rest.

On sunny days the black glutinous mud outside the door of our hut proved irresistible to a brilliant little Heliophorus. The under-side of the wings (which is often all one sees) is dull yellow, and it is only when the insect believes itself to be safe that it ventures to display its true colours. Then the wings open slowly, revealing the lovely metallic blue-green of the upper surface, but ready to snap shut at the first hint of danger. The hindwing, however, often looks black, relieved by a few red-orange spots round the border, and the tiny comma-like 'tail'; but as the butterfly pivots round, allowing the light to strike it at a different angle, it too gleams metallic blue-green like the front wing. When wallowing in the muck, this insect is not difficult to catch.

Sirhoi, 1948

Uncouth larvæ

In the rainy season many large and uncouth larvæ are abroad. The champion heavyweight was a brown hairy monster, destined to become a moth. Almost as big was a brilliant grass-green caterpillar with a leather-brown head. It was four and a quarter inches in length, its body armed with a series of paired conical turrets, from each of which projected a fascis of stiff bristles. The first pairs of turrets just behind the head were larger than the others, and more heavily armed, for from their base sprang ten diverging spikes with a single long central spike, all jet-black – a truly frightful weapon. The turrets, six to each segment, in three pairs, were distinguished by their pale yellow colour and orange base. The creature was gaudy, but not beautiful, and more frightening than lovable. It looked like one of those liassic reptiles which stalked the earth millions of years ago.

Even this creature was eclipsed in fantasy, however, by another with armament which could be instantly concealed at will. You saw a large, but ordinary-looking, caterpillar coming towards you. Suddenly it took fright; and as though it had pressed a button, two rows of ports aligned along its back opened, exposing as many tufts of bristles, each tuft countersunk in its little weapon-pit. Thus the innocent-looking larva crawled along looking as smooth and inviting as a ripe peach; the alarm being given, it suddenly unmasked its ports and displayed to the astonished gaze a dozen tufts of lethal bristles, which a minute later would vanish again with all the unexpectedness of a disappearing gun. All these armed caterpillars set up considerable irritation if you handled them, and it was hardly surprising that the Tangkhuls avoided them; nor could they understand our interest in such creatures, which experience had taught them were dangerous. However, the only caterpillar I induced to pupate became a large and rather dull white moth.

Ukhrul, 1948

A host of butterflies

We saw a remarkable sight here. On a large rock by the rushing river hundreds of butterflies, all of one species, had gathered. They were drinking from one or two rock-pools, the water in which may have been fouled by animals, or may have been there so long that it was foul anyway. Butterflies are dirty feeders. So tightly were they packed, there was standing room only for the first comers, while scores hovered close by, flying round and round, quick to take the place of any who had drunk their fill, or even trying unsuccessfully to wedge themselves in between the drinkers. They were reluctant to move, and we had much ado to stir them up. Seen with closed wings, these butterflies were a rather dusty yellow, but on the wing they looked mainly pure white, like a shower of white and pale yellow confetti. I suspect that it was the urge for salt which had attracted them to this pool of Siloam.

Hkinlum, 1953

ELEVEN

Landscapes

Nightfall over Pai-ma-shan – Hailstorm in the mountains – Sunset in the Salween valley – Atuntzu – A view of the sacred mountain – Gambolling waters – A dying glacier – Night on Laksang Bum – A break in the rains – Screes – Gompo Né – The plain of Assam – Burmese jungle – Rong Thö Chu – Pen La – Sacred turquoise lake – Ka Karpo Razi – On Tama Bum

Nightfall over Pai-ma-shan

Starting early next morning and leaving the men to pack up and follow, I rode into Atuntzu at one o'clock, to find the village bathed in brilliant sunshine; yet in the afternoon the sky grew black over Pai-ma-shan again, and we heard the thunder rolling and rumbling over that storm-riven mountain. At sunset the peaks, clearly outlined against the blue-black sky, presented an extraordinary appearance, as though recently swept by a terrific snowstorm, for they glowed with a pale reddish-gold tint, which in contrast to the darkling sky and surrounding mountains, now in deep shadow, looked like snow. Then the stars came out in their myriads, and distant lightning could be seen flickering behind Pai-ma-shan.

Atuntzu, 1910

Hailstorm in the mountains

So far the weather had kept fine, though by this time we were well up in the mountains; but no sooner did we get out on to the open plateau than I saw we were in for trouble. A nasty raw wind blew in violent gusts, and right in front of us a great black ridge of cloud hung low over the hills. We had scarcely turned southwards down the valley than the storm burst upon us with amazing fury. The whole earth seemed to rock to the thunder-claps, as the echoes tumbled from side to side amongst the hills; the hail lashed into the short turf with a sharp hissing sound, and drummed on our hats and cloaks. Rills boiled up into streams in an instant and came frothing down the grassy slopes. In less than half an hour the valley was wrapped in a shroud of hail more than an inch deep, and looking at those white mountains so bleak and bare, from which lower down a few black clumps of fir-trees stretched their grim spires up towards the leaden sky, I thought that winter had already breathed again over the grassland plateau of dreary Tibet. Yet it was scarcely mid-August.

Chianca-Mekong divide, 1910

Sunset in the Salween valley

We were now some two thousand feet above the river, and as the sun sank down behind the towering cliffs above us, the valley was filled with a glow of such wonderful colour that no description of mine can convey any idea of its spell. While all was dark and gloomy in the depth of the valley, the setting sun caught the tops of the mountains across the river, and one forgot their bare brown slopes under the waves of crimson light which they reflected. Gradually a deep blue shadow crept up out of the valley and wrapped the hills in slumber, while a soft clinging mist seemed to precipitate itself from the atmosphere and spread over the rice-fields far below. In the gloaming the crimson died down to purple, the purple became violet, and still the glorious colours of sunset played up and down the valley. Away to the south a few wisps of cloud caught the slanting rays of the sun, which flashed like the beams of a heliograph through a gap in the black wall of rock overhead, and diffused an orange glow into the deepening blue. Then a few stars shone out, and the ridge was clearly silhouetted against the eastern sky: night had come down like a curtain.

Salween valley, 1910

Atuntzu

Early in the afternoon we stood on the pass and looked down on the pale-coloured village of Atuntzu, nestling in a horseshoe of mountains. Picture the scene on a radiant afternoon, the barren valley, all steeped in sunshine, chequered with houses surrounded by shady trees and barley-fields, little oases which gleam now like emeralds in a base setting, and in autumn one by one turn to gold as harvest time creeps up the valley; the flat-topped hill, full-fledged with flowering shrubs and crowned by the white buildings of the monastery; the crescent of mud-walled houses divided by a single cobbled street rising step by step to the little fort which forms the northern gateway; the whole embraced by high mountains, their lower slopes green with a patchwork of cultivation, their summits rising amongst the frayed clouds which sail across the azure sky.

Atuntzu, 1913

A view of the sacred mountain

One evening I sat down on the mountain slope beneath bushes of rhododendron aflame with blossom; numbers of tits chirped and hopped from bush to bush, poking their heads inside the blotched corollas, seeking small beetles. When the dazzle of sunset had been replaced by violet dusk, I looked westwards across the Mekong valley to the sacred mountain of Ka Karpo, and saw cataracts of splintered ice frozen to the cliffs over which they plunged; close to the foot of the biggest glacier were several houses scattered over terraces of shining corn.

Mekong valley, 1913

Gambolling waters

While the loads and men were travelling across the rope, a business which took an hour or more, I collected plants and later seated myself on the rocks as close to the river as possible, for I never wearied of watching the rush of water. Here the surface heaves, and great pustules swell up as though gas were being rapidly generated inside them, burst with a hiss, and pass on in swimming foam; there a ridge of water dances over a hidden rock and breaks suddenly, and a little frothing wave tries to crawl back by itself over the hurrying water, but is swept hastily away, to re-form below. A stick comes frolicking down on the roaring tide, is buried for a moment, and reappears a dozen yards away; waves spring up suddenly and slap insolently against the smooth rock slabs, scored with grooves and pot-holes when the flood rose higher than it does now; and whirlpools dart gurgling from place to place like will-o'-the-wisp. It is a fascinating pastime to sit and watch all these ever-changing tricks of the gambolling, shouting Mekong waters, their voice rising throughout the summer, and dying away to a whisper in winter as the red mud sinks out of sight, and the water reflects the blue of heaven.

Mekong, 1913

A dying glacier

Continuing south-westwards in the direction of the snow mountains across undulating ground, we presently reached the summit of another ridge, and looking across several narrow, stony valleys beheld a grand sight. For the first time I saw, perfectly clear against a china-blue sky and quite close to us, the northernmost of the snow-peaks, the black buttress of Tsa-ya, a massive tower down whose near wall there crawled, its blunt arms out-thrust aimlessly like a gigantic amœba, all that was left of what must once have been a big glacier.

It was the oddest sight imaginable, that white fungus-like growth, clinging to the face of the cliff, its blunt-nosed pseudopodia protruding stiffly from its much-scratched body; with icy grip enfeebled by approaching death, it now hugged the rock it had so mauled and gashed; its tentacles clawed weakly at the face of the tower they had so wounded. And as it hung there dying, dying in the stillness, I stood spellbound.

Pai-ma-shan, 1913

Night on Laksang Bum

The evening was fine and when the moon rose over the mountains it caught the cotton-grass and splashed the whole meadow with drops of glistening silver. Fire-flies twinkled amongst the trees, some coming into my tent to examine the lantern, as though jealous of its wan beams. A deer barked close by and was answered by another, and then came a shrill scream from high up in the jungle, as of some animal in deadly fear.

The Triangle, 1914

A break in the rains

Towards the end of July there came one of those sudden and inexplicable breaks in the rains, characteristic of the hills. By night it poured as steadily as ever, but by day, in spite of the cloud blanket resting soddenly on the mountains, burying their summits, owing to some cross-current of air, some subtle readjustment of pressures, the rain held off for a week, while the sun even peeped out occasionally.

Then after a tempestuous sunset behind the Lawkhaung divide the clouds would close their ranks and, pressing heavily down on the valley, envelop the fort in drenching rain for the night. They were grand sometimes, those struggles at dusk between the retreating sun and the onswarming clouds. In a river of gold the setting sun, defiant to the last, would flash its fiery signals across the valley, and disappear, while the wicked-looking cloud waves quickly closed all loopholes and, rushing up the valley, beat furiously against the mountains.

Hpimaw, 1914

Screes

Screes are always active, some more, some less; there is no such thing as a extinct scree. Motion, swift, loud, and startling, is its very essence. As soon as rocks cease to fall, the scree begins to melt away. Transport, however slow, overtakes production; plants gain, and keep, a foothold; and the scree dissolves in fat ease. A live scree is tense and aggressive; it is all tooth and nail; all hammer and tongs.

Muli, 1921

Gompo Né

Gompo Né is little more than a name. Amongst a wilderness of gneissic monoliths, rasped and scoured by the shock of the river, then idly cast aside, their raw wounds abandoned to the sly healing jungle, stands a tor whose shape suggests a natural stupa or pagoda; while hard by, crowning another gigantic rock on whose face are cup-marks, is a real *chorten*. Leaning against this rock are a number of long poles, notched into steps, so finely cut that no human being could possibly climb them, and one might be puzzled to account for their presence, did not one recollect that we are now in the land of *nats*, those elfish spirits which live in the trees and in the lakes and rivers and mountains of the twilight forest land. Strong spirits mount quickly to the head, by these ladders. There is also an open shed where pilgrims such as ourselves sleep the night, nothing more. Once there was a monastery here, we were told, but it fell into the river; and now the great grey rocks, quarried by the river which storms by 50 feet below, lie around in confusion, while tangled mats of orchids help to conceal their bald heads, and the crawling jungle slowly buries them.

Tsangpo, 1924

The plain of Assam

It was late when we reached the saddle, and there was a bite in the air. Hardly had we begun the descent to the plain when there burst on us without warning one of the most amazing sights it has ever been my good fortune to see. The mountain is very steep on this side and the path slants to and fro in long wave-lengths, with a high bank on one side and an almost sheer drop on the other. The sun was now low down, and dead ahead; indeed we would have had it full in our eyes, but for a belt of cloud drawn tightly across the sky, its lower edge firm and hard like the sea rim. From behind this belt sprang a dazzling illumination. Right below us the hills ceased suddenly as though trimmed off with a knife, except where two long spurs flared sharply into the sunset; and there at our feet, stretching away league on league until it was swallowed up in the reeking embers of the winter's dusk, lay the plain of Assam. From this height the plain looked like a gigantic park, and across it, brazenly lit by the rays which splashed out in a golden shower from behind the cloud wrack, a maze of rivers flowed to swell the Brahmaputra. The Lohit, which we had followed for so many days through the hills, rushing out of close confinement, is suddenly checked on the plain, and proceeds to spread itself out in a network of streams covering a wide expanse of barren sand. Now all these placid channels were caught in the flame of the setting sun and shone like molten metal.

Mishmi Hills, 1926

Burmese jungle

The Burmese jungle seems deathly still. A deep, minatory gloom prevails. Listen carefully, and make no noise; presently you will begin to hear little sounds difficult to locate, such as the muffled chatter of birds, bamboos scraping together, the tinkle of distant water or the tapping of a woodpecker. A fruit hurtles down with a loud plop and startles you; or a squirrel gives a truculent cry. But most noises are low, almost furtive. There is not much movement. Suddenly, inexplicably, a leaf begins to twitch to and fro in a maddening rhythm, as a faint current of air moves it; then a banana leaf starts to flap idly. The passage of a pair of hornbills sounds quite loud. At dawn the gibbons greet the day, and as the rising sun curdles the mist they troop off into the depths of the jungle. But the baboons cough and grunt very discreetly to each other, and suddenly the trees shiver and shake to their feverish gymnastics as they take alarm and go helter-skelter.

Kachin Hills, 1930

Rong Thö Chu

A narrowing valley stretched northwards in front of us, and was cut off abruptly by the converging mountain ranges. But the river came thundering out of a deep gash, and a mist of spray hung in the air. Beyond, the cobalt sky shut down tight, like a lid. I felt rather awestruck as I gazed, noting the puffs of bright cloud shining against the violet hills. No white man had ever seen this valley before. The river was not less than a hundred miles long. . . .

After the first few miles it looked as though there could be neither villages nor cultivation. The mountains straightened their backs and approached each other more closely, squeezing the river between them till it roared. They were covered with pine forest below; but the deep shady glens and cool north slopes bore a

richer covering of oaks and maples, rhododendrons and magnolias, some of which were in bloom. The tops of the hills were
white with snow, and the air was cool and moist.

Rima, 1933

Pen La

During the ascent to the pass a mushroom-shaped black cloud
had been gathering ominously round the snow-peaks, and now
the storm burst without further warning. The hail came down
like a fluttering white curtain, quickly glazing the rocks with ice.
The blizzard had struck us full in the face just as, somewhat
exhausted, we reached the top of the Pen La, 17,350 feet above
sea level. Lightning ripped through the whirling veil in vivid
streaks, to be followed instantly by loud explosions. Flash followed flash, and the thunder-echoes rolling back and forth
amongst the mountains made a drum-fire of noise. We wrapped
our scarves round our heads, and to the accompaniment of this
Wagnerian music crossed the Great Himalayan range.

Assam Himalaya, 1935

Sacred turquoise lake

Just as I reached a grassy alp surrounded by seas of rhododendron
in strident bloom, the veil of the cloud was rent, and in a flash
there was revealed, a thousand feet below, one of the most beautiful and inspiring sights imaginable. More and more bright grew
the scene, like a swift flame, colour and form harmoniously
blended. Not that it was tame in peaceful decay, by any means;
it was grand without being savage. I was looking straight down
on to Tsogar, sacred turquoise lake. The fretted cliffs ran rivers
of gleaming ice; the largest glacier reached the edge of the water.
On its near side the lake was girdled by an emerald-green arc of
rich pasture, dark-spotted with yak. There was a smaller lake in
front of the main lake, and the stream flowed from one to the
other and so away down a valley to the south, to join the Tsari
river. In the foreground billows of rose-purple rhododendron
blossom tossed in the breeze.

The sun, though well down, fired a parting shaft of light

through a gap in the western range, illuminating the scene more brightly. Then the clouds closed in again and all was blotted out. But I was grateful for that one glimpse.

Tsogar, 1935

Ka Karpo Razi

We stood on a saddle-shaped gap between two rock towers, which might perhaps be called a pass. The men were huddled in a corner seeking shelter from the icy wind, and I crawled forward to the edge of the cliff.

Which really caught my eye first – the sheer drop over the edge into the Dandi valley two or three thousand feet below, or the grey Gothic spires of Ka Karpo Razi rising sheer into the clouds three thousand feet above our heads – I cannot say. Anyhow it was a staggering, an awful sight. I sat down on the cold rock in the bitter wind while I slowly took in the terrific scene. The view was set in a narrow frame of violent grandeur, but in spite of a bulge in the mountain on our left which hid the corner where our ridge joined the main ridge, we could see everything that really mattered to north, east and west. Had we been an hour earlier we should have had an even better view of the peak itself, for the cloud was only just beginning to gather round its head, but was gathering fast. Yet from the shrivelled glacier at its foot, whence issued the Dandi river, to the topmost jagged spire, we could see the whole 5,000-foot southern face of Ka Karpo streaked and freckled with snow, and the ice on its brow. One could almost have tossed a stone into the jinking Dandi river which showed as a white thread far below; to see the summit of Ka Karpo one had to lift up one's eyes.

Gamlang-Dandi divide, 1937

On Tama Bum

The most lasting impression I carried away from this pass was the view south-eastwards across the deep fissure of the Nmai Hka, 7,000 feet below, to the mountain ranges of the Burma-China frontier thirty or forty miles away. In May, on my brief climb to the pass, I could not see twenty yards ahead; I had no idea in which direction the track went, once I reached the top. Now I could see twenty, or forty, perhaps sixty miles over range after range. The colours, too, now that the sun was low in the west, with the shoulder of Tagulam Bum intervening and the gorge of the Hkrang Hka in shadow, were wonderful. The high peaks still glowed like hot iron, cooling off gradually to violet and indigo in the depths of the valley. Westwards the sky was bright as the sun sank in a lake of gold.

Tama Bum, 1953

TWELVE

Gardens in the Wild – 2

'Moonlight' Primula – Giant Cowslip – Silver Barberry – Rhododendron notatum – Ruby Poppy – Blue Microbe – Begonia – Rhododendron stanaulum – Magnolia campbellii – Meconopsis violacea – Carmine Cherry – Rhododendron hylaeum – Corydalis – Trees stirring to life – Primulas – Primula dumicola – An epiphytic slipper orchid – Rosa gigantea – Vitis lanata

'Moonlight' Primula

In the sunny meads, where the ground is marsh rather than bog, since treading here you do not break through the surface crust, grows the Moonlight 'sikkimensis' *Primula microdonta* (K. W. 5746), a beautiful flower, with a fragrance almost stupefying in its sweetness. The stem grows no more than 20 inches high, then spouts out on one side a fountain of rather large lolling pale sulphury flowers. It grows in sheets, in hundreds of thousands all up the wet valley, acres and acres of soft yellow radiance, distilling scent; but we saw it scarcely anywhere else.

Lunang, 1924

Giant Cowslip

The finest primula of all is the Giant Cowslip 'sikkimensis' (*P. florindæ*, K. W. 5781). Where the Moonlight 'sikkimensis' grows the Giant Cowslip is not far distant, but always in the shade and always in running water. But it has a much wider distribution than the former, for it is found on both sides of the Tsangpo, from below Nang Dzong to well within the gates of the gorge. It was most happy in the woodland brooks, which in summer overflow and flood the thorn brake. Here it manned the banks in thousands and, wading out into the stream, held up the current. It choked up ditches and roofed the steepest mud slides with its great marsh-marigold leaves; then in July came a forest of masts, which spilled out a shower of golden drops, till the tide of scent spread and filled the woodland and flowed into the meadow to mingle with that of the 'Moonlight' Primula. And all through August it kept on unfurling flowers and still more flowers, till the rains began to slacken and the brooks crept back to their beds, and the waters under the thorn brake subsided; but the seeds were not ripe till late October.

Lunang, 1924

Silver Barberry

It was here that I found the most beautiful shrub of all – the Silver Barberry. There are dozens of barberries in cultivation; every eastern tide throws up new ones, though it is often a matter of nice discrimination to tell Tweedledum from Tweedledee. Apart, however, from the incomparable Chilian species *Berberis darwinii*, and its even finer hybrid *B. stenophylla*, a few Oriental barberries really are distinct, and *B. hypokerina* can join this noble band with a good conscience, and, it is to be hoped, a good constitution. The first plants I saw had neither flowers nor fruit, so there seemed no reason why it should not be a holly – or, rather, holly as understood in England; that was what it most nearly resembled, judged by its leaves alone. But one must picture these holly leaves rather long and narrow, set jauntily on sealing-wax red stems without thorns, the upper surface not polished but of a translucent malachite green, with a delicate network of jade veins traced on it, and the under-surface softly whitened as though a flocculent film of silver had been freshly precipitated on it. The flowers, as I saw later, of a cheerful but not distinguished yellow, borne in firm clusters, are followed by little plum-purple pear-shaped fruits. The old leaves then turn scarlet, and the plant is as lovely in winter as in spring.

Seinghku valley, 1926

Rhododendron notatum

R. notatum is a winter-flowering species. I have seen it in bloom as early as November and as late as May – not the same plants, of course. The most beautiful specimen I ever saw was by the Nam Tamai, where the river comes zooming out of the densely

forested gorges above the Seinghku confluence. The water was
ice-clear, gleaming like jade where the sun smote on a deep pool,
crested with frosty foam where it slammed against the boulders,
and all the time singing, singing. An alder tree leaned out of the
forest on one side and stretched half-way across the river; from
the opposite wall another tree lurched over to meet it till the two
mingled their branches high overhead. Immediately above and
below, the river gurgled over the rocks, which bared their teeth
in a defiant grin; but beneath the arch it slid by in a smooth
trough. From either tree-trunk spouted a fountain of rhododendron blossom, the one pearl-white, the other blush, turning the
arch into a natural pergola; and from time to time a pink or white
corolla fluttered down like a hurt butterfly, and swam away on
the current. Such was *R. notatum*.

Nam Tamai, [1926]

Ruby Poppy

By this time I was clear of the larger scrub and, glancing up the
screes, I was just in time to see a flower twinkle, as a bayonet of
sunlight stabbed the clouds. Approaching, I stood in silent
wonder before the Ruby Poppy. In Sino-Himalaya, the mountain
poppies are generally blue, sometimes yellow, very rarely red.
Therefore a red poppy here is as exciting as a blue poppy in
England. Also, it was exquisite. A sheaf of finely drawn olive-
green jets shots up in a fountain from amongst the stones, curled
over, and ere they reached the ground again, splashed into rubies.
Thus one might visualize *Meconopsis rubra*, if one imagines a
fountain arrested in mid-career, and frozen. But it was not till
later, when on a stormy day I saw whole hillsides dotted with
these plants, that I really believed in *M. rubra*. As the wind
churned up the clouds, a burning brand was lit and, touching off
the flowers one by one, up they went in red flame! That was
convincing.

Seinghku valley, 1926

Blue Microbe

Above me an overhanging brow of rock cut right across the face of the mountain, and was carved into a series of towers. Beyond this the ridge climbed in lame steps up the escarpment beneath an immensity of scree. On the grey grass cliffs, strung out in flights along the fissures, was Blue Microbe (*P. fea*), an elfin primula so wee that the threadlike stem will pass through the eye of a needle, while the pagoda bell-flower is no larger than a Brownie's cap. This bell is crimson at the base, changing to blue above, and is hung from the stem by the finest silken cord. Two, sometimes three, bells nod on each stem – no more. So much for *P. fea*, another homeless orphan; but the frail beauty of this gem is almost as apparent in the dried specimen as it is in the living plant.

Seinghku valley, 1926

Begonia

A big rough-leafed begonia grew on the cliff near my camp and was now in bloom; though the pink flowers arè small, they are borne in such a rosy cloud above the harsh and handsome foliage, that I was quite pleased with the plant. You could grate nutmegs on the leaves.

Lohit-Irrawaddy divide, 1926

Rhododendron stenaulum

There was *R. stenaulum*, a gawky tree with a stout copper-red bole, almost like glass, and a crown of branches which had burst into a foam of white flowers. As a forest tree it is at its worst. The pinched flowers in floppy trusses, for all their elegance and fragrance, fall too quickly; the commonplace leaves crowded at the ends of the bare branches, and the tattered bark, also help to make it look shabby. Even so, seen from the outside across a glen, it appeared as a dome of soft blossom. But grown on a sunny or wind-swept ridge, the leggy-looking tree becomes a solid shrub with a firm outline; then, when a mantle of blossom surrounds the whole, with the scarlet of old leaves and the purple plumes of the newly born, this rhododendron takes on a very different appearance.

Delei valley, 1927

Magnolia campbellii

M. campbellii stands in a class by itself. It is incomparably the finest of all magnolias, at least in the wild state. The Tibet road through Sikkim might have been designed specially to enable travellers to see it in its *locus classicus*. The road cleaves to the face of the cliff, winding round and round, ever ascending towards the distant snows, while the valley fades beneath us. At last the air grows colder, for it is only March, and we reach the zone of oaks and rhododendrons. Everything is padded in moss; long wisps of it swing from the branches of the trees. A thin mist floats ghost-like through the dripping forest. Suddenly, round a corner, we come on the first magnolia in full bloom. It is just below us, and we look right into the heart of the tree, spouting with blossom. The sight overwhelms us. After that we see scores of trees, some with glowing pink, others with ivory-white flowers. From our giddy ledge we look down over the wide waves of the forest beating against the cliff, where the magnolia blooms toss like white horses, or lie like a fleet of pink water-lilies riding at anchor in a green surf.

Delei valley, 1927

Meconopsis violacea

Early in June 1926, in the Seinghku valley, I noticed the buoyant rosettes of a large poppy bursting vigorously through the snow. The pinnate leaves were sage-green, lined with long silken honey-coloured hairs, which glistened in the sunshine, as it might have been *Meconopsis paniculata*. Yet I felt certain it was not, and I watched it jealously as the tall leafy spire rose inch by inch from the deep crown until finally stopped by a flower-bud. Yet July came before it opened. By that time, from the axil of each bract lolled a fat bud, the topmost had thrown back their green hoods, and several silken violet flowers, piled with dark gold in the centre, fluttered out in the breeze. Such was *M. violacea*, a glorious column of bright colour, which flowered throughout July in the ice-worn valleys, being then about three feet high; throughout the rains it continued to grow, however, till in September it was over four feet high, and carried two dozen capsules, the topmost being then ripe.

Seinghku valley, 1926

Carmine Cherry

Prunus puddum, as it grows in the Adung valley, is one of the largest of the deciduous trees, only the elm outstripping it. It grows eighty to a hundred feet high, and its branches have a very wide spread. The ruby-red flower-buds appear about the middle of March, in compact clusters towards the ends of the branches, and the tree is swiftly transformed into a frozen fountain of precious stones. As the buds open, the stalks lengthen till the flowers are hanging down. Then the whole tree bursts suddenly into carmine flame. To see the setting sun through its branches when the tree is in full bloom is a thing not easily put out of one's mind.

Tahawndam, 1931

Rhododendron hylaeum

There is something rather primitive about *Rhododendron hylaeum*. A thick-set tree should not, one feels, display so sleek and almost glistening a bark; it would be more appropriate if it were cracked. One does not expect the bloom of a youthful skin on a raddled old woman. There is an uncouth contrast, too, in the shrivelled leaves and the abandonment of blossom. The flowering of *R. hylaeum* is not at all inhibited by the snow. The flowers, ten or fifteen in number, are tightly compressed to form a solid bunch; each is of a delicate rose-purple or an almost white shade with a crimson-ochre ostrich-plume printed on the upper lobe and a lighter mackerel spotting below. It is like a high, windy sky. The skeleton-like trees, covered with blossom, had an equivocal air. They were youthful, yet infinitely old, venerable and new-born. They might have stood there, crooked and crippled, from time immemorial, or they might have sprung instantaneously from the

granite rocks amongst which they grew so boldly, at the touch
of a fairy's wand. No rhododendron can be described as quick-
growing, but there is none more slow-growing than *R. hylaeum.*

Adung valley, 1931

Corydalis

The Corydalises are alpine rock- and meadow-plants, usually bi-
coloured, with flowers beaked at one end and spurred at the other;
they look rather like children's crackers tied to a sprig of foliage,
and there must have been a dozen species in the hanging valleys
above Lung Sa. Two stick in my memory. One I found on a
dreadful scree, when a thick mist hung over the mountains and
a deluge of cold rain numbed me. At every step I took, the scree
came crumbling away with a torrent of water which filled my
boots. Then I saw the baby-blue-eyed Corydalis, its clusters of
beaky flowers bobbing over the feathery foliage. In youth the
leaves are purple-tinged, but later they turn blue-green like the
shallow seas; and so finely cut are they that they reminded me of
those seaweeds which float fern-like in the rock-pools between
tides. Later in the year, the plant throws up fountains of sapphire-
and-white flowers.

A second lovely species has vaporous orange flowers, stained
walnut-brown on the spurs and on the tips of the lateral petals,
and filmy leaves.

Lung Sa, 1931

Trees stirring to life

The snow had melted, and the trees were thrilling to the stir of
life. A fairy wand of sunlight had touched them, and they had
answered, throwing off their winter covering with a delicious
crepitation of falling scales. Maple trees slowly uncrumpled the
most delicate apple-green fans and spread them without a crease.
Rhododendrons fifty feet high, which had never lost their leaves,
but had twisted them into cigars and tucked them tightly against
the branches, had burst into salvoes of crimson, primrose and
amethyst blossom. The leafless branches of the magnolias frothed

up in a lather of ivory whiteness, each flower as large as a water lily, till the grey trees were transfigured.

Giwang, 1933

Primulas

Primulas have a strong social sense. They hate to be alone. On the other hand they loathe all but their own kind. They stand for nationalism, self-determination and intolerance. They are almost as intransigent as men. If they like a place, they want it all; they can brook no rival. But if they don't like a place, they will evacuate it completely, caring nothing for what their rivals do. Dominion or downfall. Once covetous of a place in the sun the noble and haughty race of primula will strive to evict almost every other plant, and themselves cover the landscape. This they sometimes succeed in doing. They are less individualistic than most plants, more clannish. Each primula species stands up for its own rights against every other primula species; but once security is attained, it may merge its particular interest in the general interest of the genus. Then it is primulas against the world; at least the alpine world.

Lang La, 1935

Primula dumicola

Edging the muddy track through the open fields one notices, or hardly notices, a primula of sorts. As all the horticultural world knows, very few species of this incomparable genus but make us catch our breath when first we see them in all their naked loveliness; but *Primula dumicola* would be more likely to make us catch cold. One has to crawl on one's belly in the mud to see the little wretch, so tiny is it, so anaemic and paltry are the flowers – the colour might be called rusty pink, with a washy-yellow eye-spot. Though the foliage has redeeming qualities, that is not enough to raise this harijan to brahmin caste. Even after flowering the plant does not, like so many of its kind, expand while ripening its seed; rather does it shrink and, as soon as the rains begin in earnest, deliquesces into the mud. Nor must it be imagined that I saw a trace of this detestable little slut now, and I certainly did not miss her. I call attention to *P. dumicola* here as a hideous exception to a noble family, and because I believe this reach of the Adung valley is the only place in north Burma where it grows.

Adung valley, 1937

An epiphytic slipper orchid

Suddenly I stopped. What was that up in the tree seen out of a corner of my eye? Oh, an orchid! Nothing unusual in that surely. Isn't this the land of epiphytic orchids? Ah, but – why, it's a *slipper* orchid, and that *is* extraordinary! For what is a slipper orchid, an earth orchid if there ever was one, doing up a tree? And, now that I came to look squarely at it, I felt it was not entirely the unusual situation in which it grew that caused my heart to beat faster; it was rather the size of the flower and its rich though subdued colouring, the bloated honey-gold slipper of frosted porcelain texture, the broad stiff wings, sharply bisected, the upper half yellowish green, the lower half tessellated in coffee browns, the arrogant poise of the whole. I continued to stare, unwilling to move in case it was not true . . . At last I forced myself to move, climbed quickly up the tree, grabbed the prize. It was a slipper orchid *Paphiopedilum* all right, and an epiphyte. I could hardly believe my good fortune. Though several people, Farrer and Cox, Kermode and collectors from the Forest Department, Lady Cuffe and I myself had botanized along this trail during the last twenty years, there was no mention of any slipper orchid that I had heard of. Surely then it must be new – though it might turn out to be a Chinese species.

I sent a description of the plant together with pressed flowers to England, and in course of time learnt that my slipper orchid was *Paphiopedilum villosum*, no discovery, for it had already been discovered by Thomas Lobb, near Moulmein, 700 miles south of Htawgaw, many years previously. Later it had been discovered in the northern Shan States, 200 miles south of Htawgaw. However, this was at least a new locality, perhaps not far from its extreme northern limit, and I felt no acute sense of disappointment that it was not a new species.

Pyepat, 1938

Rosa gigantea

One of the most amazing sights was a huge scrambling rose, which sprawled determinedly over the trees in every lane and copse. The largest specimen we saw had what I can only describe as a trunk, as thick as a man's forearm, from which sprang several stems, each more than a hundred feet long and all heavily armed with strong flat prickles. One might hazard that it was upwards of a century old. Another veteran specimen had spread its long limbs through the surrounding thicket, growing up and pushing out from the centre until it dominated the whole. Now that it had come through the roof into the open, it greeted the sunshine by hanging out banners of flowers on every side. The chubby leaves, still soft and limp, were a deep red; the slim, pointed flower-buds a pale daffodil-yellow; but when the enormous flowers opened, they were ivory-white, borne singly all along the arching sprays, each petal faintly engraved with a network of veins like a water mark. The shock of orange-capped stamens made a perfect centre-piece, and the flower distilled a delicate fragrance. What a sight was this great dog rose throughout March, lording it over the thickets, festooning the tallest trees, and hanging from every limb in cascades of scented flowers the size of teacups! It well deserves the name given to it by General Collett, who discovered it in Upper Burma more than fifty years ago – *Rosa gigantea*.

Ukhrul, 1948

Vitis lanata

Then there were climbing plants in great variety, the most remarkable being the vines. My attention was drawn to one which bore pyramidal panicles of small flowers enveloped in a halo of auburn hair; the leaves, too, were covered with the same auburn or chestnut hair. Conspicuous though it was to us, it seemed to be far less so to the insect world; so far as we could see, none ever visited the flowers or, if they did, they were singularly ineffective as pollenators. Every single flower dropped off dead, and not one fruit did this vine set. A plague of small beetles settled on the leaves, however, and by mid-summer had reduced them to a mere skeletal network of veins. So much, then, for *Vitis lanata*, the ornamental auburn-haired vine.

Ukhrul, 1948

THIRTEEN

Portrait Gallery

The natives of Kham – A Tibetan pilgrim – A Chinese bride – A hermit lama with primulas – A Tibetan child – Two cheerful urchins – Lutzus of Saungta – Grey sisters – Chang the mandarin – Tibetan horse-traders – A Kiutzu chief and his girl-wife – A Mishmi gam – Bebejiya Mishmis – Two personages at Shergaon – A Tibetan felon – Coolies gambling – Lopas – The Jongpen of Gyamda – The postmaster of Gyamda – The Jongpen of Sanga Chöling

The natives of Kham

The native of S. E. Tibet or Kham is an extremely tall man, averaging little under six feet, though he looks even taller by reason of his slimness – unless indeed it is his height which makes him look slim for, when stripped, the great depth of his muscular chest and the set of his powerful shoulders give an indication of his unusual strength.

I found them pleasant and friendly people, though filthy. It was rare indeed to meet a man who did not salute me by spreading out both hands in front of him, palms upwards, perhaps a survival from some form of greeting indicating that the hands conceal no weapon. Less frequently they greeted me by putting out their tongues, but when they asked for anything they always closed their fists and stuck up their thumbs. Consequently I came to regard the outspread hands as an ordinary roadside greeting, the putting out of the tongue as a more humble mode of address, and the sticking up of thumbs as a sign that a favour was being asked.

The men wear a single long robe like a dressing-gown made of sackcloth, and leather-soled cloth boots reaching to the knee; in the daytime this cloak is tied up round the waist clear of the knees, forming a short skirt or kilt, and one shoulder is usually slipped out, or in the summertime both shoulders, the sleeves then being tied round the waist. At night the Tibetan wraps himself up in this long cloak and lies down to sleep whether it be under the stars or in a house. Year in and year out, night and

day, this coarse hempen cloak serves the poor Tibetan for clothing. Inside the slack of this useful garment, when tied up during
the day, a man will carry a variety of things, and it is like a
grotesque conjuring trick to see him producing, apparently from
the recesses of an enlarged paunch, such articles as a sword, a
tsamba bowl, a chicken, a pipe, and a pine-torch. From his belt
hang flint, steel, and snuff-box, and besides the things mentioned
he always carries tobacco and a bag of *tsamba*.

He wears his matted hair done up in a queue bound round the
top of his head, and frequently ornamented with a number of
coarse silver rings, each set with a big turquoise or coral; indeed
the Tibetan men are very fond of jewellery and wear several such
rings on their fingers. The women, however, do not make such
a display, finger-rings being little worn and ear-rings small. The
commonest piece of jewellery is a silver brooch, made in two
pieces fitting into each other, which fastens the collar of the jacket.

More curious still, the men always wear threaded on the queue
a section of an elephant's tusk, and I found myself wondering
why it was that both the Tibetans and Lisus wear characteristic
ornaments which are brought from other countries than their
own, the Tibetans these pieces of elephant's tusk worn in the
hair, and the Lisu women a head-dress, in shape something like
a baby's sun-bonnet, covered with cowries. There is little doubt
that this last is peculiar to the Lisus, and eminently characteristic
of them.

In country districts the Tibetan women plait their hair into
numerous thin tails which hang down behind and are collected
together into one queue below the waist; but in the cities they
wear the ordinary queue, quite half of which is artificial, piled on
the top of the head and finished off with two tassels of red or
green silk bound with silver wire.

Mekong valley, 1910

A Tibetan pilgrim

Numbers of pilgrims passed through Atuntzu every day on their
way to Doker La – long processions in single file, men and
women, with packs on their backs and bamboo wands, each
decorated with a sprig of evergreen, in their hands. I now saw
for the first time one of those extraordinary people of whom I

had often read, who proceed by measuring their length on the ground over the entire distance, thus acquiring a vast amount of merit. He was a ragged-looking man, dirty and ill-kempt, as well he might be, with a leather apron over his long cloak, and his hands thrust through the straps of flat wooden clogs, like Japanese sandals. Standing up with his arms by his side, he clapped the clogs together in front of him once, twice, then slowly raised them above his head and, clapping them together a third time, stretched himself at full length on the ground with his arms straight out in front of him. Mumbling a prayer he again clapped, made a mark on the ground at the full stretch of his arms, and rose to his feet. Then he solemnly walked forward three steps to the mark he had made, and repeated the performance; and so the weary journey went on.

Who but a Tibetan, taking no heed of time, consumed with zeal for a religion which preaches self-effacement, could devise such a method for acquiring merit? Perhaps he was travelling thus to Doker La, a journey which would take him weeks to accomplish.

Atuntzu, 1910

A Chinese bride

We passed a wedding procession, the saucy banging of a gong warning us to get out of the way. The bride, with her doll's face thickly powdered, was dressed in new silk trousers and shapeless jacket, with tiny triangular shoes above which bulged her maimed ankles. A thick black veil concealed her from view, for she was sick with shyness, so that a man must walk alongside her pony to hold her on. Followed a tawdry cabinet containing gifts of food, borne at a shuffle by ragged coolies.

Yunnan, 1913

A hermit lama with primulas

The descent by a different route to that which we had followed on the way up was fairly easy, and we found ourselves on the path again in two hours; then, instead of dropping straight down to the temple, the grey wooden roof of which rose amongst the trees a thousand feet below, we crawled round the base of a precipice and sought the hermit lama in his cave. Hither he retired periodically for contemplation. The lama received us hospitably, and offered us his best buttered tea and *tsamba*. He had just finished his prayers, behind the curtain, and all the sorcery outfit – bell, book and candle – for exorcising devils and performing other miracles was spread around the tiny cave where the lama slept and ate and prayed for days together. However, the outside of the cave was even more interesting than the inside, for on a slate cliff just above were great tufts of the lovely chrome-yellow *Primula pulvinata*, one of the Suffruticosa or woody-stemmed section of perennial primulas. It lives to a great age, even perhaps for as much as a century, forming clumps as big as a cushion. The plant was in full bloom, the stems, each bearing an umbel of four or five fragrant flowers, scarcely rising above the dense cushions of dark-green leaves which closely covered the matted stems below.

Mekong-Salween divide, 1913

A Tibetan child

Following the same route as on our previous journey, we crossed Atuntzu mountain and descended to the scorching valley, to find bare fields and women threshing the corn at Pu. The people of this village are extremely dirty and goitrous. Though friendly, they are rather shy with strangers. Yet what good-hearted creatures they really are! Shall I ever forget the scene in the *visi's* house, where I was invited to stay? A small naked child sat by the fire nursing a sick goat, on one side of him a big grey cat gazing through half-shut eyes at the embers, on the other a small wire-haired dog, like an Aberdeen terrier, half-asleep; and scuttling to and fro, now into the cool darkness of the room, now out again into the sunshine, a number of tiny fat porkers which were only just learning how to grunt in a tone calculated to disclose contentment. I have frequently seen Tibetan children hugging puppies, baby pigs, or cats, and carrying them about like dolls; for they are fond of animals, and, with the exception of their pack-donkeys, which they work to death, treat them kindly on the whole.

Pu, 1913

Two cheerful urchins

On the way down from the pass I met two little half-naked
Tibetan boys, who were looking for some yak which had strayed
over the pass from the A-dong side. It made me shiver to look
at them. Feet, legs and arms were bare, and a single goatskin, its
tatters fluttering on the breeze, partly covered the body. They
were cheerful urchins with pinched faces and hands thrust up into
the sleeves of their hairy garment for warmth. What a grand,
lonely life they led throughout the short summer, cattle-ranging
in these high valleys!

Yangtze-Mekong divide, 1913

Lutzus of Saungta

The Lutzu of Saungta – 'black' Lutzu – who recalled my journey
up the Salween to Men-kong in 1911 and were very friendly in
consequence are as wild-looking and dirty a people as one could
find. The men dress in the long Tibetan cloak (*chupa*), but wear
no boots, and do not plait their hair, which is left in a tangled
mop. Only the chief had a thin pigtail, hanging down behind. The
women, however, instead of dressing like the Tibetan women of
Jana, follow the tribal fashion and dress more like their sisters
lower down the river, the 'white' Lutzu. That is to say, they wear
a white hempen skirt, with narrow blue stripes and fringed ends,
wrapped round the waist and reaching half-way to the ankles,
and a short loose-sleeved jacket of ample width. To this is added
a hempen towel thrown over the shoulders if the weather is cold,
and used as a blanket at night. Most of the children and younger
girls, however, dress in goatskins sewn together, hair inside – a
warm and cheap garment, for large flocks of goats are kept here.
I counted five hundred on the hillside in one place.

Salween, 1913

Grey sisters

At last we halt, and camp under a cliff by the torrent, and I write
my diary by the light of the blazing logs. In the gloaming the old
women sitting in a circle round the fire, legs bare to the knees

and drawn up under their chins, skirts pulled tightly round them, wraps thrown over their shoulders, look like witches. I am reminded of the three grey sisters in the frozen cave visited by Perseus in the home of the north wind, who had but one eye between them and passed it round by hand from one to the other. Look, these people too are handing something round! – but it is only a pipe passing from mouth to mouth; a whiff here, and it goes to the next person, who in turn takes a whiff and passes it on. For now we are in the land of the tobacco plant, which does not grow in Tibet. In Tsa-rong I offered cigarettes to men who looked at them and asked what they were!

Kieunatong, 1913

Chang, the mandarin

Chang, the mandarin, came to see me off; nothing disturbed his equanimity or made him depart a hair's-breadth from his kindly courtesy. To some extent his attitude disarmed me – it was impossible to be unscrupulous in one's dealings with such a man. In the maelstrom into which rudderless China is being rapidly sucked, her rulers will do well to pause in their haste to replace tried men of the old school by hot-headed fanatics with bees in their bonnets. But Chang knew little of Western thought. He was ignorant, old-fashioned, conservative, bigoted, obstructive and – a gentleman. Tra-mu-tang is not a place of great strategic significance, and never will be; such places are best left to the wise and beneficent rule which the genius of China had evolved when, as they are fond of reminding us, our ancestors dressed in skins.

Tra-mu-tang, 1913

Tibetan horse-traders

One evening, as we rode into the village where we intended to halt for the night, we saw a party of Tibetans camped under a hedge. They took no notice of us till my cook, who spoke Tibetan well, playfully addressed them in their own tongue; immediately a dozen faces looked up and smiled at us. Later, whilst the mules were being unloaded, two of them came across to the inn and made themselves useful, then took me back with them to their

friends. Being invited to join the circle round the fire, I crossed
my legs and sank down amongst them, Tibetan-fashion. The
hubble-bubble was passed round, and every man and woman
took a pull at the coarse tobacco; they brought out wine, too,
full-flavoured and of a most villainous strength.

What a set of scarecrows they were to be sure, tricked out in
horrible horsy old check caps pulled down over their foreheads,
second-hand blankets, and frayed reach-me-downs picked up at
a Bhamo auction! They were from Chung-tien and had gone
right away down to one-time royal Mandalay, selling ponies.

Salween valley, 1914

A Kiutzu chief and his girl-wife

Tender love-scenes enacted between the chief and his girl-wife –
she looked about sixteen or seventeen years of age – were very
amusing. She was an ugly little thing, her dumpling face grotesquely tattooed with dots and crosses; and she simpered. In
spite of her dog-like faithfulness, which oozed from every pore
as she gazed on her lord and master, he treated her with disdain.
She was squeezed out of the ring round the fire and given a place
out in the cold; but she was content to lean against her lover. The
mangiest scraps of food were given to her – but she was content
to eat the crumbs which fell from her master's moustache, and
drink the dregs from his wooden cup. But sometimes he gave
her titbits, and then the love-light in her eyes would have wrung
tears from a mangle. Also she was excused the hewing of wood
and drawing of water, and our gallant always lifted her load on
to her back when we started in the morning; for the Kiutzu carry
their loads by a band passing round the forehead.

Taron, 1922

A Mishmi *gam*

Just above the village a wooden post was driven into the ground,
and from this hung a warrior's cane helmet. This I learnt was a
memorial to a murdered man. When I had persuaded the *gam*
[headman] of Meiliang to let me take his photograph, he chose
to stand by this obelisk; and though he never confessed to me, I

had dark suspicions. He always wore a necklace of human teeth, which obviously were not his own.

Peti, 1927

Bebejiya Mishmis

One morning I was surprised to see three queer dwarf men in the yard, where the paddy is husked in wooden mortars and pigs are fed and cattle milked. They were sitting on a dunghill, weaving bamboo baskets. Their hair was cropped and they wore cane helmets on their heads; otherwise they were dressed like Digaru Mishmis; that is to say, they wore a sleeveless cloth jacket and a sporran-like flap of cloth, elaborately decorated, suspended from a string round the waist. Each carried two knives, and they smoked incessantly out of long silver pipes like converted candlesticks. Two of them looked suspicious and surly, but the third, an aged headman with a well-creased mahogany face like a carved Buddha, smiled amiably. They came from the unexplored Tangon river over the snow-covered range to the west, and belonged to the Bebejiya clan.

Solé, 1933

Two personages at Shergaon

My first visitor at Shergaon was Wangia, a well-known inebriate and a great man. He is not only headman of Shergaon, but one of the 'Seven Kings of Rupa' – the ruling families of the Sherchokpa. Wangia, now in his sixties or seventies, is a somewhat lachrymose old man with red-rimmed eyes not solely due to the intensity of the light outside or to the darkness within doors. His lank white locks are greasy, his brownish skin wrinkled like a dried apple. He had dressed himself for the occasion in the greatest finery his limited wardrobe could provide – a faded Tibetan *chupa*, gaudy-coloured cloth boots, and purple skull-cap. He welcomed me fervently. Behind him came several servants bringing presents of rice, walnuts, chillies, and other local produce.

He was well pleased when I gave him two bottles of Indian country spirit. He must have tried them immediately, to make certain that they were beyond proof, since I did not see him again for two days; I was told he had met with an accident, and was still insensible.

A greater than Wangia was in Shergaon that May day; none other then Geshi Ishi Dorje, High Priest of Mönyul. Ishi Dorje is a rotund man with little pig eyes in his creased full-moon face, and he is going bald. He speaks slowly, in a thick soupy voice pitched low. His expression is benign, for he is a kindly man, a great favourite amongst the people whom he has been shepherding for a generation. He put on his canonical robes for me, that I might take his photograph, and an impressive figure he made. Perhaps the chief attraction was his hat, a gorgeous wooden steeple, lacquered and gilded. In the west the Roman church has always aimed at increasing the stature and dignity of the theocracy by crowning them with high hats, such as the mitre. In the east the Tibetan church is not far behind. And so Ishi Dorje perched on his half-bald head a miniature golden pagoda, which ended in a red glass ball. It all screwed together neatly, and in fact it took him some time to assemble the parts. He thrust his fat legs into vivid scarlet-and-green cloth boots, with snub toes, covered his ample torso in a monkish robe of dull red edged with silver braid, and throwing a brightly coloured wrap over one shoulder, appeared before me.

Shergaon, 1938

A Tibetan felon

I was not the only inmate of the dzong. Walking over the flat roofs, one could see into little courtyards where people worked outside rooms no larger than kennels. Here they lived, slept and cooked. There was a woman weaving a woollen rug, and a man in a long grey smock wearing a wide circular wooden collar round his neck. He was a big man, with a disarming smile, a ready word, and tousled hair. But his small eyes were shifty, and too close together. He was a felon, caught in some paltry misdemeanour. This man had been sentenced to wear the heavy wooden collar, or 'cangue', for a term of years. It is more familiar in China, whence it was introduced into Tibet. In many of the hill villages in Assam, small pigs are condemned to wear a triangular 'cangue'; it prevents them from breaking through the hedges and getting into the crops. My felon wandered about a free, if branded, man. He made boots – he was a cobbler by trade. He was always cheerful, and was very grateful for some cigarettes I gave him.

Chayal Dzong, 1935

Coolies gambling

No sooner had I paid off the coolies than they settled down to an afternoon's gambling. Their outfit consisted of some dice, a heap of spillikins, and a collection of brass coins, Chinese, Tibetan and Bhutanese, such as you might find in a Whitechapel pawn-shop. Every time a player shook the dice, he banged them hard down on the floor – they squatted cross-legged in a ring on the floor – with a loud cry. This was not an oath, or a prayer, but a triumphant challenge to the opposition uttered almost as a threat. Beat that if you dare! it seemed to imply. The party was still going strong, with cries and laughter, when I went to bed, the innkeeper having joined in.

Migyitun, 1935

Lopas

In spite of our long march the previous day, I was ready for the road on July 19, and we walked down the right bank of the Tsangpo in sunshine, passing through inhabited country, woods, and pasture. Villagers were cutting the corn with sickles, and I saw many Lopas at work; well set up, muscular little men with dark skins, not pygmies by any means. Every Lopa wears a round helmet, shaped rather like a British army steel helmet without the brim, on top of his head; from the back of it is suspended a small rectangle of rawhide, which protects his neck from a chance blow. The helmet, which is made of closely-woven cane, will stop an arrow and turn a sword blade: the Lopa carries a short Tibetan sword in his girdle, but that is more for adornment than for use. The Lopa weapon is the long-bow.

Tsangpo, 1935

The Jongpen of Gyamda

The Jongpen's return was an event. There was a great tintinnabu-
lation as the cavalcade swept up the narrow street, two mounted
men forming the advance guard. One of them had an umbrella
slung on his back, the other a rifle. Which was the more lethal I
cannot say; it is improbable that either of them had any ammunition. Followed a file of three ponies, each bearing a small male
child built into a saddle. They at least wore sparkling raiment
bright, for they were beautifully dressed in vivid scarlet-and-
green silks, the colour-scheme only vitiated by the fact that they
wore magenta Homburg hats. That wrecked it. Finally came the
Jongpen himself, jingling along on a gaily-caparisoned pony, and
looking as though he had just slipped round from Captain
Bertram Mills's Circus; for he was completely disguised from
head to foot as a Chinese mandarin of the first class, even to his
conical white hat with long vermilion tassel. It is curious how
the Tibetan ruling classes, who profess to loathe the Chinese,
nevertheless ape them. Their contempt for the drab dress of their
own lower orders is only equalled by their admiration for the
scintillating magnificence of that worn by the former Chinese
Amban in Lhasa. In short, the Tibetans do not like the Chinese,
but they admire and envy them.

Gyamda, 1935

The postmaster of Gyamda

I went round to the post office and talked with Mr Ma – Hsiao
Ma, 'little horse', he called himself. There was not much business,
and the tiny cubicle at the top of the rickety stair with its paper-
covered Chinese window frame, where Mr Ma slept, ate, smoked
opium and transacted postal business, was always empty. A
wooden box, about the size of a small dispatch case, with a large
Chinese brass lock, contained all the stamps, cash and accounts
that Mr Ma ever kept. You could send a letter to Lhasa, or to
Chamdo, or even to India, with reasonable assurance of its ulti-
mate arrival at destination; but you could not telegraph, or buy
a postal order, or a post office savings certificate, or a dog licence.

Mr Ma was a little man, the tightly drawn skin of his yellow
face like cracked ivory, his bright almond eyes screwed down to

slits against the glare and wind of this harsh climate. His teeth were yellow with age, and a straggling moustache and beard proclaimed his years. He wore a long blue gown, much patched, and a short sleeveless sheepskin jacket over it, short velvet boots, and a hard round black silk skull-cap with a scarlet button. His eyes and cheeks were sunken, the cheekbones almost protruding through the tight sallow skin – he seemed to be wasting away from within owing to his opium-smoking excesses.

'When does the mail leave for Lhasa, Ma Hsien-Seng?' I asked.

'The day after it arrives here from Lhasa, Hwa Hsien-Seng.'

'And when is that?'

Mr Ma shook his head; he did not know. Perhaps tomorrow, perhaps the day after. The post arrived from Lhasa when there were letters to come, and as the courier had to go back, he took letters to the capital – if any. It was a sliding service. Mr Ma was not overworked. Lately there had been a good deal of correspondence passing to and fro between Lhasa and Chamdo, and between Lhasa and Shoga Dzong, he told me.

Just then I heard a jingle of bells below. Another Jongpen arriving? Mr Ma said suavely: 'There's the Lhasa post.'

I went to the window and looked through a hole in the paper. All I saw in the cobbled street was a mangy dog scavenging, and a woman in rags shooing some pigs away from a tray of grain which was drying in the sun. Mr Ma lay down and began preparing his 'gun' – the Yunnan colloquial for opium pipe. There was a light footfall on the rickety stairs – a visitor to the post office was a rare event. However, it was only a small boy who put his head rather shyly round the corner; seeing only the two of us, he stepped into the room. Although little more than four feet tall, he was dressed in a long *chupa* and cloth boots, and carried a sword stuck horizontally across his stomach like a full-sized man. He had a round, almost cherubic face, and red cheeks, and he looked hot – which was not surprising as it was now midday and the sun beat down fiercely on the mud town. I wondered what he wanted – had he come to buy a stamp?

For a few seconds he stared at me, then at the Chinese postmaster. He said, '*Yong-song: lam yakpo mare*' (I have come: the road is bad). Then he put a grubby hand inside the ample bosom of his *chupa* and, pulling out a grubby letter, handed it to the little postmaster with an air. It was the Lhasa mail.

Gyamda, 1935

The Jongpen of Sanga Chöling

The Jongpen was a middle-sized man with close-cropped black hair and a long white scar on one cheek. His complexion was darker than it should have been without frequent recourse to stimulants. His expression was kindly, but there was a firmness in the line of mouth and chin, a thinning of the lips, which boded no good to the trifler. On the whole, a fine, strong face, I thought.

He received me like an emperor, resplendent in his official robes of purple and Imperial Heavenly gold. Two collars, one of purple and inside it a second of rich orange silk, clasped his neck, a mandarin's hat covered his head, and his long boots were of the finest leather. Nor was this all; around him as he sat cross-legged on his dais were cups of exquisite workmanship, set on scarlet lacquer tables, and on his lap lay the tiniest, most cantankerous and saucy Tibetan dog imaginable.

Sanga Chöling, 1935

FOURTEEN

Wild Aviary

Vultures – An eagle – Szecheny's pheasant-grouse – An owl – Green parakeets – Blood pheasants – Long-tailed sunbirds – Elwes' horned pheasant – More green parakeets – Birds of the Ngawchang – D'Abry's sunbird – Cinnamon sparrows – Cuckoo versus koel – A magpie – White-breasted kingfisher

Vultures

Coming down the steep slope above the village I saw a party of Tibetans engaged in trapping vultures by means of decoy birds, which are led to carrion the moment the wild birds are seen, the men hiding meanwhile. When the wild birds, circling round the cliffs at an immense height, descry from afar the feast below, they come down to join the struggle for titbits, and the tame birds at once set on them; whereupon the men rush out from cover and despatch the intruders. The birds are thus caught for the sake of their feathers, which are sold in Talifu to make fans.

Tsu-kou, 1901

An eagle

On the right bank we passed a stone hovel built on the mountain-side. It was roofed with logs and turf, with a tiny entrance leading into one small room half-underground, where the family lived. Round about, the scrub had been cleared and the ground broken up for the spring crops. Three children, the eldest seven years old, were even now working hard, dragging heavy logs and collecting firewood. A few goats wandered over the barren soil, a cat meandered carelessly distant from the hut, and a woman stood waving her arms at an eagle which soared in short circles low down over the little homestead. Suddenly it swooped with lightning-like rapidity, and next moment it was working its way up in ever-growing spirals into the blue vault of heaven. Black against the sun, with widespread pinions, it looked just like some strange Jurassic bird come to life, for from between its great claws a long tail hung down. Poor pussy had been caught napping.

Salween-Mekong divide, 1914

Szecheny's pheasant-grouse

There are many Szecheny's pheasant-grouse (*Tetraophasis szechenyii*) on the moors. This bird goes about in coveys, which scatter and run uphill, though not fast, on the approach of danger. When frightened, however, the birds take to flight, screaming noisily, with a characteristic harsh cry. In April, when snow lies on the ground, they are to be found in the upper rhododendron forest at 12,000–13,000 feet, sluggish and unafraid. At this season they feed on caterpillars. In the summer, however, they ascend to the open rhododendron moorland, above the timber line; and indeed I have seen a cock stand up on a rock, close to my tent, squawking lustily at his family on the carpet. The colouring of these birds is rather sombre, male and female being identical. Feet and beak are black; breast slate-grey, spotted black, the feathers tipped with buff; back and wings slaty brown, the upper tail coverts tipped with buff, or white; tail grey, the lateral feathers black, tipped with white, the under-feathers sienna, also tipped with white; rump silvery grey. The only bright colouring is afforded by the scarlet patch round the eye, and the buff throat.

Likiang, 1921

An owl

Every night a large owl visited us and sat, like the raven, on a branch just above our chamber door. It was not till we discovered that our camp was a hot-bed of jungle rats that we understood the reason for his visits. We trapped eight rats in two days. The rats ate the food stored in the cooking *basha;* the owl ate the rats; nothing ate the owl, at least, not while we were there. The owl was more amusing than amused when we turned the electric spotlight on him. Craning his head forward, he revolved it in circles, trying to get outside the beam, or to pierce it with his powerful vision. Obviously he was puzzled. The extraordinary thing was that he sat still under this ordeal. Sometimes his wife came, and we would hear them hissing to and kissing each other and sometimes hooting gently. Then, when we had gone to bed and the camp was in darkness, we would hear the soft swish of wings, a squawk, a dying gasp, and – silence. Sometimes at night we heard a despairing wail from the depth of the forest, but we never discovered what it was, whether bird or mammal.

Meiliang, 1927

Green parakeets

Another day we went down the river a few miles to see the green parakeets come home to roost at sundown in the teak forest. Thousands came, screeching madly, till the sky was black with them and the air vibrated with their shrill wrangling. As the main body settled down for the night like a tall storm-cloud the noise of their wings was like the rumble of thunder. At last the chaffering ceased, and it was quiet.

Myitkyina, 1930

Blood pheasants

In the bamboo thicket a pair of blood pheasants were strutting. They are gay birds with vermilion legs and apple-green breast slashed with crimson, and the throat also is crimson; the rest of the plumage is grey, but soft and full. The tail is short. These birds have a way, while pecking at insects and young shoots on the ground, of jerking up their heads as though to listen, at the same time uttering a shrill, querulous cry. Yet owing to their ignorance of man – for they live in dense uninhabited forests – their temerity amounts to foolishness. They are difficult to shoot only because they are difficult to see. Cranbrook shot one in June, on his way up the valley. In August he shot another. In November, while we were in the ten-day camp, on our way back to Tahawndam, a large family of blood pheasants stalked into the firing-line one morning, and five of them were casualties in as many minutes. It seemed unkind to shoot them; they took no notice of us, and Cranbrook knocked them over one after another like coconuts at a fair, while they took little squawking runs this way and that, trying to disperse, but not connecting their discomfiture in any way with us, and uncertain where to seek cover. The young ones had evidently never seen a man before, still less a gun; it was something beyond the range of their experience, and they were distraught.

Tahawndam, 1931

Long-tailed sunbirds

On a day of better weather I watched long-tailed sunbirds in the meadow at Lung Sa visiting irises. It was like a scene from the tropics. These sunbirds are as brilliant as humming-birds and no larger than many butterflies. So light a weight are they, so rapidly do their tiny wings vibrate, that they are able to halt, poised in mid-air, for a full minute, while with their long curved beaks they extract honey from the flowers of their choice. Amongst English birds only the skylark and, for a briefer time, certain birds of prey can hover motionless. But these flimsy flowers were made for insects, not birds: birds, however small, cannot settle on them as do insects, and it was pretty to watch these clever little creatures probing between the petals for honey, exactly like a long-tongued insect which had alighted on the flower. The iris, with its cunning contrivance of formation to ensure that the seeker after honey shall, willy-nilly, take pollen too, and transfer it from flower to flower, was no puzzle to them.

Lung Sa, 1931

Elwes' horned pheasant

Birds are ridiculously tame round Chickchar. Every morning a cock Harman's pheasant strutted majestically out of the woods and in full view of the village uttered his harsh aggressive challenge to the world. This magnificent bird, better known as Elwes' horned pheasant (*Crossoptilon harmani*), weighs as much as five pounds. The ground colour is slate-grey. The tail is short, spreading and dark; but the scarlet legs, the eye set in a great scarlet sun, a gold chain round the neck, and other minor accessories touch it up with dramatic emphasis, as lipstick touches up a woman's face. These are the decorative effects which strike one at a glance.

I became almost familiar with the crossoptilon during my short residence here. On July 4th I had the unusual experience, while on a botanical ramble, of running into a whole family of them. There were three full-grown birds and half a dozen chicks. As the parents had their children with them, children hatched a few weeks previously and therefore unsophisticated, they were naturally a little flustered. On the other hand, concern for their offspring more than counterbalanced fear of the human, even when the human was trespassing at some distance from the pilgrims' route. The mother bird, which to my untrained eye differs little from the male, ran about rather hot and bothered, trying to drive the chicks in one direction. But the chicks lost their heads and described circles, which made it difficult. The operation suggested poodles herding rabbits; there was a certain lack of co-operation. I easily caught a chick by hand; it squeaked feebly, and proved an irresistible decoy. One parent kept making advances to me, coming within five feet, then running uphill, and returning to the charge. Throughout these manoeuvres the whole family were calling on the Harman wavelength. The mother had two distinct calls, the harsh crossoptilon cry, and a shriller maternal cry, plaintive like that of the chicks. Sometimes I could scarcely distinguish between the chick in my hand, keeping the family posted as to developments, and the answering cry of anguish from the mother a few feet away. The parents' behaviour was exemplary. There was no panic. Of course, they felt they were sacred and safe; but there is always the chance of disillusion.

Chickchar, 1935

More green parakeets

Remarkable was it to see the green parakeets (*Psittacula krameri*) at dusk returning from their feeding grounds in the jungle near the foothills to their sleeping quarters in the teak plantation south of the town. They came in thousands, wave after wave in flights so large as sometimes to cover a considerable wedge of sky. They kept perfect formation, wheeling and banking together as one and, considering their numbers, speed and swift change of direction, it seemed remarkable that, so far as one could tell, they never had a collision. A master brain controlled each individual bird welding the entire flight into one organism which obeyed a single command. As they flew, hastening home at dusk, they screeched to one another – code-calls perhaps for some such general instructions to the flight as 'danger front', 'spurt', 'left incline' and so on; or perhaps mere exuberance.

One evening I walked over to the teak plantation to watch the flights come in to roost; but so thickly grew the trees and so large are the leaves of the teak that it was almost dark inside when they came, screeching and bustling and fluttering in the tree-tops where the birds must have been more congested than any ghetto. As the sun went down the noise gradually grew less, then finally ceased; and so they settled down for the night. It was difficult now to believe there were thousands of parakeets up in those trees, though they must have been sitting along the branches cheek by jowl. I believe they go off at dawn in small parties, since it is only when the day is far spent one sees the immense flocks described. How far they go to their feeding grounds is not known. It may be the fig trees which attract them to the evergreen forest at this season; at other times one finds them – or an allied species – equally abundant in the pine forests of the higher hills.

Myitkyina, 1937

Birds of the Ngawchang

Birds were still very much in evidence. Once a flock of green pigeon rocketed by. White-casqued babblers, a black-and-white magpie-robin, hoopoes and a bulbul – all black except for orange beak and claws – showed themselves. I watched with interest the wagtails – they go in pairs – strutting about, neck and tail always in motion, oscillating with the precision of a mechanical toy, a restless bird. It makes quick little darts forward or at a tangent, and will spin round in a complete circle just where it stands, like a cockchafer on a pin. At sunset swiftlets darted and wheeled, snapping up insects.

Ngawchang, 1939

D'Abry's sunbird

By 12.30 we had reached the last belt of forest, and here sat down in the sunshine beside a clump of *Rhododendron arboreum* to eat our lunch. Brilliantly-coloured sunbirds were ravishing the crimson flowers for honey, their long, slightly curved beaks probing deep into the pouch-like glands, so that they could hardly avoid entangling some of the long pollen threads in the centre amongst their feathers. This honeysucker, with gamboge breast, Prussian blue head, and deep maroon back tapering into the long, thin violet tail, is one of the most gaudy little birds in the hills, where it spends the whole of the summer, indifferent to the rain. In winter it descends to the plains. It is known as D'Abry's sunbird.*

Sirhoi, 1948

Cinnamon sparrows

On the grassy Ukhrul ridge one day we watched a flock of small finch-like birds – cinnamon sparrows, I think – flying in close formation before settling all together, smartly, as though at the word of command. Head and as much as one could see of back and wings were dark, but the under-parts were rufous or chestnut, so that when viewed from the front they took on a coppery sheen. It was their well-drilled flying – over two dozen of them in the squadron – which particularly drew my attention to them and earned my admiration.

Ukhrul, 1948

Cuckoo versus koel

At this season cuckoo meets koel, and the two compete in cheerful if monotonous rivalry – though normally the one presides over matins, the other over vespers. At Hkinlum, however, the cuckoo called every morning and evening till dusk; sometimes it even called *in* the night, thereby usurping the functions of the koel, which having taken over at dusk called *all* night. It has a slightly greater register than the cuckoo, repeating a three-note phrase on an ascending scale, until you think it must burst – and wish it would. Perhaps it thought it would, too, for after the fourth or fifth call it returned abruptly to the lowest, and again worked its

* Now known as Gould's Sunbird (*Aethopyga gouldiae dabryii*).

way up the scale to bursting point. Being quite unmusical (as Jean
tells me), I loved to hear both birds – even at dead of night.

The Triangle, 1953

A magpie

It had a very strong yellow beak, an inch and a quarter long, the
upper mandible hooked over the lower like a shrike's, with bristles at the base like a barbet; and though the bird was fifteen to
eighteen inches long, most of this was tail, the head and body
measuring only seven or eight inches. With its red-orange legs
and gamboge beak it was certainly a striking bird, in spite of its
dull plumage. The general colouring was a uniform smoky grey,
only the tail-feathers being white, broadly barred with black.

Tibu, 1953

White-breasted kingfisher

One day, the 13th July to be exact, some village boys brought
us a form of the white-breasted kingfisher which they had snared.
It was quite unharmed, and did not seem to be fussed, though it
kept very still in Tha Hla's hand. As soon as he released it, it
went off silently with a normal dipping flight, as though not in
the least surprised by the episode, and one had a second good
view of its appearance. It differed from white-breasted kingfishers
I had seen down-country in having the beak orange-brown rather
than red, and a short white eyebrow. More important, in flight
the wings appeared to be black *and* white, though at rest the
kingfisher-blue of the outer wing coverts alone showed. It was
like an amendment to the ordinary bird.

Hkinlum, 1953

FIFTEEN

Plant Hunter's Paradise
1930–31

Darus of the Adung valley – The last village in Burma – Birds of the Adung valley – Tibetan butter-making – Birds of the East Hanging Valley – A band of desperadoes

Darus of the Adung valley

The rain ceased. A party of Darus arrived, and we sent them up the valley with boxes of stores, tents, and equipment. They were the wildest and most uncouth-looking tribe I had ever seen in Upper Burma. The men were naked except for a belt composed of a number of cane rings about the thickness of packing thread round the waist, over which was draped a small square of cotton cloth, and a blanket round the shoulders against the cold. Every man wore a short hunting-knife in a half-sheath of wood supported by a string round the waist. Most of them carried cross-bows. The shock of hair was long and unkempt, but trimmed all round the head. Women and girls wore short skirts and a blanket wrapped round the body. They all smoked pipes incessantly, but did not chew *pan* like the down-river tribes. Their teeth, though not discoloured by *pan*, were foully dirty, probably owing to the miscellaneous zoological diet in which they indulge.

The Darus of the Adung valley, the last tribe in Burma, are pygmies and until recently dwellers in trees. The men average about fifty-six inches in height, the women two or three inches less, but they are sturdily built. The curious point is that these pygmies are not Negritos but quite definitely Mongoloid. Their shortness of stature may be due in part to starvation diet, or to lack of salt or to other physiological causes which could be remedied. But men (not women) over five feet high are common enough to need explanation, and there can be no doubt that the Darus are a very mixed tribe. Nevertheless, here was definite proof that there exists, in the depths of the mountain forests, a pygmy Mongoloid tribe.

The Darus are a vanishing race, doomed to extinction. Wild

men need protection when encroached on by a higher civilization, just as wild birds and wild animals do, and the Darus are not protected. Not that anyone wishes to exterminate them, but everyone wishes to exploit them, and they cannot defend themselves. So they will perish. Call them, if you will, one of Nature's unsuccessful experiments; but Nature has allowed them to survive for a time in a region where no man survives for long. Encompassed on all sides by more powerful tribes, driven relentlessly deeper and deeper into the slums of the jungle, the Darus must presently fade into the *Ewigkeit*, vanish away as though they had never been. They have bored their way into the heart of the mountains, and they can go no farther. There at present they survive, in isolation, regularly venturing forth on their own initiative, but on the whole ignored, neglected, and perhaps contented.

The last village in Burma

So we came to the Tibetan outpost of Tahawndam. Prayer-flags fluttered from a cluster of poles, and a thin spiral of smoke ascended from a pyre on which juniper branches had been ignited in our honour. I looked about me. Here and there blue pines towered above smaller trees, their powerful tawny boles contrasting harshly with their slender needles. Crimson-flowered rhododendrons (*R. magnificum*), with enormous leaves, glowed in the thickets, and there were other fat-budded rhododendrons, not yet in bloom.

Now my attention was diverted by a deputation of the local inhabitants who, with tongues stuck out and hands extended, palm upwards, to show that they neither concealed a weapon nor meditated any treachery, came to meet us. At the head of them was the Tibetan headman Tsering, a bony fellow, tall compared with the little Darus. He had a big nose and a very untidy pigtail like that of a Jack Tar of Nelson's days, and he greeted us with a lopsided smile, snatching a greasy felt hat from his disordered hair. Only his body was warmly clad in the foxy-red skins of goral; otherwise he was almost as naked as the Darus. Every few minutes he scratched himself thoughtfully, as though bearing no malice towards what was irritating his skin. With him was the village priest, a benign-looking old man, with a wrinkled face and a straggling beard, dressed in a tattered red gown and yellow sheepskin cap. He might have been a country parson in reduced circumstances. There was also a loose-limbed, horse-faced fellow with ruminant teeth which he displayed in a seraphic smile. We called him George.

While we were settling in with such luggage as we had brought with us, there arrived a procession of Daru women and girls bringing bundles of thatching grass and firewood, for us; and their Tibetan lords brought us chickens, eggs and milk. There were plenty of cattle about. Our next visitors were a collection of Tibetan women. They had clean faces with an olive complexion and rosy cheeks. Tsering's daughter, the village beauty, a buxom lass of twenty, was almost good-looking; but she had no figure. She was sack-like. She had smoothed down her sleek black hair with butter, put on her cloth boots with the scarlet and green trimming (most of the Tibetans went about barefoot), and she wore her best *chupa*, a chocolate-coloured garment like a dressing-gown, which she pulled around her ample body and tied at the waist. She also wore all her jewellery, bead necklaces, metal ear-rings and the silver finger-rings with the turquoise and coral stones in them which Tibetan women very much admire. They said they had come to see us, but I suspected that they had come to be seen.

Birds of the Adung valley

Among the first comers were the sunbirds. Perhaps they were here before us, since we noticed them immediately after our arrival. They are the jewel-birds of the temperate rain forest region. The first signalled, and also the commonest, was the Nepal yellow-backed sunbird (*Aethopyga nipalensis*), which I noted on February 6th. A month later we saw D'Abry's sunbird, but it was less common than the other. Then in June, when the wave of migratory birds had gone up into the hills where the alpine rhododendrons were flowering as fast as the snow melted (or even flowering *in* the snow), we met the Yunnan fire-tailed sunbird (*Aethopyga ignicauda*), a western Chinese species. But it was the common Nepal sunbird, with its brilliant orange breast, all iridescent blues and greens on head and throat, that I saw day after day in the bare February trees, a flying cut of a jewel from some

Aladdin's cave. Into the winter gloom and coldness of our valley it seemed to bring the joyousness of tropical blue seas and hot yellow sands.

The river itself was a favourite resort of birds. At Tahawndam the Adung is thirty yards wide and shallow, but there were days when it rose like an angry snake and lashed the banks. There was always a fast current. The white-capped redstart (*Chaimarrornis leucocephalus*), a non-migrant common on the mountain streams from the Himalayas to China, kept very late hours. Long after all good birds had gone to bed, when there was only just light enough to see by, this brisk little redstart, neat, cheeky and efficient, would speed along just above the surface of the lead-grey water, its shrill voice piercing through the noise of the cascade. The plumbeous redstart (*Rhyacornis fuliginosa*) kept almost as late hours. Both birds perch on rocks in the river, hawking flies, then skim across the ruffled water to another ambush. Cranbrook noticed that the plumbeous redstart had a trick of flying vertically upwards in the evening to a height of twenty feet or more, then swooping down in a spiral to the level from which it started – another fly-catching device. One evening I watched this bird dive at high speed to the river, hit the surface and ricochet off again like a kingfisher. It could hardly have been fishing since its beak is like a badly-sharpened pencil; but the imitation was good.

A third evening performer was a chocolate-brown dipper (*Cincius pallasi*) of retiring habits. It lurked on rocks and along the bank. When approached, it would plunge into the swift current, swimming boldly, and if necessary dive under the icy water, remaining submerged for a minute or two; then reappear in some unexpected place. It was frightened at the sight of a man. Several wagtails haunted the river or more often some rocky stream-bed hard by or even the adjacent fields. The most constantly seen was Hodgson's yellow-headed wagtail.

Other honey-sucking birds were the Yunnan green-backed tit (*Parus monticolus*) and the Nepal yellow-backed sunbird. This last must have been designed by nature for the purpose of robbing flowers of their honey. Clinging upside down to a flower stalk of *Rhododendron pankimense*, he would thrust his big, curved beak up into the pendant bell, tweeting with pleasure all the while. He also visited the pale, almost tropical-looking flowers of *R. stenaulum*, but his greatest feat was to sip honey in mid-air, hovering with a quiver of gorgeous wings like a humming-bird. His dull little mate in rifle-green could not do this. Nevertheless, she was less shy than he was. I have seen her perch herself alertly on a twig, gyrating like a fly impaled on a pin, darting off this way and that, always returning, but never precisely to the same spot.

There were many laughing-thrushes in the woods. With the gradual ascent of spring, they went up the valley in waves to the limit of trees. It seems curious that these birds should be called 'laughing'; anything less like laughter than the rather mournful, monotonous notes so many of them utter in the spring, it would be difficult to imagine. In winter, however, most of the laughing-thrushes go down into the hill jungle and congregate in large flocks on the ground under the bamboos. Suddenly a wild chortling will startle the traveller, and this outburst from twenty or thirty birds might perhaps be likened to laughter. Once I watched a flock of grey thrushes glide in single file along the branch of a tree; each bird moved with the stealth and ease of a squirrel, quickly and silently.

Tits were also numerous, particularly a little green-backed bird with a yellow waistcoat (*Parus monticolus yunnanensis*). In the early morning it was always to be found amongst the raspberry-canes eating the rather arid fruits left over from last season. Sometimes it would hover, not unlike a sunbird, pecking at the flowers of the silver-leafed *Rubus lineatus;* or it would alight on a cane and thrust its head upside-down into a flower. Later in the day it turned to a honey diet, obtained from *Rhododendron pankimense*. Not content with obtaining the honey, it pecks away at the honey-secreting tissue itself. At one time I saw four of these birds together on a rhododendron bush, the corollas of which, perforated round the base, were falling like autumn leaves.

Tibetan butter-making

The menace of dogs, savage, desperate from being kept tied up, and hungry, made me shy of visiting the Tibetan village; but the people themselves welcomed us whenever we cared to go. We paid a call one day, and watched the women making butter in a tall wooden cylinder. It is hard work forcing the wheel-shaped piston up and down through the squelching milk suds. We sat on the hard floor in the dark but too-well-ventilated room, and

buttered tea was poured out into wooden cups for us. It was a
clay-coloured, oleaginous fluid, resembling oil fuel. But the Tibetans were fond of it, and consumed several quarts a day. It was
less nauseating taken hot, with the butter well emulsified, than
cool, when the butter-drops floated to the surface and coagulated
to form a thin scum. We ate puffed corn, which was good, and
solid black millet-cakes as large as cartwheels; and in return gave
presents to our hosts, the lama and the headman. Even the Tibetan
houses are only one-roomed, but in other respects they are much
superior to the Daru huts, which would be condemned for cattle
in England.

Birds of the East Hanging Valley

While in the East Hanging Valley, I heard the musical call of the
yellow-throated grosbeak (*Perissospiza icteroides*), an unmistakable
bell-like note. These birds were going about in pairs, nesting;
there was always a pair in the patch of fir forest here, but I never
succeeded in shooting a specimen. This grosbeak is a spectacular
bird, as big as a good thrush, with a black head, back and wings,
brilliant gamboge throat and breast, and a purple beak. Though
not abundant, we saw, or more frequently heard, grosbeaks
throughout May and June. On my next visit to the East Hanging
Valley, about June 13th, I watched a sunbird visiting the crimson
flowers of *Rhododendron chaetomallum*. He was a bold bird; I stood
within a few feet of the bush while the little fellow, brilliant in
scarlet and orange, with violet throat and ultramarine cap, danced
to and fro, flickering his wings continuously, even when he settled, as though to shake off the raindrops. His wife was dressed
in dark green with a pale green breast. The corollas of *R. chaetomallum* contained small flies, and the sunbirds were probably
attracted by these; but they could hardly have failed to move
pollen from flower to flower.

A laughing-thrush with a speckled breast, and his plainer mate,
were sliding in and out through the bushes in quest of rowan
berries. From time to time these birds would hop up to the top
of the tree, and peck at the rotten fruits – never flying if they
could help it. I shot a pair for the pot, but there is very little meat
on them, and even that is tasteless.

A good many birds came round my hut in the early mornings,

and here I shot a female laughing-thrush. Afterwards I wished remorsefully that I had not; for her disconsolate male haunted me. He hung round the hut, uttering his mournful love-call, four notes repeated over and over again, until I could hardly bear it. Then he would give a despairing sort of wheezy wail and vanish like a banshee. Next morning he returned and sang again.

A band of desperadoes

How to get transport – now that we were isolated – that was the immediate problem. Visitors from Tahawndam were rare. One day we returned to camp in the afternoon, changed, had tea and were just setting down to work when we heard voices outside. Next minute Ba Kai came in and announced visitors – not from Tahawndam. At his heels entered a sturdy Chinaman and three Tibetans, one of whom I judged, from his dress, to be a man of some wealth and position. Surprised, I bade them squat on the floor. The Chinaman gave us greetings. He had come to ask if his partner – indicating the well-dressed Tibetan – and he might come into the Adung valley to dig *pai mu* (the bulb of *Fritillaria roylei*). The party, he said, consisted of some twenty men, at present camped on the other side of the mountains, who were afraid to cross over when they heard that Englishmen had come to the Adung valley. But he knew it would be all right, he said confidently, and so, accompanied by his Tibetan friend, he had come to pay us this visit. He added, by way of reference, that he came from the Mekong, that he was a Catholic and that he knew all the French Fathers there.

As I had myself travelled on the upper Mekong and had stayed at the village he mentioned, I was on home ground, so to speak; and the astute Fan Li, seeing this, made the most of his opportunity. The praise he gave to the 'good foreigners', especially the English, would have brought a blush to the cheek of more credulous listeners than myself. Meanwhile, the Tibetans, who professed to understand no word of what he said, were peering about the hut. I inquired about the Tibetan who was the head of the party and was told that he came from a village in the Salween valley, to the east of us. I had, it appeared, stayed at his house some years before, and found no reason to love him. I looked at

him and distrusted his shifty eyes, his morose silence, his perpetual peering, his nervous fidgeting – everything about him.

I was tempted to refuse these marauders permission to enter
the Adung valley, where they had no right to be, especially in
view of their avowed mission and the complaints I had heard
against them. But, after all, the bluff might have been called. If
the party intended to come over anyhow, with or without leave,
how could we prevent them? We might organize the Darus into
a defence corps, but what would happen to them next year? The
idea was fantastic. But I had more cogent reasons for making
friends with these people. We were very anxious to cross the pass
ourselves and explore the route into Tibet. Tahawndam held out
no prospect of transport, but in Fan Li I recognized a possible
ally, if rightly handled. I meant to use him. When the Tibetan
gentleman brought out his presents, therefore, and added his
request that they might come and work in the valley, I answered
in the 'diplomatic affirmative'. The presents were neither numerous nor costly – two pairs of rather gaudy, hand-woven cloth
garters, such as the Tibetans use for binding round the tops of
their long boots, into which the ends of their short trousers are
thrust. We gave them some cigarettes and an electric torch, and
they departed to Ba Kai's hut to find out what they could about
us with the aid of that young man's limited vocabulary.

Mano was still sick. The Kachins have no stomach for the high
mountains. Our visitors pitched their tent a mile up the valley,
just beyond the last patch of silver fir, at the base of a huge scree.
It was of white hemp cloth, with a light-blue border, supported
by two poles, forming a simple canopy. Then the Chinese went
back over the pass and called up the workers. Later, when I visited
the pass, I saw a line of men, high on the scree, working gradually
upwards. They were hacking up the fritillary bulbs, using a short
one-handed pick, a most useful weapon for the botanist.

A few days after that, Fan Li came again to our camp and asked
permission to take his men down the valley. They had cleaned
up the main valley, he said, and wished to visit the north main
valley above our Number One camp. The next morning we
watched the procession of thirty streaming across the bog; they
had to come by our hut, which commanded the path, and when
I saw them close to I was sorely tempted to say, 'They shall not
pass'.

They were awful. A more unsavoury lot of ruffians I have

rarely met. A mixture of Tibetan, Lisu and Chinese, the riff-raff of the highland border, they all looked capable of committing any crime. They were tall, with long hair, dressed in ragged hempen gowns hitched up round the waist. Each man carried a heavy basket of *tsamba* or corn-flour on his back, and a long thin gun with pitchfork rest. Some had knives. They carried a fortnight's rations, Fan Li told me. However, inside a week they were all back again. The Tibetan leader had had a fright and was hastening back to his own side of the mountains. Perhaps he was uneasy at our veiled hostility and our tactical position between him and his base. Anyhow, Fan Li said scornfully that his partner was afraid. It was to our advantage, because the partners wanted to sell us their surplus rations, and we were glad to buy, even at the exorbitant price demanded. When I said we had enough, moreover, the price fell to something almost reasonable.

Our Tibetan aristocrat looked magnificent in a red shirt and blue gown. He had slipped out both shoulders, and tied the arms round his waist. He wore a fur-lined cap with gold braid, and long leather boots. His thin silver pipe was thrust jauntily through his sash, at the back, and he carried a formidable, if primitive, gun. I could not help wondering to what band of reformers he had dedicated himself, but it appeared that the colour of his haberdashery had no political significance.

We inspected the contingent closely; they had the air of men who have just fought a pitched battle at long range, but we could detect nothing irregular. One of the skirmishers carried a German magazine-rifle. There was a rumour that a large body of Lisus, also in search of *pai mu*, had come up from the south to Adung Long; possibly there had been a clash, or our scouts were making a strategic retreat according to plan. The time had now come to ask the Tibetan point-blank for transport to take us to Jité. Rather to my surprise he refused. The Tibetan officials, he said, would beat him for letting us through, and he dare not do it. This was the more curious because he claimed to possess a wonderful medicine, made by the lamas, which he swore rendered swords and bullets nugatory; and, after all, bullets are more than whips, or even scorpions. The medicine was not taken internally, but was carried in a silver charm-box, encrusted with coral and turquoise, which he wore strapped round his waist. He refused to show me the mascot. Though we, in our climbing rig, dirty with wood smoke, looked shabby beside his Magnificence, I was pleased to note that he coveted our firearms, steel boxes, field-glasses, tents, furniture and other household goods. So he left us, and departed to his own country, where I hoped we should now have a good reputation, for he left behind him two or three fever-stricken men, whom we dosed with quinine and sent on after him. But Fan Li stayed with us for a while.

The next social event was the departure of Fan Li for Tahawndam. I bade him tell the headman I wanted coolies at once, but he returned three days later with a message from Tsering saying that he would send coolies when the maize was ripe. As this was the third separate reason in two months for not complying with my request, I had no further illusions as to when the transport would come. Plainly we must have patience till the Greek Kalends.

But Fan Li did not come alone. With him were two Daru coolies carrying big baskets of skins which he had purchased. I was indignant that he should be able to get two coolies while we could not get even one. But Fan Li pointed out, reasonably enough, that it was easy to get one or two coolies, but what use was that to us who wanted a dozen? As for the baskets of skins, they had no doubt been purchased in the ordinary way. Burma sends skins and medicinal roots to Tibet, the Darus supplying transport. Tibet in return sends clothing, cooking-pots, salt and *tsamba*, to Burma, the Darus fetching these things for themselves. The Tibetans pay the Darus a nominal price for what they buy; the Darus pay the Tibetans a phenomenal price for what they need. But the volume of trade between Tibet and Burma is not large.

One interesting piece of news Fan Li told us. Our hut had been overwhelmed by a landslide. A mountain had come down during the night, threatening to abolish the Tibetan settlement, but had stopped just in time. Only the Base Camp was utterly buried. This was his parting shot as Fan Li went off to Tibet with his two men, and we expected to see him no more. My last words to him were, 'Send the men of Jité to me'.

I learnt something about the mysterious *pai mu* industry from Fan Li. The bulb, or an extract of it, is reputed to cure fever. I found it, when I tasted a scale of it, if not exactly bitter like quinine, at least as pungent as red pepper. In Yunnan *pai mu* sells wholesale for eight dollars per *kin*, or about seven and sixpence a pound, at the current rate of exchange (in 1931). But it is the big seaport cities, Shanghai and Canton, which buy the stock, and by the time it reaches those distant places it is worth almost its own weight in silver. The profits of the Fan Li partnership could not have been high. Labour was cheap and it cost little to feed these hardy folk off *tsamba* and buttered tea. But they had to come a long way to get the *pai mu*, and there was no sale for it nearer than Atuntzu in Yunnan. There was a commission in kind to the diggers, too; the Tibetan said thirty-three per cent, but that seems excessive, and as the bulbs are useless to the coolies they exchange their share for food or cash.

There remains the question of extermination. But here even the well-known rapacity of Chinese medicine-mongers kept itself under control. The diggers spared small or immature plants, and when I ascended a scree behind the skirmishing line which worked diagonally across its face, I found plenty of fritillaries. Every plant produces scores of seeds, which germinate readily; there must be millions of plants in these hills.

Fan Li told me that when there is a heavy winter snowfall the fritillary crop in the following summer is good, but when there is not so much snow it is poorer. But he could not account for the connection.

SIXTEEN

Plant Hunter in Tibet
1933

*The people of Rima – Two Tibetan meals – A deserted monastery –
The people of Watak – The fight in the dzong – Perils to seeds – The
road to Ru – Visitors at Solé – Over the Dri La*

The people of Rima

Meanwhile, the people of Rima were not inactive. A troupe of
Kampa dancers arrived and enlivened the village. Tibetan dancing
is dynamic, cymbals, drums and a primitive type of very squeaky
fiddle giving rise to a medley rather than melody. There is not
much rhythm, but the dancers work themselves up into a hysteria
of gymnastic motion. Then came a religious troupe, who demon-
strated how to cast out devils, even the most stubborn. The face
of the possessed man was concealed behind a paper mask. He
gyrated violently, till even I felt giddy watching him. The devil,
as susceptible to weird music as a serpent, shook him to the
foundations, but eventually emerged, leaving the late victim
exhausted.

The Tibetans put duty to their religion before everything.
Thanks to the zeal of the lamas, Buddhist ritual has spread
throughout Zayul, and penetrated even into the Mishmi Hills.
Every householder in Rima daily offered the fragrance of imaginary burnt offerings to heaven, a rich volume of aromatic smoke,
obtained by burning bundles of an abundant weed called Artemi-
sia (Keating's Powder is made from it) in a small structure like a
clay oven, ascending into the air. Every day men, and women
too, marched solemnly round the square temple (which contained
a large image of Buddha) muttering prayers and twirling prayer-
drums. The population of Zayul consists of two distinct elements,
Tibetan and aboriginal. The aborigines must have swarmed off
some common stock long ago, and remained in undisturbed
possession of Zayul until comparatively late years. They are
pygmies, and now form the serf population. The Tibetans are
Kampas from eastern Tibet, a tall swarthy people, full of good

cheer. Kampa women are remarkably handsome, their piercing black eyes and raven hair, together with their warm colouring, suggesting a gipsy strain. They love a gay life brightened by song and dance, with plenty of drink. Much of the family wealth is invested in jewellery – large silver ear-rings set with coral and turquoise, finger-rings, and silver bangles. A collar of blue beads is often worn, and a silver charm-box suspended round the neck. In the deep warm valleys of Kam, the women can indulge their taste for bright blue cotton skirt and jacket; they are not, like the people of the plateau, compelled by the cold to dress in thick woollen *chupa*, or sheepskin. Very different are the serfs – shapeless pygmies with fat round face and wide nose. They dress in drab sacking, and for decoration wear only a multitude of bright yellow bead-necklaces – the badge of the serf, it would seem. Also it hides the goitrous lump in the neck.

Two Tibetan Meals

The white-haired abbot asked me to lunch at the monastery. He wanted me to go when they had their meal, at about 11. But Tsumbi told him that I never ate at that hour and arranged for me to go at 2 o'clock instead. This monastery, built of mud, stone and timber, was a much more substantial and magnificent building than the wooden monasteries we had seen in the forest country. The monks lived in rooms instead of in hutches.

When I entered the stone-paved courtyard, I was met by several monks who bowed and led me silently down a dark passage. A grey greasy curtain was lifted, and I went into a small, dark room, where a low stool or bench was set before a divan.

The abbot welcomed me and told a servant to bring food. He himself had taken his meal earlier and sat in an adjoining room talking to Tsumbi while I ate. I sat cross-legged on the cushion. The food was served in small china bowls, and servants, having placed chopsticks by my plate, at once withdrew, all except the tea man.

I began with a cup of reddish buttered tea, the national social lubricator. The man stood at my elbow, swilling the horrid wash round in a black teapot. I took a sip. As soon as I set down the cup, he filled it to the brim. Politeness whispered 'Drink'. Prudence shouted 'Don't'. As it grew cold, a film of butter coagulated on the surface.

One bowl contained rice, another gobbets of mutton, a third a spinach-like vegetable, a fourth the same vegetable pickled and very sour. I finicked with these drab delicacies with a pair of chopsticks; as each bowl, not much larger than a teacup, was finished it was replenished. At last I struck. The cold mucilaginous spinach defeated me. I refused further food, and presently the abbot and Tsumbi came in to talk. Amongst other things he told me that Shugden Gompa was under the patronage of Ganden Monastery near Lhasa. He remembered Bailey coming twenty-two years before; Bailey had slept a night in the monastery, but the abbot himself had not seen him.

After an exchange of courtesies, during which the abbot gave me permission to take any photographs I liked in the monastery, I returned to the dzong.

The next day, not to be outdone, the dzongpön asked me to lunch. I went again at 2 o'clock, and, as before, after being greeted by my host, I was left to eat in solitude. This meal was superior to the one I had received the day before. In addition to all that the monks had given me, I had *chang* to drink, and *tsamba* rissoles filled with chopped meat and red pepper (capsicum), Chinese brick sugar, and dried yak flesh as fibrous as asbestos and about as edible. I was waited on by the dzongpön's old servant, a reverend bald-headed, white-bearded man with a high deeply-furrowed forehead. So wrinkled was he that I began to think he had been made up in the green-room; could any man have so high and white a forehead, or was it a property wig he wore? His dingy coat clung to him in greasy folds; and he looked as if he had not undressed, even to sleep, since he reached manhood.

A deserted monastery

The evening of the day we crossed the Poyü La we came to a large village called Drongsa (officially Shoshi Dzong), at the junction of two streams. It is set in a fertile plain, an oasis among the rocks. The monastery was large and solid and very white; it looked more like a fortress. Beside it the dzong stood, looking more like a monastery. From a distance, the village seemed prosperous, rich even for these parts. But when we came close, it proved almost desolate. The houses could have held 200 people at least, but while we were there we saw no more than a score. The dzong contained only an old caretaker, and when I asked if the dzongpön was away, he told me there was no dzongpön. Apart from two figures we saw looking over the battlements, the monastery also seemed to be unoccupied. I wanted to see over it, but I was warned by the caretaker that fierce mastiffs wandered loose about the courtyard; and when I walked past I heard them making a noise more like lions roaring than dogs barking. When I went back there in October the monastery was just as deserted, so that it cannot have been that the monks were riding out.

I spent the night in the dzong. After dinner I strolled on the flat roof, watching dark clouds sail across the moon, which was almost full. For all its richness, the small plain soon ran up to screes and jagged peaks, whose outlines were sharp in silhouette against the dapple sky. Moonlight on the monastery made it look medieval; and watching it, I realized that nothing European is closer to modern Tibet than the Middle Ages. Tibetan life and culture, dominated by religion and a rich ruling class, is purely medieval. The peasants can neither read nor write. They love singing and dancing, and hold festivals and religious ceremonies. They live amidst beautiful surroundings, and are certainly not unhappy.

The people of Watak

When we reached Watak on August 4th the whole population came into the narrow fly-infested street and clamoured to do the next stage in my company. Men, women and girls seized on my boxes, each taking one article, even if it was no more than a camera. And seventeen in all distributed the loads between them. Even an empty biscuit tin, which I used for plants, had a coolie assigned to it. As usual, the heaviest loads were given to old hags, presumably on the principle that, being of no further use to the community, they might as well die in harness. The girls were dressed in patchwork skirts made of such thin rags I expected they would flake to bits as they walked. Yet they all wore fine chromatic cloth boots.

The fight in the dzong

Next day I cancelled the order for coolies, having decided to spend another day plant-hunting on the cliffs. I took Tashi, Kele, and Chimi with me; only Tsumbi stayed behind in the dzong. We spent an interesting day on the limestone crags, and it was late in the afternoon when we got back. Tsumbi did not appear when I called him, but after some delay he came, and I found fault with him. He seemed to comprehend nothing, and I dismissed him to the kitchen, telling him to hurry up with my dinner. But dinner was a long way off, and suddenly a row started in the gallery just outside my door. I went out. Tsumbi, already deep in my black books, had hold of Tashi and appeared to be threatening him. I went up to them and pulled Tsumbi roughly off. 'Stop it!' I said angrily.

He turned on me and was about to be insolent when I cut him short. I saw now that he was drunk. 'Be careful what you say, Tsumbi.' I seized his thumbs, ju-jitsu fashion; in a moment he was on the floor. He uttered no sound when I threatened to break both his thumbs if he showed the slightest sign of violence. But he was quiet enough and I let him get up.

'Go back to your room,' I said. 'I will talk to you afterwards.'

But Tsumbi was past caring about anything. I had hurt him, and he was as angry as I was. A few minutes later there was an explosion of oaths in the kitchen as Tsumbi cursed everyone in turn. Still thinking to quell the disturbance instead of letting the atmosphere cool down a little of its own accord – which might have been the wiser course – I went into the kitchen determined if necessary to have Tsumbi shut up for the night. Previous outbreaks had revealed him as noisy, quarrelsome and truculent when drunk. Tsumbi, wild-eyed and dishevelled, was sitting huddled up on a stool, shouting at everybody; his brother was on his knees before him, his head on his lap, weeping audibly; Chimi and the caretaker were cowering in a corner; only Tashi was trying to restore order. He spoke soothing words and, when I appeared, tried to drag Tsumbi to his feet. But Tsumbi would have none of it. He was far too drunk to care for anybody or anything. With misty swimming eyes he gazed at me and shouted unintelligible things.

'Tashi,' I said, 'we must get him to bed.'

'I cannot do anything with him, sahib. Only Pinzo can control
him when he's drunk.'

Then Tsumbi got up and in menacing mood advanced upon
me, though handicapped by the weeping Kele; I felt sorry for
Kele somehow.

'Tsumbi, get to bed immediately, or I shall hammer you.'

But Tsumbi was deaf to threats or to advice. It was clear that
there would be trouble. The miserable Chimi chose this moment
to start whimpering, and slunk from the room; but Tashi stood
his ground like a man. Then Tsumbi burst out, speaking curiously
enough in English: 'All ri, I know you,' he said shaking his fist
at me. 'All ri.'

I gave him one more chance, then as he advanced I hit him
between the eyes. The blow checked, but did not stop him;
recovering himself, he aimed a savage but quite wild blow at me,
grunting furiously. Kele threw himself between us, clasping me
round the knees. I absurdly imagined that he was trying to protect
me, or at any rate to part us; but as Tsumbi came on again, he
held me tight, and I realized that he had thrown his weight into
the scale on behalf of his brother; he was drunk too. Then I hit
Tsumbi hard, and he went down. At the same moment Kele
threw me, and of course I fell straight into the arms of Tsumbi,
who was now like a maniac. I saw murder in his eyes, but I
grasped his thumbs again and he was helpless. Tashi now pulled
Kele aside, and after a minute I sprang up.

'Get him out,' I panted. 'Hold him, tie him up. He's mad.' All
this had happened in less time than it takes to tell, but I was so
out of breath from the scuffle that I could only sit and pant.
Tsumbi and Kele now retired to the caretaker's room at the other
end of the gallery, and I took a padlock from one of my boxes
and locked the door, and I hoped that the incident was closed.
Half an hour later there came a loud knocking, and Tashi reported
that the drunkards were battering down the door. I went to look;
but though the blows reverberated through the empty dzong the
lock was a stout one. I believed it would hold.

Nevertheless, my position was unenviable. Tsumbi meant
murder – if he got out – of that I felt certain. Nor was I reassured
when Tashi asked me meaningly whether I had a revolver. Of
course, I had no such thing. Chimi and the caretaker had fled.
Tashi and I were alone in the fort with those two drunken maniacs
trying to get at us, and not another man near. It was now about

nine o'clock. I had not dined, nor did I want to. I told Tashi to barricade himself in the kitchen, and to call me immediately if anything happened. Then I selected a stout cudgel about three feet long which I placed at the head of my bed. Finally, I barricaded my door and set the table on its side so that anyone coming in must blunder into it and the noise would wake me. I had no mind to be murdered in my sleep. By this time I felt thoroughly frightened, and a long silence from the far end of the gallery was even more fraught with unpleasant possibilities than the hammering had been. But barricaded in my room, with the cudgel close at hand, I felt more confident. I was determined to use my weapon without hesitation if Tsumbi entered my room in the night. When everything was ready, I placed a powerful electric torch under my pillow and got into bed. In spite of a long and exhausting day it was some time before I got to sleep.

Dawn was breaking when I awoke. There was silence everywhere. There had been no dramatic turn of events. I dismantled the barricade and Tashi brought me my tea. I dressed quickly.

Suddenly a loud banging on the far side of the dzong warned me that the assault was being renewed. Tashi rushed in: 'They are breaking open the door, sahib.' No need to tell me that! With a loud splintering of wood a panel came out; the lock had held, the thick wooden door had given way. The prisoners had loosed a post and used it as a battering-ram. In a minute Kele stood before me, gesticulating and speaking rapidly, in a mixture of Tibetan and Hindustani. I spoke sharply to him, refusing to discus anything until he was sober, but though I put a bold face on it, I was feeling very uneasy. Tashi and I had to face these two thugs alone. Moreover, it now appeared that I had shut them up with the alcoholic supply – crude Tibetan rice spirit, and the sudden cessation of the assault on the door the previous night was only due to the fact that they had made this happy discovery. They had spent the hours of imprisonment very comfortably in the caretaker's room, drinking more deeply!

Knowing that Tsumbi would be upon me in a minute, I pushed Kele out of my room and walked along the gallery towards the broken door; I felt safer in the open. Before I was half way, a figure appeared coming slowly down the gallery towards me. It was some seconds before I recognized Tsumbi, and I waited while he slowly and deliberately approached. He was a dreadful sight. He had a black eye, swollen lip and a cut forehead; a smear of

blood striped one side of his inflamed face. His clothes were torn
and dusty, his thumbs which I had wrenched back were swollen
and discoloured. His pigtail had come down and his tangled hair
hung over his forehead. But the look in his bloodshot eyes was
defiant, insolent, and alarming. I had purposely brought no
weapon with me, and seeing the pitiable state Tsumbi was in, I
decided, while relaxing none of my vigilance, to give him a
chance of making peace.

'Well, Tsumbi, are you going to behave yourself?'

'Why did you hit me, sahib? I have been shamed!'

'You have forgotten something. Are you a coolie that you try
to hit me? I thought you were my *sirdar*. What will they say in
Darjeeling when they hear you were drunk and fighting with
your sahib?'

In a moment the truculent expression vanished from Tsumbi's
face. Without warning he was on his knees, clasping me round
the legs, bowing his head on my feet, and crying bitterly. 'Forgive
me, sahib, forgive me! I have a wife in Darjeeling, and a little
girl.'

So that was that. I felt an enormous relief surge over me. But
Tsumbi was far too dangerous and I determined to rid myself, if
possible, of this turbulent *sirdar*. I now raised Tashi's wages for
standing by me so pluckily during the crisis, and discussed with
him what was to be done. He agreed that Tsumbi when drunk
was uncontrollable. On the other hand, if I dismissed him, Kele
would go, too, and I would be short-handed just when I most
needed help. After turning the thing over in my mind I decided
that I would not instantly dismiss Tsumbi, but that he should
accompany me back to Shugden Gompa.

The coolies, having heard of the riot the night before and
doubtless having been warned by Tsumbi not to come as he was
unfit to travel, stayed away. I spent a restless day in the fort; and
Tsumbi, retreating again behind the splintered door, slept and
drank alternately.

I sent for the headman, and told him I must have transport for
the morrow. This was promised, and next morning the men
turned up after breakfast. Tsumbi, still looking a horrible sight,
came out of his lair and took charge. He had pulled himself
together, bound a turban on his head, washed his face, and done
what he could to tidy up.

★

'Well, Tsumbi, you are not happy with me. I will pay you your wages to date and give you money for the road, and you can start for your home in Darjeeling tomorrow. You had better go by the big road to Lho Dzong, and thence by the Lhasa road and Gyantse; you will thus meet with travellers, and be quite safe.' It was the morning after our return to Shugden. After breakfast I had sent for Tsumbi, who now stood before me.

He drew a deep breath, looked at me, and then looked down at the floor. He was smartly dressed, his black eye had mended, he bore no signs of the late fracas.

'If the sahib commands.' He hesitated and then: 'Please forgive me, sahib. I wish to stay with you. I will never get drunk again.'

'Tsumbi, you said that before. I warned you of the consequences.'

'Sahib!' – Tsumbi seized his ears and pulled them – 'you may cut off my ears if ever I drink alcohol again while I am with you. It is a promise.'

It occurred to me that during the fight in the dzong my opportunities for cutting off Tsumbi's ears had been few and uncertain; nor would the loss of them have prevented him from knifing me. However, I relented. Since we left Sangachu Dzong his behaviour had been exemplary. But then so it had been for a time in June, when I had told him that I was thinking of sending him back with my companions and taking Pinzo as *sirdar*. The threat then worked wonders; but its efficacy had gradually worn off as it ceased to have any meaning when he found himself in Shugden Gompa.

But the end of my stay here was approaching. Perhaps it would be better for us to stick together. I gave Tsumbi a final word of warning, and cancelled his dismissal. He was greatly relieved and thoroughly chastened. It is only fair to say that he kept his promise; for the next three months not a drop of alcohol passed his lips.

Perils to seeds

And now a new peril to my seeds made its appearance. Seed collecting sounds an easy occupation; anyone can collect seeds, you say. But apart from the physical difficulty of gathering seeds which ripen any time between August and December, over so wide an area, there are certain special difficulties. Slugs and larvae play havoc with them. Tragopans and other birds eat them. Rain washes them from their capsules, wind scatters them; and some are mechanically propelled from their capsules. Even those which survive all these perils may be buried under a blanket of snow, and lost beyond recall. But once I had spread the seeds out to dry on the floor of my own room I thought they were safe. Not a bit of it. A skirmish of mice descended upon them after dark, made hay with a bundle of Nomocharis capsules, and chewed up the seeds. I had to get some more and put them in a safer place. But that did not rid me of the plague, and mice continued to haunt my room, sometimes running over my face at night; I would awake with a start, thinking the devil had got me.

The road to Ru

Above our camp the valley expanded on to a bare plateau at a height of 18,000 feet. It was as well we had a guide with us, for it looked as though we could cross the range anywhere within a space of two miles. We could have reached the rim of the amphitheatre anywhere; but only one valley led down to Shoshi Dzong. There were no outstanding peaks in any direction. Passing the red mountain, we reached one which was dazzling white, and crunched over a broad saddle strewn with crystals of calcite. Near the pass was a small glacier and a lake. A saw-edged wind rasped our faces, flaying the skin. Then began the descent of another interminable valley. All day we marched, descending gradually from a lifeless region of rock and snow to alpine pastures, from alpine pastures to scrub. However, the monotony was enlivened late in the afternoon by an incident. The path here skirted the hillside a hundred feet above the bottom of the valley, where a narrow strip of pasture showed. A quarter of a mile ahead stood three black tents; and I noted the tall lanky figure of a Kampa herdsman standing outside one of them. Two dogs now detached themselves from the encampment, and bounding up the slope were lost to view behind a shoulder. I was on foot, my party some distance behind. Herdsmen and dogs – usually tied up – were familiar objects, and I paid no particular attention to them until, suddenly rounding a corner, I saw the great angular head of a Tibetan mastiff poked up from behind a rock, not twenty yards away. It looked at me without a trace of friendliness in its bloodshot eyes, and I suddenly realized my danger. Being quite unarmed, I hastily picked up the largest stone I could find and retreated backwards, shouting to the herdsman below. Then the second dog popped up its head. They were huge, hungry-looking brutes, weighing perhaps 150lb. each; these mastiffs make a blind rush, and in the first onslaught will knock a man down. At that critical moment there came a most welcome diversion. Some of the yak drivers farther back had seen and taken in the whole incident. Suddenly I heard a man running behind me, and a stone whistled over my head. 'Pönpo,' panted a stout fellow, 'look out! dogs!' He dashed past me, with drawn sword, and the mastiffs began to retreat. More men arrived, and my servants, shouting angrily to the herdsman, rushed up. Reluctantly the dogs drew off, were captured by the surly Kampa – who throughout the proceedings had displayed a truly remarkable detachment – and tied up. I felt greatly relieved; I had had a good fright.

But the incident did not end there. Both my servants and the yak drivers were furious at this wanton attack on peaceful travellers. I was angry myself; we had not gone near the tents, and anyhow it was a churlish way of greeting strangers. They all ran down the hillside, and were on top of the Kampa before he knew what was happening. I had remained on the path, thinking that they were only going to abuse him, as possibly they were; but he showed fight, and the men, now thoroughly roused, set about him.

An ugly situation now arose. Two other men came out of the tents and picked up stones; the yak drivers, going to the rescue of my men, were greeted by a fusillade, and seeing that a fracas was unavoidable, I also ran down the slope. A woman screamed and danced round the combatants: I seized a handy billet of wood, and threated to beat either of the two men who were skirmishing on the flanks, should they join in the mêlée. I also hit one man to make him drop a stone he had picked up, keeping a wary eye open lest he should try to loose the dogs on us again. Otherwise I saw no good reason why the Kampa should not get the beating he had so richly deserved.

The battle was now completely localized. The tall Kampa fought three of my men valiantly. His face was covered with blood from a cut over one eye, his hair, frequently seized by his assailants, hung matted and unkempt, his clothes were torn. The men pinioned his arms, pummelled him, and tried to throw him. He fought them silently, doggedly, and Kele at least carried marks of his displeasure. But three to one is long odds, and he had no chance; my men were too strong. He was seized, his arms bound with leather thongs borrowed from the yak drivers, and he was pushed and pulled up the hill on to the path, a prisoner. One of the young men, stung to action possibly by the imprecations of the virago, dashed up the hill to lead a rescue party; but Chimi drew his sword and, turning on him suddenly, sent him headlong in flight. It was the first really comic interlude, and I could not help laughing. The valiant Chimi – what a hero! The youth who had slunk away blubbering when Tsumbi got drunk and abused him! Needless to say it was Tsumbi, Kele, and a yak driver who had captured the prisoner. The young man, deeply concerned about his father's safety, now dived into one of the tents.

'They have gone to get their guns,' remarked the fearful Chimi.

'More likely to loose the dogs,' said I.

But the man emerged from the tent, not with gun or dog, but with a tray of *tsamba* and a large round of butter. Shouting to us, he held up his peace offering. But we would have none of it, and marched off our prisoner, who now went quietly; indeed he could do nothing else. We did however allow one of his relations inside the cordon; it was his old mother who, hearing that he would not return that night (we were adamant on the point), brought him a cloak and some spirit. Possibly his family thought they were seeing the last of him for many years; some of them certainly behaved like it, for a great wailing arose from the stricken camp. But the prisoner himself was philosophical, and only asked to be allowed to wipe the blood from his face. He was a saturnine man, not ill-looking, with a hawk-like nose and a cast in his eye.

We now resumed our march down the valley, but were told we could not reach Shoshi Dzong that night. Tempers cooled rapidly – indeed it was a chilly evening. The prisoner laughed and chatted with his captors. I took Tsumbi aside; he was still indignant as befitted a *sirdar*.

'We'll let the man go tomorrow morning,' I said.

'No, sahib. He behaved very badly. We will hand him over to the magistrate at Shoshi Dzong and have him punished.'

'I don't want to make trouble, Tsumbi, it isn't worth it; and there is no magistrate at Shoshi Dzong. Besides, you gave him a good beating, you know!'

Tsumbi beamed.

At dusk we camped. The prisoner, now unbound, helped to collect firewood. He spent a cheerful evening with his former enemies, and early next morning Tsumbi pleaded for him! I willingly let him go and he ransomed himself with a chunk of butter, apologizing for having loosed the dogs on us. His excuse was that travellers never used that pass, and he thought we must be robbers.

Visitors at Solé

The day after my arrival the headman of Modung came to see me. He presented me with a short Tibetan sword, or dagger, in a metal sheath, and a chunk of yak meat, so palpably noisome that I had to heave it out of the window. Another visitor was the widow of the late Govenor of Zayul. She, however, had not come from Rima just to see me; she was out on a financial tour, collecting the interest on agricultural loans issued by her late husband. In the rather bulky clothes of the rich Tibetan woman, wearing a striped apron, and a little fur-lined cap perched on her head, she looked almost chic. She was a merry widow; though her debtors probably did not think so. She called on me, preceded by her servants bearing two half-bricks of Chinese sugar and some walnuts, 'sent with a scarf'. She went about with an armed escort. This orderly possessed a Mauser rifle; for the wily widow had great possessions. However, he regarded his weapon as an encumbrance rather than an asset, and left it behind at my house. Tsumbi was much concerned, no doubt for the widow, and asked me if he should ride after the escort and return the rifle; but I said no, if he needed it he could come back for it. I had already observed that he had no ammunition.

The headman of Solé in whose house I stayed was an enormously fat man with a rubicund, even vinous complexion. I never saw him do a hand's turn of work. All day he hung about his veranda, leaning over the rail, telling his beads and muttering prayers. Occasionally he waddled as far as the village shrine, and sat there in the sun, talking to the oldest inhabitant. But he was very rich. He had the dirtiest house, the greediest pigs, the mangiest dogs, the leanest cattle, and the most underfed serfs of any headman in the valley. His serfs, a pleasant-looking girl, a crone and a scarecrow of a man, averaged fifty-six to fifty-eight inches high. They were always up before daylight, when a slight frost lay on the ground. Often they were at work by the light of a pine-torch at ten o'clock at night. It is no exaggeration to say that they worked eighty hours a week. Their thin clothes were in rags, they slept in kennels. Tired, hungry and cold, they lay down on the wooden floor by a feeble fire, and I could hear them talking and laughing till far into the night. One by one they drop off. The fire goes out. They awake, shivering; dawn is breaking, another day's work begins.

Over the Dri La

It was going to be a cold night. I sat by the fire until 9 p.m. toasting my feet, then crept reluctantly into my flea-bag, ready dressed except for boots and leather jacket. I slept fitfully. The men had asked to start about 4 a.m. when a waning moon rose; but I was the first up, and there was no sign of life amongst the coolies at that hour. I hated getting out of my flea-bag into twenty degrees of frost, but it had to be done. Anyhow by evening, I consoled myself, we would be in Assam. I felt cold, weary and lethargic; no sooner had I put my nose outside the tent than I almost jumped. Clouds were scudding across the moon, which gave no light at all; snow was already falling. We must hurry; now or never over the last hurdle. A wave of warm muggy air had spurted up from the depths of Assam, and was pouring over the pass. I had no breakfast, only a big bowl of hot pemmican. At 7 o'clock we started. My hands and feet were already numb.

Skirting the frozen lake, we crossed the steep valley which fed it, and started up a wide torrent bed, lined with rigid bushes of rhododendron. The water had frozen, encasing the stones in a film of ice over which lay a quilt of snow. Time and again we slipped on the ice slope, then hugged the bushes, preferring to be whipped across the face by a hard branch rather than break a limb. At last we reached the top of the fall. The slope eased off, and we trudged across an open snowfield to the foot of a couloir. The bulk of the mountain rose directly above us, buttress on buttress. The snow was piled into the couloir and plastered in fleecy layers against the cliff. At every step we sank in almost to our knees. Steeper and steeper grew the ascent, deeper and deeper the snow. I could not go fast enough to get warm. In two hours we reached the ration dump, and ten minutes were spent rearranging the loads. Then we plodded on, now sinking to our knees in the snow and tripping over unseen tuffets of rhododendron. Another rest enabled me to collect some Allium seed where the snow had partly melted. From here to the top of the mountain was completely exposed; it had caught the full fury of the last storm, and the snow had ironed out all the unevenness.

The Mishmis who had crossed the previous day had bequeathed to us a trail; yet we found it easier to make one for ourselves than to follow theirs. In places the rocks were so steep we could only clamber up them with mutual assistance. Several times I stepped into a drift and floundered waist-deep in the snow. We had now been climbing five and a half hours. Close above was the Dri Pass, a knife-edged ridge, with the wind driving the snow in our faces. Panting, I scrambled up the last few yards. At last! Assam lay right at my feet; Tibet lay behind. The Dri Pass crossed, another ambition fulfilled; but I was too exhausted to cheer.

SEVENTEEN

Assam Adventure
1935

Over the Himalayas – Across the cliff – The painted monastery – A botanist's paradise – March to the Tsangpo – Return to Tumbatse – The lost range found – The source of the Yigrong

Over the Himalayas

In the middle of the afternoon we reached Chunak, that is to say Blackwater, so çalled from the colour of a stream which rises amidst mountains of coal-black shale. It is a herd village comprising a few scattered stone houses, occupied only during the summer. There was a pleasant pasture, like a golf green. We stopped only long enough to add a yak-load of firewood to our little caravan, and went on for another hour, camping under a cliff in the mouth of the gulley, above the last trees. The altitude was about 13,000 feet. All night a cold draught off the snows poured down the gulley; we could not get shelter from the wind.

At this height there is no forest, but the south slope of the Himalayas is well covered with scrub, amongst which rhododendrons bulk large, although now reduced to a few species. By the stream, mixed with willows, barberry, honeysuckle and dog rose, grew the yellow-flowered *Rhododendron wightii* and the crimson or purple-freckled *R. aganniphum*. A more gorgeous display was made by two dwarf species, *R. anthopogon* and *R. nivale*, which covered the exposed flank of the valley, and flowed in a broad foam of crimson-rose and heather-purple down the rugged slope. *R. nivale* is a brushwood plant with very small purple flowers borne in tight little heads at the ends of the interlacing twigs, amongst the tiny nickel-plated-looking leaves. There were marmots here, popping in and out of their holes and whistling to each other; but birds were scarce. The commonest was a babbler, or laughing-thrush, of a dark rifleman green with black head and white tabs behind the ears and under the eyes. It was as big as a song thrush, and its haunting plaintive cry fitted the melancholy of these wild mountains.

Thrilled as I was at the prospect of crossing the Assam Himalayas, the weather, fair or foul, always affects my spirits; and
being cold as well as wet I felt a black depression coming on.

The sky, gloomy from the start, now began to threaten, and
soon the rain was driving down in sheets. Visibility was bad, and
under the conditions it was difficult to collect plants, or even to
see them. We reached the junction of two grey stony valleys, and
followed the torrent to the east; there was still a lot of water in
it, and I began to realize that we were a long way from the pass.
After going about a mile, the torrent divided again, and once
more we turned north. Even the scrub carpet was threadbare,
and at a height of about 15,000 feet it petered out altogether. A
wilderness of broken rocks, cracked off the high cliffs above us
and piled up in huge cone-shaped screes, barred the way.

We were in a long grim-looking valley in the cold heart of the
Himalaya. The path was steep and rough; already I was feeling
the strain. Hour after hour the yak plodded on, and I, stopping
to collect unfamiliar plants, dropped farther and farther behind.
By two o'clock I was exhausted, and also very hungry; I began
to wonder whether the yak were ever going to stop! They went
on like slow relentless machines, and the valley seemed interminable. We were still mounting steeply. Men and yak disappeared
from view, and I felt utterly lost amidst these tremendous
mountains.

At last I came up with the caravan, halted. We had now reached
a height of 16,000 feet. It was still raining, but not so heavily,
and I sat down under a rock for half an hour's rest, ate a snack,
and drank some hot tea out of my thermos flask. The valley had
broadened, and the stream wandered in several channels. We were
approaching the glaciers at its head. Snowcock cried harshly and
warningly from high up on the screes.

Resuming the climb from near the foot of the glacier, we
followed a track which slanted obliquely up a thousand feet of
soft, almost pulverized, slate towards a gap in the ridge. Snow
peaks shone dimly through the clouds to our right front. We
might have been on the moon, so harsh and bitter was the landscape. Not a blade of green did I observe until we were close to
the top. Yet I noticed that the deep hoof-prints of the yak quickly
filled with water. There was in fact no shortage of underground
water at the base of the screes, although the surface was dry.

Suddenly I caught sight of a clump of short woolly-leafed stems with spikes of dazzling sapphire-blue flowers crouched under the lee of a big boulder. It seemed astonishing that anything so lovely could survive in such a howling wilderness. This plant was *Veronica lanuginosa*, a rare Himalayan species related to our common blue speedwell (*V. arvensis*), though so different in appearance.

At this moment the sun came out for the first time, and shortly afterwards we reached the top. We were above the clouds. The Trulung La, 17,250 feet, is just a gap in the ridge between lofty towers, and we looked down into an arid valley about 2,000 feet below. That was all the view there was. The tall shadows cast by the mountains were lengthening, and presently the sun disappeared behind a range. Ahead of us, beckoning me on, a pane of glassy blue sky gleamed like a church window.

Across the cliff

At this point the Loro Chu enters a savage-looking gorge, and begins to break through the Himalayas. So far the path had been reasonably good. Now it became rougher and, after ascending a flight of crazy steps, narrowed to a ledge cut in the face of the cliff. Presently the ledge became a bracket, no path at all, just flagstones laid across wooden stakes wedged into cracks in the cliff a couple of hundred feet above the dark river. The bracket sloped upwards and disappeared round a corner; and the flags wobbled as I stepped on them. It ended abruptly at the foot of a vertical ladder thirty feet high. I had lagged behind to botanize. By the time I had sidled with faltering steps dizzily to the foot of the ladder, where the two-foot-wide ledge petered out, there was only just room to stand. Tashi, Mount Everest hero, stood waiting for me; but his presence did singularly little to restore my composure. The last coolie had gone up and disappeared out of sight, like Jack on the Beanstalk.

I went up five steps, and clung there almost overhanging the river, too frightened to go another step. So I came down again feeling sick with terror. Tashi shouted up to the coolies, and a man raced down like a jolly tar. He offered to carry me up on his back, like one of my own loads, and started putting his leather rope round me to carry out his threat. Whether I was more stung by the indignity of such an inglorious ascent, or scared stiff at the prospect, I don't know. However, the audacity of the proposal gave me an idea. I tied the rope round my body, gave the man the other end and told him to go slowly, keeping just ahead of me, and not to pull on the rope. I followed him, keeping my eyes on the ladder, not daring to look down. Thus we went to the top, as though cliff climbing. I found the other coolies on the brink of the precipice and spitting into space. They grinned when I arrived; I could afford to laugh at myself now; and did.

The painted monastery

We turned a corner, and suddenly Sanga Chöling burst into view, like a challenge. The white monastery, clapped on to a narrow ridge, looked like the superstructure of a battleship in dry dock. We walked along the stone-flagged quayside where crooked houses, with window-boxes, suggested a Georgian English sea-port; passed a stone-flagged bridge, and reached the entrance to the main monastery. Outside is a *mendong* or religious wall, a hundred yards long. We went through into the big courtyard, and I felt rather as though we were in the Piazza at Venice looking at a cruder St. Mark's. In the centre stood a flagstaff about 120 feet high, but rather cock-eyed; on its summit was perched what might have been either a fancy rocket or a ballet dancer.

Three sides of the square are occupied by residential quarters – including the public inn – with stables underneath. A wooden gallery runs lopsidedly round the buildings and gives entrance to the cell-like rooms. I was conducted to a room in the corner, and it was a tight fit. From the gallery I looked straight across the courtyard to the great temple; small wonder it fairly took my breath away. The high façade was white, with the many deep and narrow embrasures picked out in slate-grey. A flight of narrow steps led up to the massive timber doors, which were studded with iron nails. At the top of the building, just beneath the roof, a broad band of faggots formed a sort of dado; and to this were attached heraldic designs in gold on a blue ground; ornaments which looked as though they might have come out of a large cracker. One was like an Irish harp; another was like a scythe, and that of course suggested Father Time. Sombre black curtains, tattered and dingy, draped part of the façade, hanging from a wooden gallery, but a gay note was added by the window-boxes full of bright flowers.

The gaudiest part of this notable building is the flashing golden roof, its corners curled up in the best Chinese tradition. It is shaped like a motor car bonnet, with a golden radiator, and has eight cylinders, or maybe seven.

Here undoubtedly Sanga Chöling parts company with St. Mark's, but it has a piercing and sombre magnificence of its own. The village seems to be all monasteries; two of them are large, and the view of the perpendicular architecture from the other side of the river is uplifting. A closer view reminds one that here too splendour and squalor live side by side, while the many window-boxes in temple and hovel suggest a sort of everlasting harvest festival. I found Sanga Chöling an Arabian Nights palace, and the monks having greeted me as a friend, I was quite ready to stay over a day, or over a month.

A botanist's paradise

We were now in the district of Tsari. After a night spent at Chösam we continued down the valley of the Tsari river. The previous day, after crossing the pass, we had changed direction from north to east, thus we were again gradually approaching the Great Himalayan range, which trends in a north-easterly direction. The mountains were hidden in a thick mist, and rain fell steadily. Below Chösam the valley was not only a botanist's paradise, it presented a scene of almost unbelievable beauty, even on a rainy day.

The sheltered side was smothered under rhododendron bushes, most of them in flower. Silver firs appeared, scattered at first, then in groves. The valley narrowed again; and the path scrambled high up the rocky mountain where acres of alpine flowers bloomed between scattered shrubs. Abundant beneath the rhododendron bushes was the silky-petalled *Adonis brevistyla*. High up on a bastion I caught sight of the yellow-flowered *Primula barnardoana*; and *P. atrodentata*, in fruit, grew everywhere. Although the path clung dizzily to the cliffs, the valley itself had a gentle tilt, and after a couple of miles we descended again to the stream and a verdant meadow two or three miles long and half a mile wide, called Senguti. It was marshy, at least in the summer, and it must have once been a lake, which the river had silted up. Towards the lower end of the meadow was a solitary house, called Totsen, standing amidst fenced corn and grazing fields. Now the forceful beauty of the Tsari valley struck me. Across the meadow the mountains were dark with fir, with lighter patches of willow and birch by the river. Tapering tongues of forest licked their way up the sheltered gullies to meet the white tongues of glaciers which crept down out of the mist from invisible snow-fields. Somewhere behind that mist lay Takpa Shiri's sacred peak.

The lower half of the meadow itself was a sea of *Primula sikkimensis*, not the dwarf form, but typical, with dangling clusters of large daffodil-yellow bells and long narrow leaves, the blade gradually passing into the indistinct leaf stalk. Mixed with it, but far less numerous, was the grape-juice-purple colour variety of *P. alpicola*. This species has bigger and broader leaves, the oblong blade sharply distinguished from the slender leaf stalk, and puffy with a fine network of raised veins. At first a rarity, *P. alpicola* quickly increased in numbers as we descended the valley until, by the time we reached Chickchar, it was almost as common as *P. sikkimensis*. Meanwhile a third species, having milk-white flowers, *P. hopeana*, had joined in the pageant, scattered and rare to begin with, presently becoming more abundant, though never so common as *P. alpicola*. Up to within a short distance of Chickchar the riverside meadows were sunny yellow with huge drifts of *P. sikkimensis* containing millions of flowers, with a few purple strands of *P. alpicola* and *P. hopeana* lost like drops of milk in a daffodil sea. Once, where the primulas grew more scattered, I observed all three species forming a single clump, a little triumvirate; but this was exceptional. Generally, small colonies of *P. alpicola*, and separate plants of *P. hopeana*, were as flotsam in endless rocking seas of *P. sikkimensis*. And for ten miles we waded almost up to our knees through these lush flowery meadows, the damp air heavy with their delicious scent. What a scene in Paradise it was, this silent fairyland of mute bells! Now violet-shadowed with irises, now crimson-lit with Pedicularis, dappled gold with buttercups, or white on an emerald field with anemones; all familiar friendly flowers though in strange garb. Down the centre of the valley rolled the grey Tsari river, swelling as the glacier streams from the south came tumbling in. And down the valley also, enclosing the Tsari river, danced the shining band of primulas. Between silver fir forest and golden meadow came a border of shrubs and smaller trees, as rhododendron, honeysuckle, barberry, cotoneaster, rowan, cherry and spiraea; and between fir forest and snow-field another border of dwarf alpine flowers. The whole valley was a procession of glorious beauty.

March to the Tsangpo

We were now a long day's march from the Tsangpo, the headman told me; and I was determined to get there in a day. There must be no more detours before I reached the Tsangpo. If I deliberately went out of my way a third time, the prize might elude me when it was already within my grasp. A sudden panic seized me that after all my efforts I might not reach my goal. It was not reasonable, but it was insistent. I *must* not delay further, said an inner voice; on July 18th I must reach the Tsangpo and finish the journey on which so much effort had been concentrated.

The morning was far from bright, but it was not actually raining. The coolies assembled late, and it was nine o'clock before we got started. Luckily there are no villages in the gorge of the Lilung Chu, between Molo and Lilung; we should not be delayed changing transport. We had to use coolies; ponies could not get through.

In the crowd which assembled to see us off, I noticed an almost pygmy Lopa girl. Since we left Chickchar, I had seen what I judged to be Tibetanized pygmies in almost every village we passed through. Most of them were very short, especially the women. There is a constant drift of peoples northwards from the savage jungles south of the Himalayas into the pleasanter country of the Tsangpo valley. Formerly the Tibetan overlords raided and captured the Lopas for slaves, but the practice has almost died out, and the Lopas now come over the passes in the summer to work in the fields, and in early winter to trade. Some of them settle down in virtual slavery, but they are not allowed to roam about at will in Tibet. Only certain marts are open to them, and their movements are restricted. There is a good deal of mixed blood in the villages south of the Tsangpo, in Takpo and Tsari. Some of the tribes certainly appear to be pygmies, but not all. The men are almost always several inches taller than the women.

We reached Molo in ten minutes. The village, of several stone houses, stands on the right bank of the Lilung Chu immediately below the confluence and is connected with the road on the left bank by a stout bridge. Below Molo, the road keeps to the left bank for several miles, and is rough, steep and narrow. It took us four hours to do the first six miles. After an hour's rest, we crossed to the right bank by a bridge. Here the Lilung Chu is thirty yards wide, and six or eight feet deep, the stream swift and turbulent, running at ten or twelve miles an hour. Rarely is the water tranquil. Furious rapids succeed one another at short intervals, the biggest occurring where the slates characteristic of the higher mountains give place to granite as the Tsangpo valley is approached. The coolies now said it would be impossible to reach the Tsangpo that day, and I felt quite upset about it. But we went on, the path getting worse rather than better. By three o'clock we were all rather tired, and I would have given a lot to have been able to camp. I knew that from now on the magnificent scenery of the gorge would be more or less lost upon me, nor could I concentrate any longer on the plants. But still I had that feeling of panic; I must go on, and on, and on: I *dare* not halt.

The gorge of the Lilung Chu – the largest tributary the Tsangpo receives for many miles, and one of the largest on the south bank throughout its entire length – is heavily forested with evergreen trees, which clutch at the almost vertical cliffs and claw their way right to the topmost visible peaks. At Molo the forest is still predominantly coniferous, composed of Picea and Larix. Gradually broad-leafed trees, including noble specimens of *Quercus ilex*, also birch and maple, replaced conifers, at least close to the river. On the cliffs below Molo, alpines such as *Meconopsis horridula*, with Cambridge-blue flowers, and wet forest plants such as Briggsia grew side by side. Another gesnerad, *Didissandra lanuginosa*, with deep violet flowers covered the sunnier cliffs. We crossed several large tributaries on either bank, and the Lilung river continued to grow until the volume of water was terrific and the roar of the rapids filled the gorge. Looking up the narrow ravines to east and west, where one sometimes caught a glimpse of spiked ridges, I realized what a vast area of country still remained to be explored.

Along the path through the forest, and in the patches of open meadow which presently appeared, several species of Thalictrum were in flower. But by this time I was feeling so weary I could not observe anything with precision. The gorge began to widen out, and now the last and greatest transformation took place; the broad-leafed forest began to disappear, and pine forest took its place. We came to a delightful grassy space sheltered by towering cliffs; it was an ideal place for a camp, and I was greatly tempted to tarry. I particularly wanted to botanize at this end of the gorge. But again that frantic urge to push on took possession of me; I could not stop short of the Tsangpo. Besides, we must be very close to Lilung; it seemed weak to give in on the winning-post. It was now about five o'clock. At six we were high above the river on a narrow path which clung to the granite cliffs. The gorge ended. The valley was growing rapidly wider; ahead lay open country, the enormous valley of the Tsangpo. The air was balmy, fragrant with the scent of pines, and with the bewitching scent which came from great sheafs of the pink martagon lily (*Lilium wardii*) which lolled from the cliff. Its flowers were only just open, and their sweet scent in the dry air was delicious. Now the rocks were growing more naked, with twisted pine trees and a few thorny shrubs scattered about.

Dusk had fallen when at last we caught sight of an island about a mile from the Tsangpo. A bridge connects this island with either bank of the Lilung Chu, the village itself being on the far bank.

Cawdor and I had slept at Lilung and crossed this bridge in 1924. So at last I had joined up my two routes.

My tent was pitched close beside a house, in a sort of garden; but it was dark before the last tired coolie arrived, and eight o'clock before I got a cup of tea. But at least I was not shivering with wet and cold; on the contrary, it was pleasantly warm, though the altitude of Lilung is well over 9,000 feet.

I had accomplished my object. I had crossed the Assam Himalayas and southern Tibet, and had reached the Tsangpo. Other things did not seem very important for the time being.

Return to Tumbatse

By the time we reached the valley of the Rong Chu below the Temo La, I was feeling the effects of the long march. I had caught a bad cold some days before, and now felt fever coming on. The march northwards down the valley seemed interminable – I had forgotten how many miles it was to Tumbatse. I got separated from the transport, and when at last a house came in sight I crossed the swollen stream and went to it. However, there appeared to be nobody about, and it was a relief when one of my men turned up and said we were not yet arrived. Still greater was my relief when at last, after travelling another mile, we did reach the village of Tumbatse, and I recognized our house of eleven years ago. It had certainly not been renovated during my absence; but it was something that it had not fallen down. The owner, Lobsang, a typical Kongbo herd, recognized me almost before I recognized him and greeted me warmly. He brought out food and drink, and I felt as though I were the prodigal son returning to my native village after having been away in the great city.

Lobsang's daughter, who was a little child playing in the mud when I last went away, had grown into a comely lass about eighteen years old, and taken her place in the economic scheme of her yak world. In her short dark woollen skirt, undyed long-sleeved woollen jacket, and round wide-brimmed white woollen hat, she looked very pretty. All the girls of Kongbo have rosy cheeks and sparkling black eyes, and if their straight, glossy, raven-black hair does smell of stale butter, is it really more unpleasant than the smell of para-di-methyl-benzine? Little 'Rosy-cheeks' came coyly into my room to say how-do-you-do while I was having my tea, purring like a kitten. She showed me a deep scar on her arm caused by upsetting a pot of boiling water when she was still quite a child. Her father said she remembered me perfectly. I suppose it was an event to have two white men living in her house at the impressionable age of seven; anyhow, she had not seen another one since.

Looking north towards Tongkyuk in the evening, I saw for the first time the snow-peaks I sought; and if I had been eager to find them before, I was all on fire now. It seemed to me one of the most thrilling sights I had ever seen.

The lost range found

At Tashi's shout I jumped up and ran outside. Ever since we emerged from the forest, only the dribbling snouts of glaciers to the north and the dark heavily timbered ranges to the south had been visible below the cloud ceiling. Now the ceiling was breaking up in swirling eddies. Rents and holes of turquoise-blue appeared in the soft marble whiteness, and vanished, to reappear elsewhere as new eddies formed. It was as though some giant were pouring rivers of milk into a limpid sea, clouding it for an instant until the currents swept it away. The opaque fluid still hung in streaks and clots. The struggle between mist and dry air continued, but the final result was never in doubt. Quicker and quicker the air drank up the mist until, as the last shreds of curd dissolved, depths of infinite blue stood revealed. Now the whole valley was sunning itself like a gorgeous butterfly which has just cast off its chrysalis shell.

'Look, sahib! It is like the view of Kanchenjunga from Darjeeling!' Even the stolid, unemotional Tashi was moved.

I gasped. The valley, which had looked big before, had suddenly become dwarfed. A mile above our camp the slope began to rise more sharply; terrace succeeded terrace, each steeper than the last. At the head was a high jagged wall, joining two snow peaks, and one could see where the Sobhé La crossed it, if not the actual pass; it was four or five miles off. This was the only gap in a glittering semi-circle of snow, the highest peak lying to the west of the pass. I counted five hanging glaciers – none of them reached the main valley. We were clasped within the icy claws of gigantic pincers. Snow-peaks rose directly over our camp, like the spires of a cathedral above the cottages which cluster round its base. It was impossible even to estimate their height; I can only say that they were more than 20,000 feet high.

If any lingering doubt remained, it was now finally set at rest. We were in the heart of the mysterious snowy range of Pomé. The lost range was found! The enormous flight of bergs which Cawdor and I had seen far off, eleven years earlier, arching across the world for over a hundred miles, a glittering skyway joining east and west, was here in front of me. No wonder I felt uplifted!

For some minutes Tashi and Pemba, who had now joined us, and I stood there, looking up the valley. The sun had dropped behind the ridge on our left; but his last rays still shone on the peaks at the head of the valley, and on those to the east of us. Violet shadows crept swiftly over the glaciers. The valley, roofed with its ribbon of darkening sky, now looked like some wonderful fjord with the sky for deep sea, and fantastic white rocks plunging down into its depths; it was all upside down, but it was easy to believe oneself gazing into a mirror. Everything in that light was ethereal, almost spiritualized; and presently when I heard the sound of distant song I was not very surprised. There was a solemn hush about the mountains with their changing lights, the ghostly peaks shining through the oncoming darkness, the red

Maru girl

Nung woman of the Nam Tamai

A Mishmi *gam*, Delei valley

Naga girl

Daru (above) and Lisu (right)
hunters with cross-bows

Maru girl weaving

Jongpen of Sanga Chöling

Geshi Ishi Dorje, abbot of Mönyul

A Nung crossing a rope bridge over the Adung

shafts from the setting sun which still sprayed through the western wall and caught the tops of the spires opposite, and the abyss of the Tongkyuk river far below. I was in that fanciful mood when one might hear voices singing. Perhaps I was half-asleep; certainly it was all like a dream, if a dream come true. It gave me rather a shock therefore to see a group of black specks moving down the meadow beyond the next belt of trees. Not men surely! Spirits? The singing drew nearer; men's voices! They *were* men, and presently they came into camp, a happy band of pilgrims; they had been singing to scare away evil spirits as night came on. They had seen the smoke of our camp-fire and approached joyfully.

The source of the Po-Yigrong

We had started in mist, the mountain hidden behind a veil of cloud. Just as we reached the top of the scree and were entering amongst the rocks, I glanced back to the Po-Yigrong for the last time. At that moment, as though it had been pre-ordained from the beginning of time, a miraculous transformation took place. Suddenly the amorphous cloud thickened and curdled; the veil was rent, and there was revealed the most wonderful view of the actual source of the Po-Yigrong my wildest fancy could ever have painted. If I had waited, and dreamed, for ten years for that brief glimpse only, I had not lived in vain. It epitomized a life's ambition; a worthwhile discovery in Asia, truly finished.

The head of the valley was gripped in a ring of ice. One large lopsided glacier flowed right down to the floor of the main valley, at its head a broad snow-field beneath an astonishing spike of rock. Other large glaciers occupied high valleys, or were plastered to the cliff face; the cluster of rock spires and steeples suggested a Gothic cathedral, and was almost as unexpected as the cathedral would have been.

The atmosphere remained clear for several minutes, leaving blue ice, grey rock and white snow violently outlined on a turquoise curtain of sky. Then the cloud materialized again as suddenly as it had been absorbed, and the vision disappeared. It was our final glimpse of the lost range. As we reached the pass, which was perhaps 17,000 feet high, without further warning a blizzard swooped up from the other side. A low sangar, or stone wall, had been built across the gap; the men immediately crouched down behind it, and I did the same. The air was full of sharp ice crystals, whirled along at gale speed, and they stung like bees. The wind screamed amongst the towers. I had often wondered what these walls, found on many of the Tibetan passes, were for; when I saw not only the hardy Tibetans but the caravan ponies, mules, and dogs seek shelter, I realized it was not a trench behind which men fought for command of the pass, but a shelter against storm.

For twenty minutes we lay low while the wind, supercharged with snow, roared and shrieked over the bare slabs and tomb-stones which strewed the mountain. We could see nothing through the flickering veil, but the noise was terrific. Then came a lull. The caravan at once started down the opposite slope; I climbed up a steep boulder scree above the pass to get an all round view. I had barely reached the top of the ridge with much effort, a few hundred feet above the pass, when a second barrage was unleashed. There was no sangar here; so I crept behind a rock on the lee side of the ridge and waited in discomfort. After a time the blizzard went off to wherever blizzards go to, and I surveyed the scene.

I had a marvellous close-up view of the sharp tower which is the highest peak at the actual source of the Po-Yigrong; and an incredible view far down the Po-Yigrong valley to the big glacier, six or eight miles away. Far away in the east, half-buried in yeasty clouds, I could see the tops of snow-covered mountains, probably the Markandro group above Tongkyuk. But of the great snow peaks to the south-east I could see nothing; a near ridge blocked the view.

EIGHTEEN

Burma's Icy Mountains
1937; 1938–39

Adung valley – Adung river – An attempt on Ka Karpo Razi – Exploration à l'americaine – To the Panwa pass – Visit to a coffin tree – Earthquake tremors

Adung valley

On September 22nd we crossed over to the left bank by a cane suspension-bridge, thus avoiding a dangerous cliff; and shortly after came to a small Tibetan village of half a dozen wooden huts scattered in the mouth of a tributary valley. Here I learnt that the village of Tahawndam, which had served as our base camp in 1931, when we were exploring the Adung valley, had ceased to exist, and that the little colony had migrated down the valley to this point in order to escape the attentions of the self-appointed tax-gatherers who cross the mountains from Tibet, ostensibly to collect *pai mu*, but also on foray.

I bought a hunk of butter from the Tibetans, and looked forward to having buttered *chuppatties* for a change. But Marang had other ideas, and converted it into ghee for cooking before I knew what he was up to.

A tall Tibetan with a Roman nose and a shock of lank hair which fell over his forehead now appeared before me. His face was pock-marked and crimped. He wore round his neck a piece of greasy string to which was attached a leather locket containing yak hair – a charm to ward off evil. His coarse hempen *chupa* was loose above his waist, and his long legs were encased in ragged cloth boots, which reached almost to his grimy knees. Though he had aged fully twelve years in the six years since I last saw him as the gay loon of Tahawndam, I recognized him at once. It was 'George', the laughing cavalier, the last of the old brigade who had helped us in 1931, when we went to the source of the Adung. He told me that the summer after we left the bad men from the other side of the mountains came over the pass as usual, to collect *pai mu*. They had come right down to the village, and had stolen cattle and much of the food. And the same thing had happened next year, only then they had taken away one of the Daru girls who worked as slaves for the Tibetans. In the third year the crops had failed, and some of the cattle died. So they had given up the struggle and moved down the valley, to this spot, and were licking the austere land into shape for the growing of crops and the grazing of cattle. The medicine-gatherers let them alone, as they did not dare to come down the valley as far as this, and the settlers were happy. So Tahawndam was no more, and Adung Long too had gone, and the last Daru hut was only a couple of miles up the valley, on the right bank of the river.

There is not much population in this corner of the world, but life is crude and the strong prey upon the weak without correction. Man wages endless war on the jungle, he fights against the avalanche and landslide, against flood and the failure of scanty crops, coaxed from a lean soil, against pestilence and the ceaseless attacks of hordes of insects, against the wild beasts of the forest which tear down his fences and ruin his fields, and against cold and heat, and unremitting rain. For him the commonest verdict, perhaps the only verdict, is death by misadventure. Almost the only danger which never threatens him is drought.

The Adung valley, at least in spring, is surely one of the most beautiful mountain valleys on earth, but until man has found the means to quell some of the enemies which assail him there, he can earn scant leisure in which to enjoy that beauty. Those Tibetans and Chinese who, from a safer land, harass the Ishmaelites of the Irrawaddy living dangerously in the jungle, have no wish to dispossess them of their lands. Rather is it to their advantage to keep these little people alive and up to a point flourishing, that they may the more readily extract tribute from them. Just as the slave-owners took good care of their slaves, so do the people from the other side of the mountains treat the wretched Darus gently, the better to milk them. Why kill the goose that lays the golden egg?

Despite the hard living, there seems to be a steady, if slow, drift of peoples from the east into this enclave, due to pressure of population in the lands beyond the Irrawaddy.

Adung river

That night the rain ceased and next morning, the 28th, the torrent had actually dropped several feet; what was even more surprising, the water was almost clean. The tidal wave had subsided, the bridge was dry. We quickly skimmed across, though I could plainly hear the muffled thunder of the boulders dragging along the bottom.

Now we began to climb. The path along the left bank which we had followed in 1931 was fairly good; but when I had looked across to the right bank and noticed those rugged cliffs with their feet in the raging river I supposed there was no way along them; while now, from the right bank, the left bank looked hardly more passable. Up the cliff went the little Darus like monkeys, scrambling from ledge to ledge and from one hold to another. There was one awkward traverse across a smooth face high above the river and for a moment, balanced on a ledge, my heart was in my mouth; and then we were climbing down again. Presently we reached a tolerable track through the forest, close to the thundering water.

Once round the corner the Adung river defies description. It is the most dynamic mile of any in its forty-mile course. The gorge is short, full of colour and of dangerous music such as appeals to the emotions and inspires the imagination. To say that the valley is steep and that it is filled with stark and polished boulders big as Palaeolithic dolmens conveys but a poor idea of the fierce background. Above the poor little strips of cultivation around Tahawndam, where for a space the river flows swiftly indeed but almost gently, sheer cliffs suddenly hem in the waters and the gradient rises visibly. In the steepening river-bed are jumbled together in the last confusion rocks of such size and weight that not all the glaciers along the high sierra above, melting together, could budge them an inch, though the power and violence of the flood even now are awful. It is not a waterfall. Rather is it as though a giant's stairway to the terrace of his airy castle has been hit by an earthquake, and shaken, and then hit again. The enormous blocks of glistening white porphyry check the storm of water, even threaten to balk it; stop it they cannot. The highly charged river, solid, liquid and gas in one, pouring over, under and round the rocks, batters its way down the slope, roaring with rage. Looking upstream from the mouth of the gorge, it is impossible to see the level terrace at the top of the slope, perhaps half a mile distant and two or three hundred feet above; only an irregular line of sabre-toothed rocks, like the mouth of a shark, is visible against the wedge of grey sky. The angle of slope in the gorge is about 15°. Dense forest, now sombre in colour, lines the river at flood level. But in spring the rising note of the water is matched in melody by the clash and ring of colour on colour – the hot breathless glow of rhododendron against the faltering greens and brave yellows of unfurling maple leaves, the sharp green bristling larches studded with crimson cones like prehistoric sea anemones, the cold marble-white globes of magnolia which glimmer in the darkness with an unearthly light. Add to these, slim fairy-like catkins swinging gently in the breeze, the stiff pyramidal jets of bird cherry, the rebellious aquamarine tassels of *Decaisnea*, and it will be realized that form as well as colour mingle in the magic of the scene.

Dimly one senses the terrible power of the Adung river as it moulds its deep wrinkle on the earth's hard crust. Yet after ascending a few hundred feet one finds it flowing, swiftly indeed but placidly, down a long gently-sloping terrace humming to itself, no longer raging, its bed clear of big rocks.

An attempt on Ka Karpo Razi

When at 6 a.m. on October 9th I found the minimum temperature down to 37° and the sky crystal-clear, with a nip in the air, and long shadows striping the honey-coloured cliffs, I decided to go up the valley once more, taking a light camp, and make a final attempt the following day.

Marang and I, therefore, set out with four coolies, carrying my Whymper tent (less the outer fly), bedding, a few supplies, collecting outfit and camera, and in the afternoon pitched camp on the last bit of flat ground below the screes, at an altitude of about 13,500 feet. The coolies returned to the main camp. The sky had become completely overcast by midday, and the weather did not look set fair; but I could at least see the cliffs and ice-falls. My plan was to tackle the glacier again next day. As there was no snow, I could hardly fall into a hidden crevasse, and might get higher than I had done previously. However, it was certain that I could not reach the top of the glacier by myself, and I had come on a forlorn hope really, the object of which could only be to confirm what I already knew.

Leaving Marang to look after the camp and get the oil-stove going, I went for a scramble. While searching the north-east cliffs through a field-glass, I noticed a gulley which led right up to a sort of ice ledge, not far below the lowest gaps in the ridge. After a long scrutiny I came to the conclusion that I could climb the gulley and that, once having reached the ice ledge, I could follow it along to the extreme north-east corner. (The ice ledge referred to was a smooth gently-sloping platform of varying width, some-times very narrow, which jutted out between the upper cliffs and the thousand-foot drop into the valley formed by the main cliff. It was a sort of high-water mark, or rather ice mark, all that remained of the floor of the original glacier valley, before water took a hand and cut out the present valley.) It might even be possible to reach a gap in the ridge; if I could, I should be less than a mile from the summit of Ka Karpo.

Moreover, it would be less dangerous in a mist than the glacier, and it certainly looked a more promising route; there were gaps in the wall at 15,000 to 16,000 feet, so I only had to climb about 2,000 feet to reach the crest of the ridge here.

Marang and I had supper inside the tent, which the stove warmed a little, and turned in early. I slept reasonably well, but was troubled with horrible dreams. I was up before daylight. At 6 a.m. the temperature was 40° – much too warm for fine weather, and already the sky was heavy with cloud; nor did we see the sun all day. It took us a long time to cook breakfast, and I did not start on my climb till 8.30. I carried a fairly heavy rucksack containing food and clothing in case of accident.

The gulley proved to be more difficult than it had looked. There were one or two awkward places where a large boulder had jammed, but I surmounted or 'turned' these and reached the ice ledge in quick time. I was now at the foot of the second line of cliffs, which were set back. Colonies of *Primula serratifolia* and of a small 'Petiolares' *Primula* like *P. albiflos* grew here: they were not in flower. The altitude of the ledge was perhaps 15,000 feet. It slanted up towards the corner more steeply than I had supposed. After a short rest I turned in that direction, hugging the base of the cliff. The valley seemed a long way below me now. I passed several snow cones which had slid down gulleys in the setback cliff. Eventually I reached a big gulley at the bottom of which

flowed a stream. This also I crossed. Then came a deep gash in
the cliff with a gulley above, and I could see the sky beyond.
Unfortunately, to get into the gulley I had to scale a smooth
eight-foot granite wall, and this was beyond my powers. Had I
been able to surmount that obstacle it might have been a simple
matter to have ascended the gulley to the crest of the ridge, from
where I would have had a close-up view of my peak, less than a
mile away. Meanwhile, the clouds had gathered again: already
the main sierra ridge above the big glacier was hidden, though I
could hear the clatter of falling séracs and rocks. The going
became harder, and as I approached the corner where the Gamlang-Dandi ridge joined the main ridge, I was dismayed to see a
deep dark gulley chiselling the cliff; it yawned below me. I clambered over more loose boulders piled on top of one another, and
then abruptly everything came to an end. There was the blank
wall of the cliff as before, but now it was no longer set back; it
went straight down as well as straight up, without any ledge to
walk along. Across space was the upper part of the steep gulley;
even had I been able to struggle across the vertical cliff face and
reach it, I knew I could never ascend it. A stream of water from
invisible snow poured down it. I could just see a bit of the main
ridge above the top of the gulley; it was still hundreds of feet
above me, and my own altitude could not have been less than
16,000 feet. Somehow I felt that an experienced climber would
never have got himself into my position – I had not made a
sufficiently detailed study of the route. Well, there it was: I was
stymied, and would have to go back – the way I came. I was
feeling the weight of the rucksack; and a drizzling rain had set in.

I reached camp soon after four, wet through and tired out.
Marang met me with hot tea and the news that two Daru coolies
had come up. I had intended to spend a second night here, but
the prospect of a warm bed and a camp-fire was too much for
me; we packed quickly and hurried down the valley, getting in
just before dark.

Exploration à l'americaine

Arthur was keen to shoot a takin, and had offered a reward to
anyone who could locate a herd and lead us to it. Several parties
of scouts were alleged to be tracking them. Meanwhile we settled

down to our first spell of steady field-work. With two or three guns out every day, and the long trap-lines Harold set every evening, specimens began to pour in, and the skinners worked overtime to keep pace with us. I went through the crops of many of J. K.'s birds, in order to discover what they ate, and thus was able to identify favourite seeds and types of insects making up their diet.

By this time I had collected about 200 herbarium sheets, and seeds of over 40 species. But already somewhat divided councils prevailed, what we should do and where we should go. Both Arthur and Suydam were restless, and neither of them cared to spend any length of time in one place. They wanted to visit all the passes into China, but had only the haziest idea of how long this would take. Harold, who gave his opinions in vigorous and picturesque phraseology, wanted to spend more time collecting and less time travelling, but was generally for going to some better – but unspecified – place than the one we happened to be at. J. K., who was always in good spirits and full of energy, spent long days in the field with glasses and gun, and got results wherever he was. So also for that matter did Harold with his traps. As for me, the only member of the expedition with first-hand knowledge of the country, the more ground we could cover the better pleased I was, though I liked to explore a few selected places in detail, the higher the better. It seemed obvious to me that with the immense quantity of gear we had brought – much of it was never even unpacked – our best plan now would be to make Kangfang our permanent base and choose a few high-level camps, spending a week or ten days at each. I wanted particularly to go up the main valley as far as the last Lisu village, as this was practically virgin territory; also it was reasonably high without being under snow. Visiting all the passes, and spending only five days at each, would have consumed most of the available time, half of which would be spent travelling; though by splitting into two or three parties we could have covered them all with ease, including perhaps even the distant Sajang pass, far to the north at the source of the Ngawchang river. We did in fact visit four of them, though they were little more than flying visits; but unfortunately not the Sajang.

As the Chawngmaw hut was already built and waiting for us, I played up the idea that we go there first, and this was agreed to. Meanwhile, scouts arrived with news that takin had been located; and it was decided that Suydam, Arthur and I should hunt takin, while Harold remained at the base camp and J. K. went on a bear hunt.

Life at the base camp, under the perfect weather conditions, was pleasant enough, and so long as we got results it was worth while staying on, even though most of the surrounding country was rather 'lived in'. The camp was well-organized, and the expedition well found in every respect – thanks to Suydam and Arthur we lacked nothing. It was cozy at night, with the pressure lamps sizzling and the fire flickering on the floor in the centre of the room, and the wind howling outside, in spite of the draught through the bamboo-matting walls. Supper finished, the tables were cleared and we sat round telling yarns. J. K. was a good raconteur, and he kept the Americans in roars of laughter with his stories of a Burma Civil Servant's life. Over the fire was suspended a bamboo rack on which rested my plant presses and paper, drying in the smoke. On the mat walls hung field-glasses, water-bottles, cartridge belts and such like gear, and all round the room stood specimen boxes containing trays full of stuffed birds and mammals. In one corner were stacked the guns and rifles, in another corner was a table with the radio. But no one ever listened to *that*. The hut certainly gave the impression that work was being done.

On January 6th Suydam, Arthur and I started, marching a few miles up the Hpawte valley towards the Chimeli pass before turning up a side stream and camping close to the Lisu village of Sadulau, 6,500 feet. It is a wretched village. The people, especially the women, were dirty, diseased, undersized and certainly under-fed. To scratch a bare living from this ungracious soil needs unremitting work, as hard, though probably not as monotonous, unhealthy or dangerous, as coal-mining. There is rough culti-vation up to 7,000 feet, and it is amazing that these steep slopes, with great outcrops of granite bulging up here and there, yield any return at all. The people were cutting the long grass, instead of burning it; it is used for thatching and bedding. After supper we sat out by a big wood fire under the tawny light of a full moon, until our backs froze.

Next morning we continued up the little valley, whose singing stream threaded its way through the brown hills; progress was slow. At one point we came upon three deserted wooden huts; the inhabitants, finding it too cold to live there, had gone to live further down, preferring the long daily climb to their fields. When we finally camped at 7,000 feet there was still one clearing just above us. Camp was pitched by the stream.

We were now close to where the trackers had said they had located takin, but though five days had passed since they had found them, nobody seemed to be in any hurry, so presumably the takin were supposed to be static. The Lisus said we would hunt next day. My belief is that in winter, when the takin are driven by snow to seek food at lower altitudes, the herds break up, and that it is almost impossible to find solitary animals, or small parties, in this dense forest. In summer, when they gather in large herds above the tree-line, they are easy to spot. I felt sceptical about our Lisu hunters – perhaps they did not really want us to find a takin. However, we know very little for certain about this strange creature, half-goat half-ox; possibly small herds *do* stay within a limited area throughout the winter.

If I had good reason to doubt the stories put out by our guides now, I had better reason after the first and, so far as we were concerned, last day's hunt.

The following morning we set out after breakfast with these Lisu trackers, crossed a difficult patch of second growth, clambering over huge charred logs which lay at all angles down the steep slope half-buried in the rank growth, and entered the forest. The leading tracker now laid his cross-bow on the ground, struck an attitude, repeated a number of incantations, then cast his bread upon the waters – in other words, flung a handful of rice into the forest. But whether he was praying that a takin be vouchsafed us, or for the safety of the herd, was known to few.

We followed the bed of a steep rocky torrent, and after an hour came on the first authentic signs of takin in the neighbourhood; a heap of dung. Everything now became hush-hush, speech was whispered, or conveyed by signs. We split into two parties. But as we crept upwards through the heavy undergrowth we made so much noise that the cloak-and-dagger business seemed rather like children playing robbers – make-believe. On the other hand it was real takin country, of that there was no question, and we came on various clues. But you cannot shoot a clue; and I felt that long before we could possibly see a takin it would have heard us and reached the next valley. Though we climbed to 9,000 feet, we got no nearer our quarry, and it was a rather exhausted party which, after scaling an almost vertical cliff, at last reached the crest of the ridge. Here the forest was impenetrable, and we sat down on a rock in the sunshine to eat some lunch.

We decided to call it a day. There was no chance of surprising even so dull an animal as a takin in heavy forest the way we were going about it. Let the Lisu hunters go by themselves! So we returned to our camp, and the Lisus went off next morning while we explored lower heights for lesser game; we collected several small birds, including a sibia, a grey nuthatch, and a little bright green bird (*Chloropsis*). The Lisus returned empty-handed, and we prepared to return to Kangfang, reached on the afternoon of the 10th.

We found both Harold and J. K. at the base camp, the latter triumphant with a bear which he had hunted and shot. It was the common black Himalayan bear (*Ursus torquatus*), an awkward customer when cornered, and a brute for destroying the hillman's crops.

To the Panwa pass

Dressed in a style which was really a compromise between the more practical garb of the Chinese women and the more picturesque fashion of the hill women, comely Lisu girls visited our camp from time to time, bringing chickens and eggs for sale, so that we were able to take colour photographs both of them and of their Lashi cousins; for Hpimaw village is the metropolis of the Lashi tribe.

Though the rain had ceased there was a great deal of cloud about and the high ranges were hidden. There were comparatively few birds, but Harold trapped a good series of long-snouted shrews (*Neotebracus*).

Four days later Arthur, who had rejoined us after taking the specimen bones to Htawgaw, decided that we must visit the Panwa pass; so on February 27th, just as we were beginning to know our way about, we went down the hill and on to Black Rock. It was the first fine day we had had for a week and even Imaw Bum showed up momentarily through the frothing clouds, well caked with snow. Down below, the sun was shining, trees were bursting into flower and leaf, birds singing; a thin carpet of green, spangled with the mauve of primulas, was mantling the charred hillside. Not far from Black Rock a red flame showed on the river bank like a volcanic fire, glowing with a peculiar intensity against the porcelain-blue of the sky and the quick green of the surrounding forest. I clambered over the rocks towards this dazzling billow of flame, to find the first carmine cherry in full bloom. For the next hour I basked in the radiance of its superb colour.

This was the largest specimen of the carmine cherry I had ever seen, and it hung poised over the foaming river like an unquenchable fire. Thousands of bees hummed amongst the blossom, which had attracted a multitude of brightly-coloured birds. In an ecstasy of enjoyment, with much twittering and fluttering and squabbling, they probed roughly into the flowers in their search for insects, thereby causing a gentle rain of glowing petals, buds and bud-scales to fall about me. Amongst frequent visitors were *Yuhinas, Ixulus, Ixos* and *Emberiza*; never could there have been less than a dozen birds in the tree together, and when I shot one, momentarily driving most of them away, they soon returned, irresistibly attracted by the overpowering scent and colour.

At Black Rock *Michelia floribunda*, recovered from the buffeting by rain, had opened a fresh lot of flowers, and these too were sought after by birds, though not to the same extent as the carmine cherry. Some potters were at work in a field where a buffalo puddled the clay. The potter's wheel worked to and fro, with a treadle. The pots had no top or bottom, were in fact more like chimney-pots; bottoms are put on afterwards. They are used for fermenting grain.

Visit to a coffin tree

A Chinese merchant who lived in Htawgaw, hearing that I wanted to see a coffin tree, admitted that he owned one, and now volunteered to show it me. The coffin tree was said to be quite close, only about three miles away in fact, but of course it proved to be further away than that. Lupting and I left Htawgaw in the late afternoon, retraced our steps down the hill towards Hkamkawn, crossed the Ngawchang by a high cane suspension-bridge, and at dusk reached a village at the foot of the mountain. Here we spent the night.

A full-sized *Taiwania* may be 200 years old, perhaps twice that age, and will yield sixty or eighty planks. A Chinese businessman will pay as much as Rs 100/- to the owner of a tree – probably a Maru – or to anyone who, in the course of his travels, has found one in the forest. The purchaser, however, may hold on to it for years before cutting it down. So long as nobody else cuts it down on the sly – and that would not be easy – it is a sound investment. Every few years Chinese contractors from T'eng-yueh bring over carpenters who with saw, wedge and adze fell, and cut into planks, those trees which have been marked as ripe for felling.

Apart from the fashionable angle, and the desire of every rich man to have the best obtainable, there is a good and proper reason why the mandarin wishes to own a coffin of durable timber. For the Chinese after death is first buried and then burned; and the interval between burial and cremation may be two or three years. Nay, the interval between death and burial may likewise be long. According to Chinese belief, it is important for the body (or at least the skeleton) to be complete at the time of cremation; otherwise it will be incomplete at the resurrection also and enter the shadow-world a cripple. Unless the coffin can be guaranteed to hold together, which it can only do if made of some resistant, usually scented, wood, there is every likelihood that some of the bones will be lost, as almost invariably happens with the poorer classes who are buried in cheap coffins.

Ever since the first decade of this century, rumours of the Chinese coffin tree have come out of this remote corner of Burma, the timber being at one time identified with *Juniperus recurva*, and possibly with other species. That the Chinese, who monopolize the trade, fearing competition, should attempt to hide the identity of the tree, is hardly surprising. But there is no longer any room for doubt that it is in reality identical with the tree discovered in Formosa in 1906 (and subsequently 1500 miles distant in the Htawgaw hills), known to botanists as *Taiwania cryptomerioides*.

The next day, that is on March 7th, with my guide and a man to carry my camera and other effects, I started off to find the coffin tree, following a scarcely visible track. Our path led through high grass and second growth, but we were soon ascending steeply along the crest of a ridge which sloped up at about 60°. The village from which we had started was not much more than 4,000 feet above sea level, so I reckoned we had some height to climb before we should meet with any *Taiwania*. After a couple of hours, however, in the course of which the path had degenerated into a deep rut down which water coursed furiously during the rainy season, and logs of wood were dragged during the dry season, we were well into the upper pine forest, and, as I should judge, some 7,000 feet above sea level. In places we had to bend double to get through the bushes, particularly where there were small cliffs to clamber up – and here in the damp gloom I noticed colonies of *Primula dictyophylla* with unusually large leaves. At last the forest began to grow a little thicker, with other trees besides pines, and a lot of bamboo undergrowth. Then came veteran trees of *Rhododendron stenaulum* in flower, and a smattering of large granite boulders, over which sprawled bushes of *R. bullatum*, their beautifully crimped rose-pink buds here and there expanded to scented ivory-white flowers with the faintest blush. I noticed also *Michelia floribunda*, *Rhodoleia forrestii*, *Magnolia nitida*, *Bucklandia*, *Litsaea* and *Schima*; bunches of the crimson-flowered *Agapetes lacei* hung like mistletoe from some of the trees.

Suddenly the guide, who for some time had been looking carefully about him, halted, and parting the bushes which grew thickly on our right concealing, as I now discovered, a deep glen, pointed dramatically.

'Look, duwa!'

At first I could see nothing, or rather I could not see the trees for the forest, which was dense enough. But when he had hacked away some of the bushes I found myself looking down a steep slope into the crown of the trees below, and presently made out a single tree which towered high above the canopy; its pyramidal top, seen against the sky, had rather the look of an idealized Christmas tree. Meanwhile, the guide was cutting a path down the slope to the base of the tree, and when I had cleared out a few intervening shrubs, I got a very fair view of the trunk as well as of the top. Thus at last I found myself gazing in awe on a full-grown Chinese coffin tree; and presently I scrambled down to examine it more closely. The tall slender trunk – it was six to seven feet in girth five feet above the ground, with no trace of plank-buttress roots – rose unbranched for about fifty feet, a splendid pillar of timber, straight as a dart. I estimated the total height at about 125 feet, possibly more. The reddish bark was rough and stringy and reminded me of the Californian redwoods. I had no means of guessing what its age might be, but it could not have been less than 150 years, and might well have been nearer 250 years. I was interested to observe that one solitary specimen could be found growing in the midst of broad-leaved forest, consisting largely of oaks, magnolias, laurels, chestnuts and so forth – temperate evergreen rain forest, as I have called it elsewhere – although almost pure stands of *Taiwania* are said to occur further north. That there still exist a number of specimen trees in these mountains seems probable; but that the Chinese will extract every one they can find is certain. On the other hand, I was informed that the Marus, who are politely regarded as the real owners, having become alive to the value of this asset, are planting more trees for the benefit of future generations; a piece of foresight which, if true, is not a little surprising.

Earthquake tremors

Across the torrent the steep sheltered side of the valley was still covered with forest, chequered with little bare patches where the soil had slipped; it looked rather as though it were pitted with small shell-craters. Even as I stood there wondering what had caused these scars, a shiver seemed to pass down the valley, accompanied by a loud booming noise, which startled me. It was not a sudden explosion, however, but more like the prolonged roll of thunder echoing through the hills. An hour later when I had reached the rest-house at Zuklang (or Sanlang), the same thing happened again, and now the bungalow shook, and the windows rattled; the muffled roar which accompanied the tremor – for earth-tremor it undoubtedly was – seemed to proceed from under the ground. At first these little quakes were alarming, some more so than others; but we very soon grew so used to them that we took no notice, and this will not sound surprising when I say that during our short stay in this area we experienced several hundred shocks. On some days there would be a dozen or a score, at the rate of perhaps one an hour, and no day passed without our experiencing several. But though some of the strongest and noisiest quakes startled us not a little, I never saw any rocks fall or any slip occur, or felt any wind, though the mountains all round the Panwa pass were, as already remarked, scarred with earth slips. The whole area within which these shocks occurred covered no more than two or three hundred square miles; and judging from the bareness of the slips – most of which probably take place during the rainy season when the soil is saturated and loose – I fancy unrest had only recently broken out at the Panwa. Some years earlier, however, Htawgaw itself had been the focus of these shivering fits, which had split the little stone fort asunder, and caused considerable alarm, so that Htawgaw was abandoned as the headquarters, which were shifted to Lawkhaung. Yet during the months we were in the immediate Htawgaw area, never once did we feel a quake until we went to the Panwa pass. It would appear, therefore, that the epicentre had shifted southwards.

NINETEEN

Plant Hunter in Manipur
1948

A trying day – In search of tea – The Manipur Lily – A journey delayed – The glorious fifth of June – Forest in rain – Caught in a thunderstorm – Naga harvest

A trying day

We stayed at Chammu on the 12th while we repacked the loads. It was a fine, hot day and all the peaks were clear of cloud – just the sort of day we should have been standing on the summit enjoying the view and seeing a number of interesting trees. In the evening we walked to the edge of the Phow Khong valley. Looking across the 3,000-foot-deep chasm we could see a black wall of rock a thousand feet high crowning the eastern range. Though none of the peaks south of Hkacha Bum, where the frontier turns south, is so much as 7,000 feet high, this line of straight black cliffs running on for miles – the 'Great Wall of Burma' – is very impressive; it recalls the Rift Valley of Africa.

The Phow Khong rises in Hkayam Bum and flows south through the Valley of Tea to join the Nam Panga. It is, in fact, one of the two source streams of the Nam Panga, the other (and larger) source stream rising, appropriately enough, on Sirhoi. The wide valley of the Nam Panga gives easy access from the Chindwin valley into Manipur, and has no doubt been used for very many centuries. Buddhism does not appear to have been brought into Assam by this or any other route; at least it never flourished there, although the twelfth-century Shan conquerors were, theoretically at least, Buddhists. But I was not a little surprised by the number of Burmese gongs, especially the spinning axe-blade gongs used in Burmese monasteries, seen in the Phow Khong villages from Khaiyang southwards.

On May 13th we started. We had been promised two fairly tough marches to Mollen, in the heart of the tea district, and this proved to be no exaggerated description.

Chammu, like other villages along the border, comprises two

separate parts, Kuki and Tangkhul, besides out-villages of a few
huts. It was a long, steep descent through pine woods to the
river, a rushing torrent about two and a half feet deep. In the
rains it would be unfordable, but now it was comparatively easy
to cross, as an island divided it into two streams, each ten or
twelve yards wide. Sub-tropical jungle fringed the bank and filled
the gullies with an assortment of trees alien to the ridges, for the
river-bed was not much more than 1,500 feet above sea level. A
tall tree with a crown of white blossom was perhaps *Derris robusta*;
I noticed also Indian horse-chestnut (*Aesculus assamica*) and *Duab-
anga sonneratioides*, which is quite the gawkiest and most unlovely
tree in the jungle; even the large white flowers are gauche.

Unfortunately, we had no sooner reached the river than it
began to rain, gently at first, then harder, finally in torrents. We
halted on the far bank for a snack lunch, and found the path up
to Kasung slippery. Just below the village we passed a huge
champak tree (*Michelia champaca*) in full bloom. Its trunk towered
up, pale, smooth, unbranched like a cathedral pillar, for perhaps
a hundred feet, so there was no possibility of getting a flower. It
scented the air all around. We had collected a single plant of the
'red Vanda' (*Renanthra coccinea*), which is a lovely colour like red
morocco leather, but the flowers are somewhat spidery, as though
waiting motionless to trap the unwary.

The Kukis put a hut at our disposal, so we did not have to
bother with tents.

It was unfortunate that we nearly always started the day's
march, when we were fresh, by descending one or two thousand
feet, and ended it with a long climb up to the next village when
we were not so fresh. It had been so in marked degree this day,
hence it was not surprising I felt tired out. But we were not to
get off too easily. After supper we were just settling down to
write our diaries before turning in, when there came a knock on
the door of the hut, and in walked the headman, holding aloft a
pine-torch which spluttered and smoked like a firework. He was
followed by a woman carrying a black earthenware pot, and a
man grasping a long bamboo water-vessel or *chung*. It was obvious we were in for an alcoholic session, and Jean would be
expected to hold a midnight clinic with all the mystery and ceremony of a midnight Mass. I braced myself for the ordeal.

Our visitors squatted down, poured some water from the *chung*
into the pot, which contained fermenting rice, brought out a long

bamboo siphon, and proceeded to draw off some of the hissing liquor into glasses. It tasted like a milk-shake made with flat soda. We now perceived through the open door a sea of dimly outlined faces; evidently most of the village were gathered round – the night air was warm and fragrant with the cloying scent of champak – watching their opportunity. It was the children's hour, and as soon as we had quaffed 'wine' the mothers began to arrange their children as though setting up a baby show. Most of them were still suckling, and several resented this departure from routine. One tiny tot was brought in and, with no outside help, stood up boldly for inspection. Somehow Jean managed to elicit the nature of the symptoms, or a colourful imitation thereof, prescribed the right (or, just as likely, the wrong) medicine, and – what really mattered – gave the proud mothers confidence. In due course the infantry inspection ended, the headman and his young wife departed (taking the still with them), and we were left in peace. It had been a trying day.

In search of tea

Wild Tea was reported from Manipur so long ago as 1885, but its occurrence there has never been confirmed. Indeed, nobody knows what really wild Tea looks like, or even if it exists. What has, in the past been called wild Tea has, on closer investigation, always turned out to be abandoned Tea, or cultivated Tea run wild and self-sown – a very different thing. There is plenty of Tea in the foothills round Imphal. It grows in the jungle, and nobody bothers to manufacture tea from it; but even so it has the hallmark of the cultivated Tea bush, though the trees grow thirty feet high, and one would need a ladder before one could pluck them.

Across the Manipur frontier, in the Chindwin valley, Tea has long been cultivated by the Shans. At Tamanthi, where tea is still manufactured (as in Yunnan), it looks no more – and no less – wild than does the so-called wild Tea of Assam. Our informant spoke of 'forests of Tea', and presumably this was it. We had been told by a Kuki that Tea grew wild all along the Burma frontier, and perhaps it did. We were further told that it occurred in several villages, including Mollen, Kasung, Chatrik, Maokot and Chahong (the last named, if Chinese, might well mean 'tea factory' or 'tea company'). We worked out a homeward route via the frontier range and the valley of the Phow Khong, in which most of the above villages are situated.

After a short rest and a snack we set out, still with our guide, for the Tea. The descent into the valley, under a brazen sky, was rather tiresome, and as we had to circle the isolated pyramid from the south, I began to realize that we had a long day before us. In fact, it took us over two hours to reach the dry bamboo jungle where the Tea grew, mixed with a variety of small trees and large shrubs. The Tea trees were not more than thirty or forty years old, and fifteen or twenty feet tall. There had probably been cultivation hereabouts at some earlier period, though there was no sign of human habitation now.

As for the Tea, it was not unlike the variety known to planters as Assam Indigenous, or Dark Burma. It might well have passed as wild Tea, to the uncritical; but I came to the conclusion that it had formerly been cultivated here, in the casual way in which Tea *is* cultivated on a cottage scale – that is to say, permitted, even encouraged, to grow at the expense of other trees, but not receiving any favoured treatment. I saw neither flowers nor fruits. It may be remarked that we were now in the valley of the Nam Panga (or at any rate in the valley of the Phow Khong close to its confluence with the Nam Panga), and so within easy reach of the Chindwin. What more natural than that one should find a chain of Tea plantations, in all stages of disuse, dotted along this ancient trade route? The Shans, who seem to have been largely responsible for the spread of the Tea bush in early history, passed this way; and it appeared to me a fact of no little significance that, not merely Tea, but the tea-drinking habit, should be found here.

It was now long past midday and unbearably hot. Our one desire was to reach the camp as early as possible, and I had pictured to myself an easy walk of perhaps three miles beside the river. The path, so far as I could judge, set out in the right direction. We crossed several dry rocky *nallas*, and presently came to a stream, which made me more than ever convinced that there had formerly been cultivation nearby. The river was now less than a mile away, but this was the nearest we got to it. For the next hour we had to struggle up and down – but chiefly up – through thick jungle, till we had almost completed the circuit of the sugar-loaf hill. There was no path.

Finally we found ourselves close to Mollen again, and it was in a chastened mood that we started for the river a second time, now following a steep ridge. At 4.30 we reached it, and found our tent pitched on a sandbank on the far side. I had been slogging up and down these steep hills under a grilling sun for eight hours, and was dead beat. The inside of the tent was like Arabia in July, but it was pleasant outside. We had tea, then walked downstream to find a quiet bathing pool. After a swim I felt better, and we lay on the rocks carefree, drying in the sun.

The Manipur Lily

The acceptance of a plant into the Temple of Flora, backed by authority for the new name, by valid description (in Latin), and inclusion in the Kew Index, is one thing; its coming out like a *jeune fille* into the great horticultural world is quite another. It is the difference between being born into Debrett, and getting there.

In October, when we visited Sirhoi for the last time, Jean suggested that we introduce the lily [*Lilium mackliniae*] into England in a big way, by sending mature bulbs home; popularize it, so to speak. So, after giving a demonstration of how to hack up bulbs with an ice-axe without damaging them, I commissioned Yarter to dig up a few, and by the end of the month we had nearly three hundred bulbs laid out. Of these we selected the largest and best, about two hundred in all, packed them in two bamboo baskets with a handful of moss round every individual bulb, and had them carried down to Ukhrul, whence they reached Tocklai safely in December.

Early in January 1949 we flew to Calcutta, taking with us the bulbs, now packed (still in moss) in three wooden boxes. With little delay these were dispatched to London by air, where they arrived inside a week, thanks largely to my friend Mr A. Simmonds, Assistant Secretary of the Royal Horticultural Society, who telephoned to Paris to get them put on to the London plane immediately, instead of lying neglected on the airfield for a week, and then persuaded the British Customs authorities to boost them over the last hurdle.

Thus it came about that nearly two hundred fine lily bulbs reached my old friend Colonel F. C. Stern, greatest living expert on lilies and famous in the botanical no less than in the horticultural world, about the middle of February, that is, some three months after they had been exhumed. Fred Stern grew them on for eighteen months, and when he exhibited a plant in full bloom at the Chelsea Flower Show in 1950, like a debutante at a coming-out ball, *Lilium mackliniae* received the Royal Horticultural Society's blessing, in the shape of the coveted Award of Merit.

The final step was to get the surviving stock – which still amounted to well over a hundred finely grown plants – into the hands of a nurseryman who would put them into circulation. The well-known firm Messrs R. W. Wallace & Co. of Tunbridge Wells, lily specialists, bought the whole issue; and there we may safely leave our débutante, so lately 'presented', to come out and make history as *Lilium (née Nomocharis) mackliniae*, known to its friends as the Manipur Lily.

A journey delayed

We dared not delay our proposed journey to Sirhoi much longer; unless we went in the first week of June, at latest, we would be too late. Our Ukhrul plants were in flower before the middle of May; on Sirhoi's green top they would be at their best in early June – or so we reckoned. But when we tried to get porters to carry our loads, we found everybody so busy they hardly had time to say no, as they hurried off to the rice-fields.

On June 1st we walked to the West Mountain again, repeating our walk of April 1st. Our main object was to discover whether the magnolia which grew on the col was the same as the one I had found in flower above Kangkoi on May 19th or not (*Manglietia insignis*). A comparison of the herbarium material suggested that it was, but it needed confirmation.

As usual, there was thick cloud over the ridge in the early morning; we decided to wait and see before starting. But the day turned out fine, and starting at eleven, we walked so fast that we were over the col and into the precious shade of the forest before one o'clock. As I had expected, the West Mountain magnolia proved to be *Manglietia insignis*, but the flowers were almost all over. Few magnolia flowers last long, at any rate in this climate. They grow so rapidly that the outer petals are sometimes falling by the time the innermost are fully expanded. The American *Magnolia grandiflora* grows quite well in Upper Assam, but the pink stamens are dropping, and the milk-white petals beginning to turn brown, on the third day; and it is only the fact that the magnificent blooms open in long succession – coupled, of course, with the very beautiful glossy evergreen foliage, foxy-red beneath – that makes it worth cultivating there.

Our giant maple, draped with thousands of little crimson tassels, looked more beautiful than ever.

It was pleasant in the cool, damp forest with the greenish light drifting through the lace-like canopy, exquisite ferns carpeting the banks, and a stream tumbling over the rocks where forktails, barred with black and white, flitted suddenly through the gloom, screeching. We heard the English cuckoo again, too.

So the first rapturous days of summer slipped by, and we began to grow seriously alarmed. We talked to Mangalay, told him how important it was for us to camp at Sirhoi *now*, told him he *must* get us porters. When would the urgent work in the rice-fields be over? He did not know. In a week? Certainly in a fortnight. It did not matter . . . it would be too late.

One sunny afternoon we walked along the ridge to Humdum, where so many good trees and shrubs grew; we felt despondent. Sirhoi was clearly visible, its open slope flashing green.

It was like early summer in the country in England. The day was warm, but not too hot, and daylight lingered on into fragrant twilight. The sky was blue, but not cloudless; the air soft and caressing, sweet with the scent of flowers and the clean smell of fertile earth. Morning and evening birds sang, whistled, and called, mate to mate. Never had the mountains to north and south, to east and west, looked so close, so colourful, or so desirable. Already ten days had passed since we first beheld our poor lilies, battered and splashed with mud. Unless we returned to Sirhoi immediately, what hope had we of seeing those green slopes as we had pictured them, gay with lilies – even of seeing lilies in flower at all? The chance was slipping from us; we should have to wait a full year before it came again. And we *knew* the lilies were there in their hundreds – had we not seen them in April?

Nevertheless, the heavy and continuous rains of May might have been disastrous to them, unless (possibly) they had delayed flowering till the fine weather returned. Otherwise the fate which had overtaken our garden might be theirs too. We *must* go and camp on Sirhoi and see for ourselves – and we must go at once.

Now for the first time we had come up against the hard facts of peasant life; that is, against the urgent need of the primary producer. It was the rice-planting season, and every man, woman and child in the village was at work in the fields from dawn to dusk. No one could spare so much as a day off – their very lives depended on the work they put in now. Money meant less than nothing to them, for it would not buy food – only the earth produced that. And after days of vain inquiry, we had learnt emphatically that we should not get transport till the paddy had been planted out from the nurseries to the *khets* – the terraces of running water – which meant for two more weeks, no matter what we offered.

The glorious fifth of June

Shortly afterwards came the greatest discovery of the day. We had been peering at some plant growing by the side of the path, when I glanced up to see Jean staring in a startled way at something growing on a rock a short distance up the slope. From the ecstatic look on her face I guessed it was something out of the ordinary, and following the direction of her gaze my eyes were immediately riveted by a star cluster of pale flowers which seemed to radiate a phosphorescent blue light. The plant was growing on a rock, and there was only one thing it could possibly be; nevertheless, for half a minute I stared, unbelieving. It seemed impossible.

'*What* is it?' Jean whispered in an awe-struck voice.

'By God, it's a *primula*,' I whispered back (as though it might overhear us and run away). 'It can't be – *here*! But it *is*!'

We rushed up the slope and knelt down in front of the little rock as though before a shrine. Growing out of a crack was a rosette of soft crinkled green leaves glistening with silky hairs, and from the centre rose a short mealy-white scape bearing three flowers. It was a primula all right – one I had never seen before in my life, wild or in cultivation – and of almost unearthly beauty. For a minute we knelt there enchanted, dumb with adoration in the face of so exquisite a flower, savouring too the delicate scent which came from it. The whole plant was only about four inches high, and each corolla about an inch across, of a pale lilac-mauve shade with a white star of powdery meal in the centre. But what most astonished us was the extraordinary length of the slender tube, which was fully two inches long! One would have thought that a primula of any shape and colour, whose slender tube reached a length of two inches, would have an almost giraffe-like ungainliness; to stick one's neck out like that, even though wearing a frilly pale-green collar, is asking for laughter. But there was nothing ridiculous about this sweet flower – it was as near perfection as a rock primula could be.

I have said that I had never seen its like either in the mountains or in cultivation, and I have seen several hundred species of primula growing. But suddenly I remembered I had seen a photograph of it. That immensely long tube, as though no insect other than a butterfly or perhaps a hawk moth could possibly pollinate it, was unique. Only one known primula possessed it – a species discovered by that fine plant-hunter Major George Sherriff in Bhutan some years previously, and named after his wife. That was the picture I remembered, and I had little doubt that our plant was *P. sherriffiae*, turned up again on the south side of the Assam valley.

Feeling almost as though we were in church, we tiptoed the few hundred yards to the summit of Sirhoi and sat down to take in the view, while Jean once more opened the press to preserve our new treasures. In a shallow gulley a close colony of taller irises were coming into flower, a very different plant from the dwarf species which was richly scattered over the slope amidst a sea of pink lilies. Below us the southern slopes of Sirhoi fell steeply to the forest lining the mountain scuppers; and far away to the south the sun gleamed on the Chindwin river of Burma, which shone dully like pewter. Eastwards the frontier mountains were higher and bolder, almost menacing. Westwards we could still see Ukhrul, smaller now, a row of dark conifers like a file of blackshirts marking the site of the old red-roofed hospital and the Military Police post. It looked an immense distance away.

It was important to find more plants of *Primula sherriffiae* for seed in due course, and I cast around from the rocky summit of the peak. There were several shallow furrows here between what may have been ancient moraines. Searching every likely place, I presently found whole colonies of our plant plastered on the hard rocky outcrops and against the steepest, stoniest slopes, in the teeth of the wind and in the direct path of the monsoon rain. It

was curious choice of ground for so delicate a plant, but it grew
nowhere else.

Forest in rain

The rain did not prevent our carrying on botanical exploration;
it merely made it more uncomfortable. Sometimes the mist was
so thick we could hardly see where we were going. Nor was it
cold outside, not even when, as invariably happened, we were
soaked to the skin. The forest insured us against the wind, but was
otherwise depressing. It was colder on the open slope, exposed to
the wind, but altogether lighter and more cheerful. The path,
however, composed of red clay derived from igneous rocks was
very slippery.

We explored the magic glade, but it was now a bog. An intense
gloom had settled over the forest. No longer did spouting buds
pour forth a wealth of colour from flower and scrolled leaf. The
bent trees, heavily festooned with moss, looked like giant green
candles guttering in the wind, suggesting immemorial age and
neglect, a vast antiquity. The bowed bamboos leaning in every
direction, the dripping ferns, the furrowed trickling slopes, all
these helped to intensify a feeling of ruin and decay. The undergrowth, such as there was, surged waist-high, heavy with water.

The cave-like dimness deepens as the mist spreads like a dark
stain, and the grotesquely swollen branches of trees, their frilled
outlines uncertain against the canopy, are half-seen, while the
wind in the tree-tops sounds like far breakers. Even the steady
drip, drip from the moss-bearded branches might be the sea-
wrack bubbling as the ebb tide runs, leaving it bare. Spectres of
wrecked ships with broken spars and battered hulls peer through
the greenish half-light. A bird calls suddenly, a monotonous one-
note call, shrill-edged. Inside the forest one might indeed be
drowned five fathoms deep. And as though to emphasize the
washed-out colour of everything, I found the big lopsided leaves
of a Chirita whose long, narrow, tubular flowers, with pouting
mouth, were the pale violet of a reflected rainbow. A single tree
Symplocos, crowned with a veil of blossom, rode the tossing
green seas above our heads like a snow-white ship.

Caught in a thunderstorm

It was on the 26th that, not for the first time, it looked as though it might be fine all day. We reached the summit in good time, then decided to follow the Mapum path which plunged steeply down the north-east ridge. But the cloud came up more quickly than we could go down, and soon began to mass itself between us and the top. We went down several hundred feet, then plunged once more into forest. Trees and undergrowth were the same as we had seen on the other side of the mountain.

While we were eating a snack lunch it began to rain, gently at first, then more heavily; finally in sheets. The noise was amazing. Soaked to the skin and shivering, we made our way back up the ridge. At the top we suddenly found ourselves right inside a thunderhead, everything blacked out. We had just left the summit when there came a blinding flash, accompanied by a terrific explosion. Instinctively we ducked, covered our faces. The path, here traversing the steep southern face, had become a rushing torrent in which we had difficulty in keeping our balance, as the stones were being torn out from under our feet and rolled along; but we went as fast as we could, for it seemed that the top of the mountain had been struck by lightning. Frightened and half-deafened by the explosion, we threw caution to the winds and fairly ran down the path into the shelter of the next bit of forest.

Naga harvest

We could not start till the harvest was in. All day from dawn till sunset men, women and girls were at work in the rice-fields or trudging up the steep footpaths to the village with heavy burdens on their backs. Dusk had fallen by the time the last tired parties came along the ridge, girls in the lead, bent from the hips and chanting as they walked, women next, men in the rear, echoing in deep voices the leaders' refrain. Sometimes by the light of the moon, when a thin pearl-white mist spread like a bridal veil over the tree-tops, a ghostly procession would toil past, dimly outlined against the star-spangled sky, and we would hear the musical, monotonous 'hey . . . ho . . . hey . . . ho' growing louder for a time, then fading slowly away. Nothing is more characteristic of the Naga Hills than this rhythmical chant that accompanies all hard labour. They are masters of syncopation, too, but however complicated the pattern of the chant, the basic rhythm is never lost, and it is a great help to walk in step with one's porters' guttural music, especially when one is tired at the end of a stiff march.

TWENTY

Assam Earthquake
1950

On 15 August 1950 my wife and I were camped in the village of Rima, on the left bank of the Lohit River, approximately lat. 28° 30'N., long. 97° 00'E., at an altitude of 5,000 ft. Rima is not really the name of a village, but rather of a small district containing five or six villages of rude timber houses and granaries, with a total population of a few hundred people.

Between the Rong Thö Chu-Zayul Chu confluence, a mile north of Rima, and the Indo-Tibetan frontier to the south, the Lohit gorge suddenly opens out, causing a sort of amphitheatre, some three miles from north to south, mainly on the east bank, where the villages are situated. The river itself is here more than 600 yards wide, twisting as though it were flowing across a flood plain. All around, the mountains rise very steeply from the flat terraces, a cluster of snow-peaks on the Burma frontier, more than 19,000 ft high, lying within the twenty-five mile radius; but only four miles from the river they are already 15,000 ft high. Hence Western geographers might speak of the 'Rima basin'.

We had been several days in Rima, and had just concluded arrangements for sixteen porters to take us three marches up the La Ti torrent which, crashing down from the Burma frontier, flows into the Lohit immediately below Rima. We were to start early on the morning of 16 August for the alpine pastures. It was about 8 p.m. by (our) local time, roughly three-quarters of an hour after dark on a hot, close night, the stars shining brightly up and down the arid gorge. My wife was in bed, our two servants were in their tent, and I was seated writing my diary near the entrance to our tent.

Suddenly, after the faintest tremor (felt by my wife but not by me) there came an appalling noise, and the earth began to shudder violently. I jumped up and looked out of the tent. I have a distinct recollection of seeing the outlines of the landscape, visible against the starry sky, blurred – every ridge and tree fuzzy – as though it were rapidly moving up and down; but fifteen or twenty seconds passed before I realized that an earthquake had started.

My wife shouted 'Earthquake!' before I did, and leapt out of bed. Together we rushed outside, I seizing the oil lantern which I placed on the ground; I was conscious of fearing that the tent would catch fire. We were immediately thrown to the ground; the lantern, too, was knocked over, and went out instantly.

I find it very difficult to recollect my emotions during the four or five minutes the shock lasted; but the first feeling of bewilderment – an incredulous astonishment that these solid-looking hills were in the grip of a force which shook them as a terrier shakes a rat – soon gave place to stark terror. Yet my wife and I, lying side by side on the sandbank, spoke quite calmly together, and to our two Sherpa boys who, having already been thrown down twice, were lying close to us.

The earthquake was now well under way, and it felt as though a powerful ram were hitting against the earth beneath us with the persistence of a kettledrum. I had exactly the sensation that a thin crust at the bottom of the basin, on which we lay, was breaking up like an ice-floe, and that we were all going down together through an immense hole, into the interior of the earth. The din was terrible; but it was difficult to separate the noise made by the earthquake itself from the roar of the rock avalanches pouring down on all sides into the basin.

Gradually the crash of falling rocks became more distinct, the frightful hammer blows weakened, the vibration grew less, and presently we knew that the main shock was over. The end of the earthquake was, however, very clearly marked by a noise, or series of noises, which had nothing to do with falling rocks. From high up in the sky to the north-west (as it seemed) came a quick succession of short, sharp explosions – five or six – clear and loud, each quite distinct, like 'ack-ack' shells bursting. It was the 'cease-fire'.

After about half an hour we returned to the tent. I noticed that the travelling clock on the table and my watch were both going; the altimeter still registered 5,000 ft exactly, and the thermometer outside under the fly showed 73° F. Nothing inside the tent was disturbed, except that a glass of water had been upset. Not a dog in the village barked. The tents were pitched on a small sandbank about 600 yards from the high bank of the La Ti torrent, rather more from the Lohit River. The nearest mountainside was 300–400 yards to the east of us, and, as it happened, that particular face did not slip badly; at any rate, no boulders reached us, or even the village. We could not have selected a safer site in an earthquake!

Within two hours the air was so thick with dust that every star was hidden; we breathed dust, it gritted our teeth, filled our eyes. Within a week every leaf of every tree and bush was caked with dust. Violent tremors continued all night, and twice we rushed outside – though the tent was perfectly safe. I slept intermittently for three hours; my wife not at all.

As soon as it was light, we dressed and went out to see what had happened. In the village every house had lost its roof of wooden slats, and every lean-to had been thrown down. The main irrigation channel was blocked, and the paddy-fields with their standing rice would soon be dry. Farther afield, the small wooden monastery lay on its side, a bottle-shaped *chorten* had been stripped down to its axis, and a *mani* wall of flat inscribed stones had collapsed. I noticed that most of these structures had been thrown down towards the east, as though the push had come from the west.

Long fissures cut across the stony fields, running for the most part parallel with the river bank, past or present. In some places numerous fissures lay close together; elsewhere far apart. It appeared to depend on the nature of the soil, whether sandy or clayey. These cracks were rarely more than a few inches wide and two to four feet deep. Every well-trodden path was cracked throughout its length. Here and there a small block of land had sunk bodily.

The La Ti torrent was an extraordinary sight. The previous day the sparkling water, of a beautiful blue-green tint, revealed every boulder as it flowed swiftly down its rocky bed. Now it was dark coffee-coloured, but so thick with foam that it looked like *café-au-lait*. It had risen nearly four feet, and the muffled grinding of submerged boulders sounded ominous. The water smelt unpleasantly of mud, but I could detect nothing sulphurous about it. Three watermills, housed in timber cabins, had been smashed.

The Lohit had also risen, and the swift stream carried along great quantities of pine logs, which were already beginning to jam. The Rong Thö Chu was bringing down much more debris than the Zayul Chu, and the visible destruction up the former valley seemed to be greater than in the latter. (I have long held, contrary to the maps, that the Rong Thö Chu, which rises among glaciers, is the main stream. Its valley is also more thickly forested.) However, following up the Zayul River for half a mile, I soon reached a road-block where a cliff had come down.

Day after day, night after night, tremors followed one another. Many of them were severe, and were always preceded by a short roar, like a distant thunder-clap. The weather was sultry, the maximum shade temperature often more than 95°, until a wet spell between August 23 and 27 brought it down; the minimum was usually about 65°. On fine days a breeze blew from the south, but in the Rima basin it was so charged with fine dust, and so hot, that it brought no relief. By midday, as the rock avalanches began to fall, a vast dust cloud hid the sun, or dimmed it until it looked like a copper plate. Dust also mingled with the gathering thunderheads, and visibility was reduced to a mile or two.

No one was killed in Rima, but cattle and pigs were injured or killed by falling timber; in the river, great numbers of fish were killed, though few were taken from those raging waters. All the hens stopped laying. The indifference, or fatalism, of the local population (nominally Buddhist) was superb. The day after the earthquake they went about their work in the fields. Yet many of them seemed to think there would be a repetition of the major shock, and that next time they might all be killed. We could find no one who recollected a previous earthquake. With their houses exposed to the weather, they slept in temporary shelters made out of boards; and mending their roofs in the evenings, our village at least looked normal again after a fortnight.

The rope-bridge across the Lohit had been broken, and until another rope was constructed and fixed in position we could not leave Rima. Our chief anxiety was potable water, and this proved something of a problem until we discovered a spring in the bank of the Lohit.

As for the mountains which enclose the basin, they had everywhere been badly mauled. Wide belts had been ripped off, carrying trees and rocks; whole cliffs had crashed down, deep wounds scored; and everywhere rocks continued to cascade down hundreds of gullies. The damage done in the main Lohit valley was bad enough; that done in the tributary valleys, where every stream had to break through a narrow gorge thousands of feet deep, was infinitely worse. The destruction extended to the very tops of the main ranges – 15,000–16,000 ft. above sea level. No wonder the mountain torrents began to flow intermittently as the gorges became blocked, followed later by the breaking of the dam; whereupon a wall of water 20 ft high would roar down the gulley, carrying everything before it and leaving a trail of evil-smelling grey mud.

Everywhere the scraped cliffs glistened white in the sunshine. Fallen boulders showed that by far the most abundant rock is granite, containing tiny nuggets of black mica evenly distributed through it; occasionally the mica is in excess. Quartz veins ramify through the rock in all directions and are of frequent occurrence; and an abrupt change in the size and nature of the crystals, without any cleavage plane, is not infrequent. Not far from our camp was an outcrop of sandstone and schist with secondary white mica. A cliff of this had broken away and buried the main irrigation flume. But this type of rock was not met with elsewhere.

The Rima men made several attempts to fix the rope-bridge and establish connexion with the right bank; but it was not until 6 September that they succeeded. Meanwhile, no news came, and only a few wild rumours (based on occasional conversations shouted across the Lohit) reached us. When we left for Walong on 7 September, together with a patrol of the Assam Rifles who had joined us a fortnight after the earthquake, we had only a few days' food in hand.

We reached Walong Outpost on 11 September after a risky journey, and any hope that below Rima the earthquake might have done negligible damage was quickly dispelled. (We did not yet know, of course, that we had been at the epicentre, or that we had survived one of the greatest earthquakes in history.)

It would be incautious at this stage to state categorically that the annual burning of the pine forest for the last fifty years, between Walong and Rima, was responsible for the huge damage done in the arid Lohit valley; but it seems certain that any further burning will prove completely disastrous. Even without the annual fires, the Lohit valley is likely to be a perilous place for some years.

Return to the Irrawaddy
1953

An ancient forest – Ordeal by rain – A change in the valley - A view of snow mountains – The rarest conifer – Myitkyina

An ancient forest

The sun was already shining fiercely, and after a long and dull ascent through second growth only a few years old, we were thankful to reach the shelter of the forest, above all cultivation – past, present or future. The only plant of interest with any claim to beauty we met with in this zone was the climbing Veronia with tight plumes of florets, like small shaving-brushes, purplish-pink in colour. We first saw it at Sumprabum on the 22nd February, just beginning to open its buds, and again in full bloom at Arahku on the 4th April. Now it was over.

We were now on a ridge and could follow the much-used path without difficulty. We ascended gradually, with several descents, and gained height slowly to start with. At about 7,000 feet we found ourselves in the midst of forest which was old when the Talaings ruled in Pegu, and Rangoon was a village in the marshes of the Irrawaddy delta – forest which had probably not sensibly changed in 5,000 or 50,000 years. The trees, of many species all mixed up together, though hoary with age were yet upright and virile. They looked enormous, in height, and especially in bulk and girth. The maples festooned with thousands of slender red tassels made a notable display; in autumn, when the fruits had turned crimson and spread their wings, they were magnificent. Besides these there were oaks, chestnuts, hollies, magnolias, laurels, cherries, birch, rhododendron, and many others.

Though the overhead canopy was unbroken, it was thin in places, and enough light came through to sustain a variety of shrubs and small trees, which could hardly be described as a second tier, but ranked rather with the herbaceous plants which grew beneath them. Two shrubs which deserve mention were a spindle (Euonymus) twinkling with hundreds of tiny chocolate-drop flowers on long stalks; and a much rarer dwarf hydrangea bearing terminal heads of powder-blue flowers. Each inflorescence was clasped by a lace collar of four paper-white sterile flowers.

Then, on the dark mouldering leaf carpet, under the dripping canopy, came the third tier of vegetation – the herbaceous layer – of which two plants immediately attracted our attention. They grew close to one another in scattered colonies, as though for self-defence. One was an Arisaema, a *de luxe* model of a cuckoo-pint. The magnificent dark liver-coloured spathe, narrowly ribbed with silver, looks like a drinking horn. It is whorled on either side, and from a little distance these side rosettes look like bat's ears, or even ammonites; while the triangular tip, pulled well down over the rim of the vessel, is narrowed abruptly into a whiplash tail which reaches the incredible length of four to five *feet*, and of course trails on the ground. But not directly. Each spathe is accompanied by one solitary compound leaf, which like the spathe, springs directly out of the ground. The leaf blade is composed of three separate leaflets, the whole being almost fan-shaped, borne aloft on a strong stalk. It is taller than the spathe, and shelters it like an umbrella.

As Jean pointed out, the 'tail' almost invariably lies along the midrib of the central leaflet, which may be as much as a foot and a half long; and from its pointed tip hangs down to and trails on the ground.

How, then, was the 'tail' laid with such mathematical precision along the midrib of the central leaflet, when the leaf itself was taller than the spathe? Jean asked. A fair question. One thing seems obvious: the 'tail' was accurately laid down before the leaf stalk grew up. First the 'flower' – strictly, the spathe sheltering the flowers which are crowded on a spadix – appeared, followed later by the solitary leaf, whose stalk grew faster. It carried aloft the 'tail', already placed on the central leaflet. The 'tail', however, grew fastest of all, till it trailed on the ground, and still continued to grow.

But why? To what purpose? Was it in order to lift at least the tip of the close-fitting hood sufficiently to permit the entrance of some creature? (I have read that slugs pollinate Arisaemas, but have never caught them in the act.) Or was it to act as a guide to some creature seeking the interior of the hood?

Unfortunately, on our return in November we didn't find a single plant which had set any seed; so if the scheme is as postulated above, it met on this occasion with scant success; nor did we ever discover what the hypothetical creature was.

The second prominent herbaceous plant was a squat ground-orchid (Calanthe), which from the centre of a lettuce-like clump of broad leaves sends up a short spike with white flowers having a violet lip. They looked as dainty as butterflies crowded on a stick.

Ordeal by rain

The path was exceedingly steep, with boulder steps so high that it was impossible to take them without using one's hands; but a small stream, rapidly swelling to a torrent, cascaded down the obvious channel. At this level the bamboos had recently flowered and died, leaving a hideous tangle of blackened haulms leaning at all angles. The forest was very open, the big trees rather far apart; they included *Magnolia rostrata* and *Michelia doltsopa*, at its highest limit (about 8,000 feet), *Quercus lamellosa*, Tetrameles, and white-beam (Sorbus). It looked rather as though somebody had tried to open up the forest by fire-raising, though with very limited success. Still, one must suppose that this track had been in use for a century or two.

When presently the slope eased off we emerged again from the cover of the forest on to a fully exposed slope. On the steep part, the torrent, now rushing down the path like a mill-race, had washed the rocks from under our feet as we trod on them, making a foothold very insecure. Here the path was simply a trench, and it was stagnant water we had to deal with. Also, it was overgrown with dense thickets of thin-stemmed Arundinaria, whose feathery branches met overhead. Pushing our way through this, over our ankles in mud and water, or slopping almost knee-deep into invisible pools, we were drenched to the skin in a matter of minutes. All the time we were exposed to a wind which in the bamboos sounded like an express train running through a junction. It sucked the warmth out of our bodies in no time at all.

There followed a descent, and presently we were under the protection of forest again, on a more level section of the ridge. But it was too late. The intense chill had set up an uncontrollable shivering, and we felt wretched. At the next steep ascent I was almost 'all in'. The porters had gone ahead and Tha Hla's party

also. But Jean, who was not feeling good herself, stayed behind
to keep me company, though she could easily have kept up with
the porters.

Under these tiresome conditions, with the rain streaming down
and the track a butterslide where it wasn't level and a bog where
it was, we could hardly take great interest in the plants we saw.
But it was impossible to ignore them completely. The massed
rhododendrons to some extent compensated us for the misery we
suffered. The finest sight was Jean's yellow 'Grande' rhododendron, clumps of veteran trees growing together along the ridge,
and all in full bloom. It was like a sudden blaze of sunshine
through the streaming rain.

As the slope became easier, new rhododendrons burst on us –
the blood-red *R. euchaites* and white-flowered *R. bullatum* high in
the trees. But there was nothing to compare with a tall rather
fastigiate shrub, so profusely covered with large bell-shaped
flowers that one could hardly see any leaves at all. They were of
several shades, usually a pale primrose-yellow, but often salmon-
pink or faintly tinged blue-violet, and sometimes pure white. The
bushes lined both sides of the ridge forming an avenue of blossom
which was startling. This species was related to *R. triflorum*, and
it so dominated the ridge that for two or three hundred yards it
made a double wall of contrasting colours, with here and there a
splash of crimson *R. euchaites* or the splendid purple of a shrub
like *R. oreotrephes*.

During the last part of the ascent the ridge was riddled with
wide holes filled with liquid mud, though they looked deceitfully
solid. We went in knee-deep. Jean had now gone ahead to help
prepare the camp and some hot tea. She sent back a man with a
tot of brandy for me, but perhaps I looked a little (hardly much)
worse than I felt. Anyway, I didn't need the brandy, which was
precious on the post, so to speak.

Quite suddenly I came upon a lot of disconsolate porters huddled together on the path, with our two servants looking dis-
tressed, and Jean with an expression of near-despair on her face.
'There's no camping ground,' she said, 'only this!' – indicating
the forest in general. 'We can't pitch the tents. The only thing to
do seems to be to return to Tibu camp. What do you say? I don't
think you can do it, can you? We're all so frightfully cold. We
must at any rate rest and have a meal first.'

I said I didn't feel like going down and we'd stick it out. We managed to clear enough space to put up the small tent, though it sagged like an old sack, with the guy ropes tied haphazardly to tree-trunks, and the uneven ground broken by projecting stumps. After that we strung tent-flies and 'waterproof' sheets along the path, and managed to give some shelter to our servants and to their fire. Tha Hla's party pitched their outer fly – one could hardly call it a tent – on a muddy platform in the dip of the col; but the roof was full of holes and let in a lot of water. Their bedding, like ours, was soaked through.

We lit the stove in our cramped tent, and after a couple of hours, during which time we had changed into dry clothes, Joi Wa Naw brought us some hot tea. Jean, always at her best when things are going badly, then made tea for everyone, for which the porters were very grateful; and presently we all began to revive.

It was hard labour changing all the plant-paper, with three days' collecting in the presses, and we soon realized that it would be impossible to work under such conditions for a week on end. The collection would suffer. We must return to the more spacious Tibu camp. Our little tent was already full of sodden clothes, wet plant-paper, several fat presses which we hoped to keep dry, together with our camp-beds and wet bedding. All other loads stood about outside, in pools of water, it being quite impossible to put them under the fly. The more important ones had their waterproof sheets spread over them; but half our sheets were out on loan to the wretched porters. If we wanted anything, we had to go outside and burrow around for the right box, then open it in the pouring rain – the height of discomfort. We christened this Dismal Camp.

We presently learnt that the porters wouldn't budge next day unless the rain ceased. The path, they said, was too difficult to carry loads down while the rain continued. If they went down without loads, leaving us behind, we might be here for a fortnight before they returned. We pondered this and agreed to feed them for one day if they would carry our loads down the following day, wet or fine. There was at least a chance the weather might improve.

Unfortunately it didn't, and we stayed put in some discomfort, chiefly owing to the fact that Jean had to change all the presses. Every sheet of paper – about 300 of them – must be hand-dried singly over the cookhouse fire, and this thankless task our good-natured girl porters performed.

A change in the valley

By the end of July a profound change had come over the valley. With the fading beauty of the forest the very air had changed. When we arrived in the spring, the scent of the fresh earth, purified by frost, of the swelling buds as they strained and cracked open, of the baby-fingered leaves as they uncrumpled, and of the slowly opening flowers, was sweet. Now, after weeks of rain and darkness, the fecund mouldy soil had broken out into noisome blights, blisters and excrescences. The forest was a shambles of low life, parasitic and saprophytic, locked with nobler forms of vegetation in merciless nibbling warfare; and the stench of battle, of the living and of the slain, hung heavy in the air. I noticed it most when I went into the forest to look for orchids. Rotting leaves, flowers long dead, fallen bud-scales and the broken limbs of trees, stank to high heaven. No less did overripe fruits, fluffy with mildew, stink. Unripe fruits, plucked from their hold by birds or squirrels and now abandoned to hordes of hungry insects and worms, lay on the ground half-buried in the festering mould. To stroll through the forest in the damp midsummer heat is quite pleasant. Compared with the breath-taking air of spring, the smell of the grave is odious; compared with the crisp lilliput crackle of new life as the bud-scales are forced aside, the poignant rustle of the shroud is macabre.

A view of snow mountains

I know nothing so inspiring as a clear view of limitless mountains, with snow-peaks pricking the blue dome of heaven, and deep shadow-filled valleys. I gazed in awe on the scene, while I tried to recognize in various directions peaks I had visited, passes I had crossed, and valleys I had explored, during thirty years of travel.

From north-west to north-east the horizon was now an almost complete arc of snow-peaks; but Ka Karpo Razi, Burma's Icy Mountain, about 125 miles distant bearing 15° or 20° west of north, was outstanding. At the eastern end of what looked like a

single range rose a dazzling white pyramid, while the western
peak was more rounded. This cluster of somewhat isolated peaks,
fused together by distance, looked superb against the cloudless
cornflower-blue of the sky. It dwarfed everything else in that
direction.

Further away, to the north-east, three sharp snow-peaks stood
up from a jumble of mountains, brooding and disdainful. They
must have been beyond the Salween, perhaps on the Salween-
Mekong divide, or even beyond the Mekong river. It was impossible to say for certain. Then, much closer, but in the same general
direction, was another snowy peak rising a head above the supporting ranges. This was almost certainly on the Taron-Salween
divide; it may have been the Gompa La, which rises above
Chamutang on the Salween, pointing the way to India. I hoped
it was that. I had crossed the Gompa La on my journey from
China to Burma thirty years previously, and had an affection for
it.

Westwards, about seventy miles distant, the Assam-Burma
frontier range was clearly visible. It is not so high as the ranges
further north and east, and was not yet snow-clad. So we were
looking into three countries – China, Tibet, Assam – I reflected;
but all we saw was mountains, range on range. We might have
been looking at the moon for all the signs of man's presence
that we could see. And yet, hundreds of beautiful trees, shrubs,
climbers, and rock meadow plants – especially alpines – had been
rescued from that savage but inspiring landscape, for man to
study and enjoy. But hundreds still remained as yet unrevealed –
of that I felt certain – and revealed they would be, one day.

The rarest conifer

A day or two before, Tha Hla had got hold of a man who knew
of a full-grown 'Taxodium' which grew beside the path to Laja,
and had gone to see it. He told us it was easy to reach, and we
were all agog to see it too; and in order to make sure we didn't
miss it, took the man with us. It was 10.30 before we started,
after saying all our goodbyes, and the march began.

The path runs northwards to begin with, then curves gradually
west to cross the northern branch of the Hkrang Hka and reach
Laja, on the right bank, below the confluence of north and south

branches. The first five or six marches would be over new ground, and though we were only on the other side of the river, almost within hailing distance of the left bank, it was surprising how different the country looked, simply because we hadn't been over it before.

When we reached the crest of the ridge which forms the divide between the two main branches, north and south of the Hkrang Hka, our guide turned aside into the forest, and fifteen minutes later, after a difficult scramble up and down precipitous slopes, we stopped at the foot of a tree. It was a fairly big tree, about 100 or 120 feet high, reaching the canopy but not rising clear above it; and it had a smooth straight pillar-like trunk, which kept the same diameter up to the first branch about fifty feet from the ground. That certainly was a thrilling moment, and I stood gazing in awe for almost a minute, silenced by the sight of a full-sized 'Taxodium', the rarest conifer in these forests; it was the first time I had seen one. The crown looked a bit sickly, as though some of the limbs were dying; and there seemed to be rather too many epiphytes on them. But this appearance may have been only because the leaves had changed to a brownish-yellow before dropping – almost the colour of a larch in the autumn before it turns brighter yellow.

In the middle of the forest, and on a difficult slope, it was impossible to get an all-inclusive view of this strange tree. The girth near the base was eight and a half feet, giving a diameter of thirty-four inches, which for a 100-foot tree isn't much. The blaze is red, and without fragrance.

The crown was rather open, comprising a few thick, spreading limbs and branches. It was not so dominating as the solitary Taiwania I had seen (also in North Burma) some years previously; *that* stood up clear of the canopy. Nevertheless, the 'Taxodium' was an outstanding tree.

We seemed to have come to the right spot, for shortly after we got back to the bridle-path, having spent three-quarters of an hour on the quest, about a hundred yards on I spotted another specimen close beside the path. It was only about fifty feet high, and not full-grown; but it was no sapling. The guide seemed surprised at my success, and also pleased. As mentioned before, it is a valuable tree, and he had not known of this one before. The Hkanung name for it is *di kum* or *di krum*.

Myitkyina

We spent the next five days in Myitkyina, making up packets of seeds and finishing off the botanical work. We had no reason to go into the town much; when we did, we noticed that it was full of young people – boys and girls – in semi-European dress, who seemed to have nothing to do. Chinese and Burmese girls, wearing conical limpet-shaped straw hats, rode bicycles – as shocking an exhibition to an older generation, no doubt, as the first girls dressed in bloomers were to Victorian matrons.

But the point is: Myitkyina, no longer the sleepy little riverside village it had been before the war, was now a bustling town, and riddled with thieves. The Catholic priests had been burgled three times; and while we were there, Tha Hla's clothes, hung out on a line to dry, were all stolen in the night, and with them Jean's expedition sweater which she had leant him. Are the young, who have nothing much to do, turning into a race of spivs; and are the thieves recruited from the spiv ranks?

After dark the town becomes noisy and is garishly lit up. Only at the northern end is it quiet; and such sounds as one hears – the slow squeak and creak of a bullock-cart, the cawing of crows, and after dark the shrill whistle of the train as it comes round the bend – are not unpleasant.

Index

Birds — General — Insects — Mammals & reptiles — Mountains — Passes — People — Places — Plants & Shrubs — Races — Rivers — Trees